The United States Army
in the War of 1812

ALSO BY JOHN C. FREDRIKSEN

The B-45 Tornado:
An Operational History of the First
American Jet Bomber (McFarland, 2009)

The United States Army in the War of 1812

Concise Biographies of Commanders and Operational Histories of Regiments, with Bibliographies of Published and Primary Resources

JOHN C. FREDRIKSEN

Foreword by Richard V. Barbuto

McFarland & Company, Inc., Publishers
Jefferson, North Carolina, and London

LIBRARY OF CONGRESS CATALOGUING-IN-PUBLICATION DATA

Fredriksen, John C.
  The United States Army in the War of 1812 : concise biographies of commanders and operational histories of regiments, with bibliographies of published and primary sources / John C. Fredriksen ; foreword by Richard V. Barbuto.
    p.   cm.
  Includes bibliographical references and index.

  ISBN 978-0-7864-4143-3
  softcover : 50# alkaline paper ∞

  1. United States — History — War of 1812. 2. United States — History — War of 1812 — Biography. 3. United States. Army — Biography. 4. United States — History — War of 1812 — Sources — Bibliography. 5. United States. Army — History — 19th century — Sources — Bibliography. 6. United States. Army — History — 19th century. I. Title.
  E354.F74   2009
  973.5′242 — dc22   2009012377

British Library cataloguing data are available

©2009 John C. Fredriksen. All rights reserved

No part of this book may be reproduced or transmitted in any form or by any means, electronic or mechanical, including photocopying or recording, or by any information storage and retrieval system, without permission in writing from the publisher.

Cover image: 25th U.S. Infantry, 1813 ©2009 Historical Art Prints

Manufactured in the United States of America

McFarland & Company, Inc., Publishers
  Box 611, Jefferson, North Carolina 28640
    www.mcfarlandpub.com

To Mr. Madison's warriors

Table of Contents

Foreword by Richard V. Barbuto   1
Preface and Acknowledgments   5

COMMANDER-IN-CHIEF   9
SECRETARIES OF WAR   15
MAJOR GENERALS   29
BRIGADIER GENERALS   70
VARIOUS DEPARTMENTS   153
ARTILLERY   161
CAVALRY   179
ENGINEERS   187
INFANTRY   193
RIFLES   280

Archival and Manuscript Depositories   291
Index   299

Foreword

by Richard V. Barbuto

Years of perceived insults, interference and, indeed, an armed clash on territorial waters persuaded Congress to declare war upon the British empire in June 1812. President Madison expected that the seizure of Montreal in Canada would convince Britain to cease impressing American seaman and to quit arming hostile natives on America's frontier. The "War Hawks," the ardent supporters of a war with Britain within Congress, clearly understood that the minuscule American regular army was not up to the task of invading a foreign land. In January 1812, Congress and the President began an enormous expansion of regular forces. Prior to the expansion, the army was comprised of eleven regiments of infantry, rifles, light dragoons and artillery. From that January onward throughout the war years, Congress added forty-five more regiments of all arms, an increase of more than 400 percent.

Authorizing an increase was one thing; finding officers and men to flesh out these new formations was quite another. Hundreds of young men, motivated by the tales of glory of the Revolutionary generation and anxious to likewise make their mark in the world, applied for commissions as officers in the new units. While some had military experience or training, most did not. The secretary of war and the president chose potential officer candidates for military and sent nominees to the Congress for approval. The successful acquired uniforms, swords, and equipment and traveled to their rendezvous points or began the task of recruiting the men to fill their companies.

Young men, lured by the potential for adventure or to make a living and motivated at least in part by the promise of land and money at the end of their enlistment, responded to martial music and patriotic speeches. Slowly and in small numbers, these citizens mustered into federal service and began the arduous training and socialization to become American soldiers. These partially trained and equipped troops were led by inexperienced officers and generals of mixed quality, and they marched into the Canadas in an attempt to force Britain to treat the United States as a sovereign power. The results were either disastrous or farcical.

Detroit and much of the Michigan Territory were lost in a matter of weeks. The debacle at Queenstown Heights was heart-breaking. Generals Henry Dearborn and Alexander Smyth made lamentable, even laughable, attempts to gain toeholds in British territory. However, throughout the failures, natural leaders emerged. Slowly, and not without shortcomings and continued defeat on the battlefield, these leaders shaped their companies and regiments into effective fighting forces. By 1814, many Americans regiments were trained, hardened, and the equal of British forces in North America. True, the American regiments did not equal the centuries-long tradition of the British counterparts. Yet, somehow, unit cohesion and pride and an unwillingness to yield emerged and exhibited itself on battlefields such as Chippewa, Lundy's Lane, Fort Erie, Plattsburgh, and New Orleans. One anecdote is both inspiring yet typical of the American units after two years of struggle and suffering.

When in his thirties, Jarvis Frary Hanks recorded his wartime exploits as a teen-aged drummer boy for his family and friends. Hanks served in the 11th Infantry, a regiment recruited in Vermont that saw hot action in the last year of the war. The 11th was part of Winfield Scott's famed brigade which served in Jacob Brown's renowned Left Division. At Lundy's Lane, Scott marched the 11th and two other regiments directly into a maelstrom of British artillery and musketry. The combatants exchanged furious fire. As a regimental musician, Hanks stood close by the regimental color party, the officers and non-commissioned officers charged with holding high the regimental flags.

Hanks reminded his readers, "It is one of the first objects of contending armies, to break the centres of regiments and lines, and thus throw them into confusion. This is done as effectively as any other way, by aiming at the colors, which are stationed in the centre of their respective regiments." Hanks went on to tell the story of his regimental flag and color party. "During this engagement, nine different persons were shot down, under this flag, successively. At last, this sergeant Festus Thompson, took it and threw its proud folds to the breeze. He was wounded in the hip, and the staff was severed into splinters in his hand. But he again grasped it by the stump, and waved it triumphantly over how own, and his fellow soldiers' heads, until the close of the battle."

Thompson's bravery, while extraordinary, was certainly not unique. The American soldier of the War of 1812 exhibited gallantry and physical courage not unlike his peers in the Revolution, the Civil War, and the World Wars, yet the formations that fought these other conflicts are far and away better documented than those of 1812–1815. Morgan's Riflemen, the 54th Massachusetts, the Stonewall Brigade, the Lost Battalion, the Screaming Eagles, the Third Army, all enjoy certain acclaim, even celebrity. The stories of the regiments and leaders of the Second War of Independence, however, have largely remained untold. There are fine operational histories to be sure, stirring narratives of battles and campaigns. But regimental histories are few and far between. One of the problems has been a lack of foundational research guides. *The United States Army in the War of 1812* fills that need.

Virtually every regiment that fought in the Civil War has its history recorded. However, fewer than 5 percent of War of 1812 regiments are documented in a scholarly, comprehensive fashion. The work of more than three decades, *The United States Army in the War of 1812* provides the researcher with a treasure trove of archival, manuscript, and secondary sources which are the fundamental basis for units' histories that need to be shared. John C. Fredriksen has also provided much-needed biographical data on the president, the commander-in-chief, his secretaries of war, and his generals. Dr. Fredriksen's painstaking attention to detail is evident on every page, as his is obvious dedication to America's fighting men.

The United States Army in the War of 1812 rounds out a trilogy of Fredriksen's powerful reference works. *Free Trade and Sailors' Rights* (1985) remains the foremost bibliography of the conflict and *War of 1812 Eyewitness Accounts* (1997) lists a host of published primary sources from American, British, and Canadian participants. Armed with these potent research tools, the historian can craft comprehensive narratives that chronicle the military formations which were home to tens of thousands who came forward to defend their country. Mr. Madison's warriors, perhaps; America's finest, for certain.

Richard V. Barbuto is the deputy director of the Department of Military History at the U.S. Army Command and General Staff College at Fort Leavenworth, Kansas. He is also the author of *Niagara 1814: America Invades Canada* (2000).

Preface and Acknowledgments

One of the most enduring anomalies of War of 1812 historiography is the near-complete lack of studies on the U.S. Army, either as a fighting instrument or a social institution. Compared to that vast body of literature on America's military establishment during the Civil War or World War II, this lacuna is as puzzling as it is glaring. The state militias of this period, which constitute the bulk of manpower assembled for the war effort, have also been better covered, with several excellent essays and monographs extant. Recently, detailed campaign studies have also emerged from authors on both sides of the border, and which perform useful work highlighting our appreciation and comprehension of the many variables at play on the field of battle. Nonetheless, as far as the regular army is concerned, historians and students of this conflict still contend with a handful of relatively recent articles on recruitment trends, officer appointees, and uniforms, with little else. Analytical discourse as it applies to regiments, supply, training, equipping, combat, and biographies of military leaders remains relatively unexplored. The apparent lack of interest on the part of the historical community, however, is somewhat easy to fathom: the War of 1812 was hardly a successful conflict and, in a strictly military context, usually downright vexing. Simply put, who wants to dwell on defeat, particularly those of the most embarrassing variety? Moreover, ever since the first decades of the 20th century, the best and most erudite research invariably focused itself upon politics, ideology, or diplomacy. Non-military historians seem to blithely ignore the reality that the War of 1812 was, first and foremost, *a war*, not a social, political, or diplomatic abstraction. It is hoped that the approaching bicentennial in 2012, coupled with the invariable wave of revisionism such events engender, will stimulate new military inquiries and afford the U.S. Army the coverage it lacks and so richly deserves. To devotees of this conflict, it is a debt of obligation we owe "Mr. Madison's Warriors."

Why study the army from this war when there are other, larger, and more successful events in its aftermath? I maintain that the War of 1812 was a rite of passage for the U.S. Army, for reasons political as much as military. It entered that conflict after years of supine neglect from the Jeffersonian Republicans, was committed to battle while still raw and untested, and suffered accordingly. Two years of embarrassing setbacks and humiliations lapsed before the hard and unforgiving school of war weeded out incompetents at every level of command, while laying the groundwork for greater military competence. These improvements, highly touted in the history books, were a necessary change but occurred far too late to greatly alter the course of events. They did, however, occasion some impressive battlefield performances which were a far cry from the halting efforts of 1812–1813. Scant consolation, perhaps, in light of the greater strategic failure, but still a welcome boost to military and national morale.

So, in a very direct sense, the army's experience in the War of 1812 stimulated the rise of military professionalism in the postwar period, and bequeathed to the fledgling force meaningful traditions of victory that it heretofore lacked. These lessons, painfully accrued and fully inculcated, were essential for creating the more potent military machine that triumphed in 1846–1848, and even 1861–1865. Equally important was belated recognition, by both the political establishment and the American polity in general, that cherished notions regarding state militias were dangerously unrealistic when pitted against adversaries of the caliber of Great Britain, and required dramatic revamping. True, victories like the Thames and New Orleans did much to salvage and perpetuate the militia myth but, after 1815, the nation was demonstrably more at ease with its standing military establishment. However small by European standards, regulars gradually supplanted state levies as the nation's first line of defense — something unthinkable before 1812. In sum, the lessons accrued during the Revolutionary War had been quickly forgotten; after the War of 1812, these same lessons, painfully relearned at considerable cost, were finally absorbed by the national polity and occasioned far more rational policies respecting the army and its central role in national defense.

Despite a fair share of setbacks, the U.S. Army did produce some outfits and leaders worthy of attention and study. The 2nd and 3rd Regiments of Artillery, the 11th, 21st, and 25th Regiments of Infantry, and the Regiment of Riflemen all emerged as superb combat formations, equal or surpassing many European counterparts. The Corps of Engineers, itself a nascent clan, likewise performed with a consummate professionalism that belied its minuscule numbers. In terms of military leadership, the initial senior cadre can best be described as ossified, but men like Jacob J. Brown, Winfield Scott, and Andrew

Jackson afford ample proof that the Jeffersonian military system could produce outstanding combat leaders. Recent books on these figures abound, while accomplished officers such as George Izard, Eleazar W. Ripley, Joseph G. Swift, and Alexander Macomb await biographical coverage of their own. Lesser lights such as Joseph Bloomfield, Thomas Flournoy, and Thomas Parker also beg attention. Such a rich and varied field afford excellent lines of inquiry for enterprising graduate students and historians alike, and would go far in promoting a fuller picture of the military equation as it manifested in 1812–1815. May the gauntlet be picked up soon, and in earnest.

The book you hold is the product of 33 years of painstaking work, and is specifically designed to facilitate the kind of research so lacking in this field. It is a hand-crafted assemblage of archival, manuscript, printed primary, and secondary sources, all carefully organized and arrayed to impart a maximum of information within the barest minimum of space. Thus disposed, it is now possible for researchers and students to quickly identify the requisite empirical evidence, along with the most recent secondary texts, needed to compose studies on the commander-in-chief, his secretaries of war, major generals, brigadier generals, various departments, artillery, cavalry, engineers, infantry, or riflemen. The archival and manuscript sections are delineated by corporate authorship, the nature of the materials, their holding depository, and their call number, dates, and selected information where possible.

Uniformity is stressed throughout with two important exceptions: manuscripts are listed alphabetically by author and archival information for regiments is listed alphabetically by institution. The end product is a very useful cross section of primary and published materials available for prospective researchers. Regrettably, the listing is not yet definitive. Constraints on time prevented the author from extended stays at the Lilly Library, Indiana University, Clements Library, University of Michigan, and the Burton Historical Collection, Detroit Public Library, where many more individual letters reside; several significant entries from these institutions are listed but more work remains to be done. Perhaps a second edition can be expanded to include such materials.

The author extends thanks to his distinguished colleague Richard V. Barbuto for providing a useful foreword to this book, and to noted War of 1812 scholar Donald R. Hickey for reviewing the manuscript. Readers are also indebted to Kelly M. Kennington of the Perkins Library, Duke University, for her help in tracking down individual letters at the splendid facility. David Haugaard of the Historical Society of Pennsylvania and Olga Tsapina of the Huntington Library also performed yeoman work in this regard. Finally, I acknowledge Donald E. Graves and Rene Chartrand for granting me access to their own unpublished manuscript on the U.S. Army, 1812–1815, a useful compilation whose time has come. If the present effort assists those pursuing the military establishment of this conflict, and promotes meaningful historical coverage of the same, it has exceeded the author's fondest expectations. Should it do justice to a lost generation of American soldiery, the historical flotsam of a long-neglected conflict, I am all the more grateful.

COMMANDER-IN-CHIEF

James Madison

James Madison was born in Port Conway, Virginia, on March 16, 1751, the son of a planter. He passed through the College of New Jersey (Princeton University) in 1771, developed an interest in politics, and in 1776, won a seat at the Virginia Convention, where he helped compose the new Virginia Constitution and Bill of Rights. Madison, diminutive physically but intellectually intense, subsequently played a pivotal role in United States history by attending the Constitutional Convention in Philadelphia in 1787, and promulgating the so-called "Virginia Plan," for stronger, centralized governance. This document became the intellectual framework for the new U. S. Constitution, and he has been hailed as the architect ever since. Madison gradually sided with fellow Virginian Thomas Jefferson during the ideologically-charged political battles of the 1790s, becoming an exponent of strict constitutional constructionalism to restrain federal power. He subsequently served as Jefferson's secretary of state during a period of increasing friction with both Great Britain and Napoleonic France, primarily stemming from their harassment of American shipping at sea. Madison supported Jefferson's economic coercion to outright war to curtail these abuses but no measure, including the famous "embargo," could force England to relent. After 1809, these excesses continued into Madison's first term as president, despite a series of well-intentioned bills and agreements aimed at the British government which, again, came to naught. Especially galling to Madison was their practice of impressment, whereby the Royal Navy boarded American vessels at sea, then culled their crews for possible "deserters" and service aboard His Majesty's warships. Resentment at home crested in the election of the 12th, or "War Congress," in the fall of 1811, whereby peaceful coercion gave way to demands for war to avenge national honor. Madison, though pacifistic by nature, did little to discourage the political machinations and heated nationalistic rhetoric of many Southern and Western politicians over the following

President James Madison. The Colonial Williamsburg Foundation; gift of Mrs. George S. Robbins.

six months, and on June 18, 1812, having exhausted all avenues of negotiation, he agreed to the first declared war under the Constitution. As daunting a prospect this posed to Madison, the notion of submission to Great Britain, and its inherent threat to republicanism, was worse. Ironically, the British Orders in Council, which Madison cited in his war message as an underlying cause for war, would be repealed by the British government on June 23, five days after the declaration.

Rarely has a commander-in-chief gone to war with the national polity in such fractious disarray, for sectionalism and factionalism were rife. The Federalists, largely centered in New England, stridently opposed renewed conflict with Great Britain and did everything within their power to compromise military efforts aimed at invading Canada. Madison's own Republicans were likewise riven by strife, with northern party members coalescing around former New York governor DeWitt Clinton in the fall of 1812 in an attempt to deny the Madison presidency. Only Southern Republicans evinced interest in seizing and possibly incorporating Canada into the union as a possible outcome of the war, although they were equally fixated upon the Spanish domain of Florida. But the biggest obstacle to success in the War of 1812, from start to finish, proved the sheer military unpreparedness of the country. Republican dogma looked askance at standing professional forces on the European model, holding them to be a threat to personal liberty, and instead placed greater emphasis on state militias and volunteer forces as the bulk of national defense. However, both the army and the militia had suffered from the neglect and economy of the Jeffersonians, and were wretchedly trained and equipped. The searing experience of war and several humiliating defeats gradually removed the deadwood from the officer corps and, by 1814, American forces had acquired the veneer of professionalism but, once Napoleon had been vanquished, the British were deploying thousands of crack troops for service in North America. The most startling example of Republican military ineptitude occurred in August 1814 when 4,000 British professionals routed twice their number of militia at Bladensburg, Maryland, whereupon the national capital was occupied and burned. This single act underscored a decade of Jeffersonian unpreparedness and also represents the nadir of Madison's political fortunes. Fortunately, the nation was buoyed by a string of defensive victories at Plattsburgh and Baltimore while American peace negotiators in Europe, heartened by the good news, stood fast against any territorial concessions based on conquest. Fortuitously, their British counterparts, facing an explosive situation at the Congress of Vienna, decided it was time to end the American sideshow and concentrate on more threatening matters closer to home. The resulting Treaty of Ghent, signed December 24, 1814, was in many ways a Christmas present to the young republic, for it ended the War of 1812 on the basis of *status quo antebellum*, and sans concessions or reparations. Ironically, impressment and other maritime issues, major causes for the war, went unmentioned. Furthermore, General Andrew Jackson landed a black eye at New Orleans that was as spectacular as it was unexpected, which further boosted national morale. The fact that the war's largest battle unfolded three weeks after the peace treaty had been signed wilted in the face of the hoopla it engendered.

Human memory being a selective thing, Americans basically overlooked the humiliations of the previous two years and embraced the recent conflict as a kind of moral victory over a blustering bully. National relief became enmeshed with a joyous, almost irrational sense that the United States had "won," after all. This afterglow ushered a period of intense nationalism and political unity lacking in the prewar period, which entered the political lexicography as the "Era of Good Feelings." This was a far cry from popular perceptions of only a few months previously, when the president was mockingly lampooned as "Poor Jemmy," and his conflict derided as "Mr. Madison's War." Madison, for his part, was rehabilitated politically in the afterglow and ended his presidency on a high note in 1817 by passing the torch to James Monroe, the third and final member of the "Virginia dynasty."

Whatever the political course and ramifications of the War of 1812 it was, in military parlance, a brush with disaster. By the conflict's end Canada lay unconquered, the nation's capital was in ruins, and the Royal Navy gripped the nation's economy in a stranglehold. A fair portion of this misfortune can be ascribed to Madison's halting performance as commander-in-chief. As father of the constitution and a strict constructionist, he felt strongly that executive leadership was based on a partnership with Congress. However, he did send numerous recommendations to Congress and tried prodding them into compliance. Yet, Madison seemed more or less unwilling to exercise the command prerogatives required of national leadership during wartime. Shackled by his own constitutional scruples, he declined to press the political establishment to do more. Madison, given his intellectually detached proclivities, basically remained aloof from the process and was highly dependent upon his secretaries and political allies to get things done. Moreover, the president's cabinet was beset by incompetence and internecine feuding that mirrored the entire war effort. His first secretary of war, the amiable Dr. William Eustis, was forced from office after a string of disasters that marked the first six months of the war. His successor, John Armstrong of New York, was marginally more competent, but he harbored presidential aspirations of his own and openly feuded with the secretary of state, James Monroe. Worse still, Armstrong allowed military actions to drift westward and away from strategic Lower Canada, where a quick military strike in overwhelming force may have proven decisive. All told, the war at the cabinet level was a litany of mismanagement and strategic misdirection that made any projected conquest of Canada by undermanned and poorly trained American forces, already difficult, virtually impossible. Few nations had embarked on war so unprepared as the United States in 1812; fewer still escaped the consequences so lightly. Madison, nominally America's least successful commander in chief, emerged for better or for worse with his efficacy intact. He retired from political life and reposed on his farm at Montpelier, Virginia, serving as an elder statesman until his death there on June 28, 1836. Hailed as the "Last of the Founding Fathers," Madison remains best known and justly celebrated as progenitor of the U.S. Constitution; his missteps during the first war waged under that seminal document are seldom mentioned.

Manuscript

Madison, James. Letters. Alderman Library. #2988, Madison Family Papers; 1812–1815.
Madison, James. Papers. Alderman Library. Box 1; 1812–1815.
Madison, James. Papers. Alderman Library. #1661, James and Dolley Madison Papers.
Madison, James. Papers. Chicago Historical. James Madison Papers; 1812–1815.
Madison, James. Letters. Chicago Historical. Edward Coles Papers, personal secretary.
Madison, James. Letters. Gilder Lehrman. 1812–1815.
Madison, James. Papers. Historical Society (Pa). 2 bound volumes; 1812–1815.
Madison, James. Letters. Historical Society (Pa). Daniel Parker Papers, Box 4, 5, 16.
Madison, James. Letters. Historical Society (Pa). Jones Papers, naval affairs, 1813–1814.
Madison, James. Letter, 1813. Houghton Library. Autograph file; to Gov. William Plumer.
Madison, James. Papers. Library of Congress. James Madison Papers; 1812–1815.
Madison, James. Letters. Library of Congress. Misc. Mss. 3649, Key-Cutts-Turner Papers.
Madison, James. Letters. Library of Congress. William Eustis Papers; 1812.
Madison, James. Letters. Library of Congress. James A. Bayard Papers; 1812–1815.
Madison, James. Letters. Library of Congress. Misc. Mss. 094, William Lowndes Papers.
Madison, James. Letter, 1813. Manuscript and Archives. Mss 1095, Van Sinderin Collection.
Madison, James. Letters. Massachusetts Historical. Cutts-Madison Papers; 1812–1814.
Madison, James. Letters. Massachusetts Historical. Thomas Jefferson Papers; 1812–1815.
Madison, James. Letters. Morristown National. Micro. Reel 33, 776–782; 1812–1814.
Madison, James. Letters. Mudd Library. CO0037, Edward Coles Papers; 1812–1815.
Madison, James. Letters. Mudd Library. CO0082, Crane Collection; 1812–1814.
Madison, James. Letters. New York Historical. Albert Gallatin Papers; 1812–1815.
Madison, James. Letters. New York Public. James Monroe Papers; 1812–1815.
Madison, James. Papers. New York Public. Box 2; 1812–1814.
Madison, James. Letter, 1814. New York Public. James Barbour Papers.
Madison, James. Letter, 1814. Perkins Library. William H. Crawford Papers.
Madison, James. Letters. Swem Library. Edward Coles Papers; Madison's secretary.

Printed Primary

Rutland, Robert A., et al., eds. *The Papers of James Madison*. 16 vols. Charlottesville: University Press of Virginia, 1994–.

Select Secondary

Brant, Irving. *James Madison: Commander in Chief, 1812–1836.* Indianapolis: Bobbs-Merrill, 1961.

Craughwell, Thomas J. *Failures of the Presidents: From the Whiskey Rebellion to the War of 1812 to the Bay of Pigs to the Iran Contra Affair.* Beverly, Mass.: Fair Winds Press, 2008.

Hickey, Donald R. *The War of 1812: A Forgotten Conflict.* Urbana: University of Illinois Press, 1989.

McAuley, R. Bryan. "President James Madison and the War Congress of 1812." Unpublished master's thesis, Southwest Texas State University, 1995.

Rutland, Robert A. *The Presidency of James Madison.* Lawrence: University Press of Kansas, 1990.

Smith, Aaron E. "Into the Great White North: American Strategy and Objectives in the War of 1812." Unpublished master's thesis, Temple University, 2000.

Stagg, J. C. A. *Mr. Madison's War: Politics, Diplomacy, and Warfare in the Early American Republic, 1783–1830.* Princeton: Princeton University Press, 1983.

Stagg, J. C. A. "James Madison and George Mathews: The East Florida Revolution of 1812 Reconsidered." *Diplomatic History* 30, no. 1 (2006): 23–55.

SECRETARIES OF WAR

William Eustis

William Eustis was born in Cambridge, Massachusetts, on June 10, 1753, the son of a noted physician. He graduated from Harvard College at the age of 19 and studied medicine under the celebrated Dr. Joseph Warren. Eustis sided with the Patriots when the Revolutionary War commenced in 1775 and fought at Bunker Hill as a voluntary surgeon. He served in this capacity until the end of the war, then opened up a successful practice of his own. In 1786–1787, Eustis again took to the field as an army surgeon during Shays's Rebellion, during which time he developed an appetite for politics. In 1788 he gained a seat in the state legislature and subsequently served two terms in the U.S. House of Representatives as a Democratic-Republican. He was finally defeated by Federalist stalwart Josiah Quincy in 1804, but his party proclivities were noted by President James Madison, who appointed him secretary of war to succeed Henry Dearborn on March 7, 1809. Madison did so out of concern to shore up Republican support in Federalist-dominated New England, so Eustis's actual qualifications for the post were not deemed essential. As an administrator, he was sincere and diligent, but lacked meaningful military experience. Like his predecessor, he pursued frugality to extremes and eliminated such innovations as the army's only horse artillery team on account of expense. On the other hand, he was cognizant of enlarging the military establishment in light off escalating tensions with England, and in 1810 he advocated raising a force of 30,000 volunteers to augment the small standing army. He also recognized the need for artillerists and riflemen to compliment the regulars, and suggested recruiting 6,000 for the new force. Eustis next perceived the necessity for overhauling existing functions of the War Department and, on the very cusp of renewed hostilities, made known his desire to create a superintendent of ordnance, a commissary general, and a quartermaster general's department. Congress did, in fact, pass legislation creating these departments in the spring of 1812, but these could neither be

Secretary of War William Eustis. Metropolitan Museum of Art, bequest of Eustis Langdon Hopkins, 1945 (46.28).

adequately staffed nor their procedures and authority clearly defined before the hostilities commenced that June.

In the absence of a commanding general, Eustis and his eight clerks at the War Department became responsible for juggling the manpower, combat, and logistical considerations of nine military districts. The last six months of his tenure in office were a litany of major and minor disasters, although the ineptitude of American generalship in the field was equally culpable. The fall of Mackinac, Fort Dearborn, and Detroit, coupled with a stinging defeat at Queenston Heights and a stumbling attempt against Montreal, caused a public uproar and politicians called for his resignation. Madison, however, loyally clung to his secretary until the fall elections, after which both the president and the secretary felt that the needs of the nation would be better served by his departure. Eustis accordingly resigned on December 3, 1812, only to be replaced by the politically ambitious John Armstrong. In 1814 Madison appointed him minister plenipotentiary to the Netherlands, where he remained until 1818. That year he returned home, successfully stood for a seat in Congress, and in 1823 gained election as governor of Massachusetts. Eustis died in office on February 6, 1825, a talented, congenial, and moderate political figure of some merit, but untrained and unsuited for high-level, military decision making.

Archival

Military District No. 1. Order book. Boston Public. **C.33.15; 1812.
RG107. Letters. National Archives. Secretary of War's Office; 1812.

Manuscript

Eustis, William. Letters. Alderman Library. 10029-c, Richard Cutts Papers; 1813–1814.
Eustis, William. Letter, 1812. Connecticut Historical. Ms 8413, New London fortifications.
Eustis, William. Letters. Chicago Historical. James Wilkinson Papers; 1812.
Eustis, William. Letters. Danvers Archival. PR/PO/C, Moses Porter Papers.
Eustis, William. Letters. Historical Society (Pa). Parker Papers, Box 10, 23, 25, 26, 28, 33, 40.
Eustis, William. Letters. Historical Society (Pa). Richard Rush Papers; 1812.
Eustis, William. Letters, 1812. Houghton Library. bMS Am 1569.6 (30,72); Hull, Dearborn.
Eustis, William. Letters. Indiana Historical. Arthur G. Mitten Collection; 1812.
Eustis, William. Papers. Library of Congress. William Eustis Papers; 1808–1812.
Eustis, William. Letters. Library of Congress. William H. Harrison Papers; 1811–1812.
Eustis, William. Letters. Library of Congress. Anthony Lamb Papers; 1812.
Eustis, William. Letters. Library of Congress. James Madison Papers; 1811–1814.
Eustis, William. Letters. Library of Congress. William Eustis Papers; 1812.
Eustis, William. Letters. Library of Virginia. 41557, James Barbour Papers; 1812.
Eustis, William. Letter, 1812. Lilly Library. To Henry Dearborn on diversionary move.
Eustis, William. Letter, 1812. Manuscript and Archives. Mss 783, Joseph Wheaton Papers.
Eustis, William. Letters. Massachusetts Historical. Eustis-Langdon; 1812–1813.
Eustis, William. Letters. Massachusetts Historical. Henry Dearborn Papers.
Eustis, William. Letters. Massachusetts Historical. W. Eustis Papers, 1812–1814.

Eustis, William. Letter, 1812. Massachusetts Historical. Norcross; to Henry Dearborn.
Eustis, William. Letters. Massachusetts Historical. C.E. French; June–December, 1812.
Eustis, William. Letter, 1812. New York Historical. Misc Mss P, to William Plumer.
Eustis, William. Letters. New York Historical. Henry Dearborn letter books; 1812.
Eustis, William. Letter, 1812. New York Historical. Gallatin 1812 #119A, Detroit surrender.
Eustis, William. Letters. New York Historical. Misc Mss E, to Henry Dearborn; 1812.
Eustis, William. Letters. Oberlin College. Nos. 8, 9, 10, Orrin June Collection, 1812.
Eustis, William. Letters. Ohio Historical. Vol. 1232, Fort Fayette Letter book, 1812.
Eustis, William. Letter, 1812. Perkins Library. William Eustis Papers.
Eustis, William. Letter, 1812. Perkins Library. Campbell family Papers.

Printed Primary

American State Papers. Military Affairs. 2 vols. Washington, D.C.: Gales and Seaton, 1832–1861.
Carter, Clarence E., ed. *The Territorial Papers of the United States: Vol. VI, The Territory of Mississippi, 1809–1817.* Washington, D.C.: Government Printing Office, 1938.
Carter, Clarence E., ed. *The Territorial Papers of the United States: Vol. VIII, The Territory of Indiana, 1810–1816.* Washington, D.C.: Government Printing Office, 1939.
Carter, Clarence E., ed. *The Territorial Papers of the United States: Vol. X, The Territory of Michigan, 1805–1820.* Washington, D.C.: Government Printing Office, 1942.
Carter, Clarence E., ed. *The Territorial Papers of the United States: Vol. XIV, The Territory of Louisiana-Missouri, 1806–1814.* Washington, D.C.: Government Printing Office, 1949.
Carter, Clarence E., ed. *The Territorial Papers of the United States: Vol. XVI, The Territory of Illinois, 1809–1814.* Washington, D.C.: Government Printing Office, 1948.

Select Secondary

Ayres, I. "Sketch of William Eustis, M. D., 1753–1825." *New England Magazine* 15 (February 1897): 749–754.
Jacobs, James R. *The Beginnings of the U. S. Army, 1783–1812.* Princeton: Princeton University Press, 1947.
Porter, G. W. "A Sketch of the Life and Character of the Late William Eustis." *Lexington Historical Society Proceedings* 1 (1890): 101–109.
Stagg, J. C. A. *Mr. Madison's War: Politics, Diplomacy, and Warfare in the Early American Republic, 1783–1830.* Princeton: Princeton University Press, 1983.
White, Leonard D. *The Jeffersonians: A Study in Administrative History.* New York: Macmillan, 1951.

John Armstrong

John Armstrong was born in Carlisle, Pennsylvania, on November 25, 1758, the son of a noted Indian fighter. He attended the College of New Jersey (Princeton University) for two years before the onset of the Revolutionary War in 1775 prompted him to enlist in the Continental Army. An attentive soldier, he served as aide-de-camp to General Hugh Mercer at Trenton and Princeton, then joined the staff of General Horatio Gates in time for his victorious Saratoga campaign of 1777. Armstrong was not present during Gates's debacle at Camden in 1780, and by 1782 he was serving at Newburgh, New York, awaiting a discharge. It was here that Armstrong revealed his uncanny knack for intrigue by penning the so-called "Newburgh Addresses," which anonymously called upon the Continental Army to coerce Congress over the issue of back pay. The matter became serious enough to warrant General George Washington's personal intervention before it subsided, and Armstrong's authorship, when it became known, forever branded him as an intriguer. After the war he served in the Pennsylvania legislature before relocating to New York, joined the Democratic-Republicans, and campaigned on behalf of Thomas Jefferson in 1800. Armstrong also served as a U.S. Senator from New York until 1804, when Jefferson appointed him ambassador to France. There he clashed with Napoleon over the latter's seizures of American shipping, which were quite as rapacious as the British. When he resigned from the post in 1810, Armstrong strongly recommended that the United States declare war on both France and England.

After the War of 1812 commenced in June 1812, Armstrong was touted by Republican Governor Daniel D. Tompkins and President James Madison appointed him an army brigadier general on July 6, 1812. He commanded the defenses of New York City for six months until the resignation of Secretary of War William Eustis prompted Madison, who needed to shore up his political support in New York, to nominate Armstrong as a replacement. Armstrong, who fancied himself a military expert and harbored presidential ambitions of his own, welcomed the appointment over the objections of Secretary of State James Monroe, who was a bitter personal rival. Moreover, Armstrong's pungent personality and imperious demeanor militated against him in political circles and he had surfeit of enemies. The senate nonetheless confirmed him on January 13, 1813, and he immediately went to work overhauling the War Department. In this respect, Armstrong was a distinct improvement over his predecessor, and he authorized compilation of the *Rules and Regulations of the Army* to bring about uniform procedures. He then divided the country up into nine, self-contained military districts to better promote smoother, more efficient administration. He also established the nucleus of a general staff by creating a quartermaster department, refining the adjutant general's department, and re-instituting the inspector general's office. As a military strategist, however, Armstrong proved an intrusive influence by constantly meddling in his generals' matters, allowing the war effort to drift westward towards Niagara instead of against Montreal or even Kingston, and treating the capable General William Henry Harrison so shabbily that he resigned from command. Armstrong then filled the vacancy with militia general Andrew Jackson without first securing Madison's approval. In the fall of 1813 Armstrong also grossly erred by allowing two vitriolic adversaries, James Wilkinson and Wade Hampton, to jointly command the ill-fated St. Lawrence expedition. Armstrong compounded the problems by personally venturing to Sacketts Harbor to confer with Wilkinson and superimposing his strategic vision on its operations. This muddled, divided endeavor collapsed at the defeats of Chateauguay and Crysler's farm, whereupon a torrent of criticism about his leadership arose. Though increasingly isolated within Madison's inner circle, Armstrong continued in office over the next ten months for want of someone better to replace him.

In the spring of 1814, Armstrong made his single-most important contribution to the war effort by appointing a bevy of younger, more vigorous generals to replace the politically-appointed deadwood of the past two years. Among them were George Izard, Jacob Jennings Brown, and Andrew Jackson as major generals, with Winfield Scott, Eleazar Wheelock Ripley, Edmund Pendleton Gaines, Alexander Macomb, Daniel Bissell, and Thomas Adams Smith serving as brigadiers. All of these leaders wielded significant impact on subsequent military events, with many performing valuable service up through the Antebellum period, four decades hence. Armstrong's strategic grasp, however, remained muddled as ever and, once again, he allowed the war effort to drift from Kingston and launched Brown on the spectacular, if futile, Niagara campaign. Worse yet, in August 1814, he directed General Izard's army away from Plattsburgh to reinforce Brown, just as Governor-general Sir George Prevost was posed to launch a huge invasion of New York from Lower Canada. But Armstrong's biggest miscalculation was his refusal to fortify Washington, D.C., from amphibious attack, under the belief that the capital was too insignificant to be a target. He also opposed Madison's intention to create the new 10th Military District to defend both the capital and Baltimore, Maryland. When General William Henry Winder was selected to com-mand here over Armstrong's choice of General Moses Porter, his behavior became one of sullen uncooperativeness. The seriousness of all these factors was famously underscored at Bladensburg on August 24, 1814, when 4,000 British troops easily stampeded 7,000 militia, then burned all public buildings in the capital. The brooding Armstrong, who had refused to cooperate

Secretary of War John Armstrong. National Portrait Gallery, Smithsonian Institution.

with Winder, was unceremoniously forced to resign and never again held public office. He retired to self-imposed exile at Red Hook, New York, penning vindictive memoirs and castigating his enemies with pointed and poisoned commentary. Armstrong died there on April 1, 1843, a talented polemicist who made important contributions the War of 1812, seemingly in spite of himself.

Archival

Military District No. 1. Order book. Boston Public Library. **C.33.15; 1813–1814.
RG107. Letters. National Archives. Secretary of War's Office; 1813–1814.

Manuscript

Armstrong, John. Letters. Chicago Historical. James Wilkinson Papers; 1813–1814.
Armstrong, John. Letter, 1814. Cincinnati Historical. Mss VF3907; to George Izard.
Armstrong, John. Letters. Danvers Archival. PR/PO/C, Moses Porter Papers.
Armstrong, John. Letters. Hay Library. Russell Papers; 1812–1813.
Armstrong, John. Letters. Historical Society (Pa). Parker Papers, Box 2, 20, 24, 28, 29, 30, 31.
Armstrong, John. Letters. Historical Society (Pa). Irvine Family Papers; 1813–1815.
Armstrong, John. Letter, 1813. Historical Society (Pa). William Jones Papers, Lake Ontario.
Armstrong, John. Letter, 1814. Historical Society (Pa). Gratz Coll., Box 32, to Gov. Isaac Shelby.
Armstrong, John. Letters. Indiana. Historical. Arthur G. Mitten Collection; 1813–1814.
Armstrong, John. Letters. Indiana Historical. No. 34; John Armstrong Papers.
Armstrong, John. Letters. Library of Congress. Folio Volume; 1812–1814.
Armstrong, John. Letters. Library of Congress. 3212, Jacob Brown Papers; 1814.
Armstrong, John. Letters. Library of Congress. James Madison Papers; 1813–1814.
Armstrong, John. Letters. Library of Congress. William H. Harrison Papers; 1813.
Armstrong, John. Letters. Library of Congress. Duncan McArthur Papers; 1814.
Armstrong, John. Letters. Library of Congress. Andrew Jackson Papers; 1814.
Armstrong, John. Letters. Library of Congress. Christopher Van Deventer Papers; prisoner.
Armstrong, John. Letters. Library of Virginia. 41557, James Barbour Papers; 1813–1814.
Armstrong, John. Letters. Lilly Library. 1813–1814.
Armstrong, John. Letters. Manuscripts and Archives. Mss 544, Eli Whitney Papers, 1813–1814.
Armstrong, John. Letter, 1814. Massachusetts Historical. C.E. French; to Dearborn.
Armstrong, John. Letters. Massachusetts Historical. Henry Dearborn Papers; 1813–1814.
Armstrong, John. Letters. Massachusetts Historical. Jacob J. Brown Papers, 1814.
Armstrong, John. Letters. New York Historical. William Astor Chanler Coll., 1812–1815.
Armstrong, John. Letters. New York Historical. Henry Dearborn letter book; 1812–1813.
Armstrong, John. Letters. New York Historical. John W. Taylor Papers; 1813–1814.
Armstrong, John. Letter, 1812. New York Historical. Misc Mss A, to Simon Snyder, militia.
Armstrong, John. Letter, 1814. New York Historical. Rufus King Papers, Vol. 1814–1815, #18.
Armstrong, John. Letters. New York State. Charles K. Gardner Papers; 1813–1815.
Armstrong, John. Letter, 1813. Ohio Historical. VFM654; militia deficiencies to Congress.

Armstrong, John. Letter, 1814. Perkins Library. Campbell Family papers.
Armstrong, John. Letter, 1814. Perkins Library. John Vinton Papers.
Armstrong, John. Letter, 1814. Regenstein Library. Butler-Gunsaulus Collection; to Snyder.
Armstrong, John. Letter, 1814. Rowan College. 973.52 Safe Ms; to Gov. Simon Snyder.
Armstrong, John. Letter, 1813. Virginia Historical. Mss1 P9267 d 7-255 (AL); Preston to 23rd Infantry.

Printed Primary

American State Papers. Military Affairs. 7 vols. Washington, D.C.: Gales and Seaton, 1831–1861. Vol. 1.
Armstrong, John. *Hints to Young Generals.* Kingston, N.Y.: J. Buel, 1812.
Armstrong, John. *Notices of the War of 1812.* 2 vols. New York: Wiley and Putnam, 1840.
Carter, Clarence E., ed. *The Territorial Papers of the United States: Vol. X, The Territory of Michigan, 1805–1820.* Washington, D.C.: Government Printing Office, 1942.
Carter, Clarence E., ed. *The Territorial Papers of the United States: Vol. XIV, The Territory of Louisiana-Missouri, 1806–1814.* Washington, D.C.: Government Printing Office, 1949.
Carter, Clarence E., ed. *The Territorial Papers of the United States: Vol. XVI, The Territory of Illinois, 1809–1814.* Washington, D.C.: Government Printing Office, 1948.

Select Secondary

George, Christopher. *Terror on the Chesapeake: The War of 1812 on the Bay.* Shippensburg, Pa.: White Mane Books, 2000.
Hooks, Jonathan. "A Study of the Rivalry Between James Monroe and John Armstrong." Unpublished master's thesis, East Carolina University, 2002.
Pitch, Anthony. *The Burning of Washington: The British Invasion.* Annapolis, Md.: Naval Institute Press, 1998.
Skeen, C. Edward. *John Armstrong, Jr., 1758–1843: A Biography.* Syracuse: Syracuse University Press, 1981.
Whitehorne, Joseph W. A. *The Battle for Baltimore, 1814.* Baltimore, Md.: Nautical & Aviation Press, 1997.

James Monroe

James Monroe was born in Westmoreland County, Virginia, on April 28, 1758, and he was enrolled at William and Mary College when the Revolutionary War erupted in 1775. He quit school and joined the Continental Army as a lieutenant, fighting with distinction at Harlem, White Plains, Trenton,

Brandywine, Germantown, and Monmouth. He eventually joined the local militia to study law under Thomas Jefferson and was elected to the Continental Congress in 1783. Monroe then settled upon a career in politics, and between 1794 and 1811 he functioned as a Democratic-Republican apparatchik. These included stints as U.S. Envoy to France and Great Britain, and governor of Virginia. In 1808 he campaigned for the presidency against fellow Republican James Madison, lost, and on March 29, 1811, accepted the appointment as his secretary of state. In this capacity he informed British minister Augustus J. Foster that, unless they relented from seizing American vessels and impressing crew members, war would be the inevitable result. These entreaties failed to gain the desired results, so Monroe worked tirelessly behind the scenes to shore up Republican support for renewed conflict with Great Britain. After war arrived on June 18, 1812, Monroe sought out a military commission, but Madison balked at granting him a rank with greater seniority than the generals already extant. The poor performance of the army and the militia led to the resignation of Secretary of War William Eustis in December, 1812, at which point Monroe temporarily filled that post while serving as secretary of state. On February 13, 1814, John Armstrong of New York became the new secretary of war, which set both secretaries on a collision course for the rest of the war. Both men harbored political aspirations for the White House and Armstrong and Monroe evinced a thinly veiled contempt for each other. The former went so far as to actively deny the latter a military commission or any chance for distinction in the field. In August, 1814, British forces landed in Chesapeake Bay, marched on Washington, defeated a large militia force, and humiliated the capital. Monroe was on the battlefield and constantly interfered with the orders of General William Henry Winder, but the political outcry drove Armstrong from office. Short on viable or even willing candidates, Madison again asked Monroe to resume the duties of acting secretary of war on September 14, 1814. The secretary of state, eager to jockey for political advantage, readily acquiesced.

The new secretary's immediate concern was the security of Baltimore, Maryland, and he energetically set about raising troops, coordinating construction efforts, and appointing General Samuel Smith, a militia leader of some repute, to head up the city's defense. The net result convinced the British not to attack the city on September 14, 1814, which, in concert with the repulse of enemy forces at Plattsburgh three days earlier, shored up the nation's diplomatic hand during negotiations at Ghent (modern-day Belgium). Monroe then busied himself with trying to improve and enlarge the U.S. Army, which, despite an authorized strength of 60,000 men, barely mustered half that. Like many Republican elders, he now believed that the party's reflexive reliance upon state levies was impractical, and that only a sizable and well-disciplined

Secretary of War James Monroe. National Gallery of Art.

force of regulars could carry the war into Canada. He the embraced an even bigger political taboo by suggesting a limited form of conscription to flesh out its ranks. The Republican majority in Congress, however, considered this an anathema; that December, despite the presence of Royal Navy forces off the American coast and 30,000 British Peninsula veterans in Canada, they effectively squelched Monroe's plan. The secretary also endured his share of qualms in dealing with General Andrew Jackson. By the fall, Monroe had very good intelligence that the British were embarking on a major expedition against New Orleans and he ordered Jackson to defend that city at all hazards, but the general remained obsessed with a small British force at Pensacola. The single-minded Jackson made no attempt to garrison New Orleans until he first drove the enemy from Pensacola, which was aggressively accomplished, then marched for the defense of that city only days before the enemy appeared in force. Further north, dissatisfaction with the war also culminated in the infamous Hartford Convention, whereby Federalist delegates openly flirted with secession. Monroe firmly responded by dispatching Lieutenant Colonel Thomas S. Jesup and his 25th Infantry to the town, ostensibly for recruiting purposes, but with orders to suppress any attempt at disloyalty. In the spring of 1815, Monroe also held several meetings with the aggressive General Jacob J. Brown, who concurred with the secretary's plan to raise 15,000 regulars and 40,000 volunteers to capture Montreal that fall. The stratagem was completely unrealistic, given the British manpower present, but it demonstrates Monroe's determination to wage offensive war. The effort was made moot by ratification of the Treaty of Ghent on February 16, 1815, and Monroe was succeeded at the War Department by Alexander J. Dallas.

The War of 1812, while a brush with disaster, enhanced Monroe's reputation within the Republican Party and in November 1816 they helped elect him president. He thus became the final member of the "Virginia dynasty," and was also the last Revolutionary War veteran to serve as chief executive. His accomplishments in office closely mirrored his political career in general, being more solid than distinguished. He was reelected in 1820 and gained a measure of fame by enunciating the "Monroe Doctrine" (actually conceived by his secretary of state, John Quincy Adams) which placed the Western Hemisphere off limits to further European colonization. Monroe, last of the so-called "Cocked Hats" due to his predilection for wearing 18th century gentlemen's garb, died in New York City on July 4, 1831. His relatively brief tenures as secretary of war were but footnotes in a long and distinguished public life but, on balance, not without merit.

Archival

RG107. Letters. National Archives. Secretary of War's Office; 1814–1815.

Manuscript

Monroe, James. Letters. Alderman. 10029-c, Richard Cutts Papers; 1812–1815.
Monroe, James. Letter, 1815. Buffalo and Erie. A66-19, to Peter B. Porter, Niagara.
Monroe, James. Papers. Burton Historical.
Monroe, James. Letter, 1813. Cincinnati Historical. Mss VF3094; retaliatory captivity.

Monroe, James. Letters. Danvers Archival. PR/PO/C, Moses Porter Papers.
Monroe, James. Letter, 1815. Gilder Lehrman. GLC05280; Hartford Convention, trouble.
Monroe, James. Letters. Hay Library. Russell Papers; 1811–1814.
Monroe, James. Letter, 1814. Historic New Orleans. William C. Cook Collection.
Monroe, James. Letters. Historical Society (Pa). D. Parker Papers, Box 5, 12, 23, 26, 28, 30.
Monroe, James. Letter, 1813. Historical Society (Pa). Society Collection; quartermaster matters.
Monroe, James. Letter, 1813. Historical Society (Pa). William Jones Papers, Washington a target.
Monroe, James. Letters. James Monroe Museum. 1814.
Monroe, James. Letters. Library of Congress. 3212, Jacob Brown Papers; 1814–1815.
Monroe, James. Letters. Library of Congress. Andrew Jackson Papers; 1814–1815.
Monroe, James. Letters. Library of Congress. James Madison Papers; 1812–1814.
Monroe, James. Letters. Library of Congress. Duncan McArthur Papers; 1814.
Monroe, James. Letters. Library of Congress. James A. Bayard Papers; 1812–1815.
Monroe, James. Letters. Library of Congress. William Eustis Papers; 1812.
Monroe, James. Letters. Library of Congress. 0316u, Samuel Smith Papers; Baltimore.
Monroe, James. Letters. Library of Congress. Christopher Van Deventer Papers; prisoner.
Monroe, James. Letters. Library of Congress. James Madison Papers; 1812–1815.
Monroe, James. Letters. Library of Virginia. 41557, James Barbour Papers, 1814.
Monroe, James. Letters. New York Historical. Albert Gallatin Papers; 1812–1815.
Monroe, James. Notes. New York Historical. Misc Mss Monroe, musings on the war.
Monroe, James. Letter, 1813. New York Historical. Rufus King Papers, Vol. 1810–1813 #101.
Monroe, James. Letters. New York Historical. Thomas Barclay Papers, prisoners; 1813.
Monroe, James. Letter, 1814. New York Historical. Misc Mss M, to Henry Dearborn.
Monroe, James. Papers. New York Public. James Monroe Papers, 1812–1815.
Monroe, James. Letters. New York Public. James Barbour Papers; 1814.
Monroe, James. Letter, 1814. Oberlin Library. No. 61, Orrin June Coll.; caustic comments.
Monroe, James. Letters. Perkins Library. William H. Crawford Papers; 1813–1814.
Monroe, James. Papers. Swem Library. 01/Mss.39.1M75; 1812–1815.

Printed Primary

Carter, Clarence E., ed. *The Territorial Papers of the United States: Vol. X, The Territory of Michigan, 1805–1820.* Washington, D.C.: Government Printing Office, 1942.
Hamilton, Stanislaus M., ed. *The Writings of James Monroe.* 7 vols. New York: G. P. Putnam's Sons, 1898–1903.
Izard, George. *Official Correspondence with the Department of War Relative to Military Operations of the American Army under the Command of Major General Izard on the Northern frontier of the United States in the Years 1814 and 1815.* Philadelphia: Thomas Dobson, 1816.

Preston, Daniel. *A Comprehensive Catalog of the Correspondence and Papers of James Monroe*. Westport, Conn.: Greenwood Press, 2001.

Stacey, Charles P., ed. "An American Plan for a Canadian Campaign: Secretary James Monroe to Major General Jacob Brown, February, 1815." *American Historical Review* 46 (January 1941): 348–358.

Select Secondary

Hooks, Jonathan. "A Study of the Rivalry Between James Monroe and John Armstrong." Unpublished master's thesis, East Carolina University, 2002.

Pitch, Anthony. *The Burning of Washington: The British Invasion*. Annapolis, Md.: Naval Institute Press, 1998.

Whitehorne, Joseph W. A. *The Battle for Baltimore, 1814*. Baltimore, Md.: Nautical & Aviation Press, 1997.

Major Generals

Jacob Jennings Brown

Jacob Jennings Brown was born in Bucks County, Pennsylvania, on May 9, 1775, descended from a long line of Quakers. By turns a teacher, surveyor, and one-time secretary to Alexander Hamilton during the Quasi-War with France, he settled upon land speculating in upstate New York, and also served as a county judge. Highly energetic, Brown became relatively prosperous through smuggling potash into Canada after the Embargo of 1808. Yet, he evinced genuine interest in military affairs and in 1809 he served as a colonel of Jefferson County militia. Brown conducted his affairs ably and two years later he became a brigadier general entrusted with defending a 250-mile strip of land from Sacketts Harbor, on Lake Ontario, to Ogdensburg, down the St. Lawrence River. Brown's first challenge as a war leader came on October 4, 1812, when his cannon and militia easily repulsed a cross-river raid against Ogdensburg by aged Colonel Lethbridge.

A more severe test occurred on May 29, 1813 when Governor-General Sir George Prevost launched a surprise amphibious raid against strategic Sacketts Harbor, home port to Commodore Isaac Chauncey's Lake Ontario squadron. Chauncey being absent at the time, Brown could only summon 500 raw militia and 500 untested regulars for its defense. The British landed 700 battle-hardened veterans, who easily routed the levies and drove the handful of regulars into slap-dash fortifications ringing the harbor. Brown, meanwhile, galloped after his militiamen, insisted they were winning the battle, and led them back against Prevost's left flank just as a series of attacks upon the American blockhouses failed. The governor-general, wary of being cut off from his fleet, hastily sounded the retreat and reembarked for Kingston. As a reward for this dramatic victory, Brown was commissioned a brigadier general in the U.S. Army as of July 19, 1813, and placed in charge of the new 2nd Brigade (15th, 22nd, 23rd Infantries).

Throughout General James Wilkinson's ill-fated St. Lawrence Expedition of 1813, Brown capably spearheaded the army's advance, scouring the river banks of enemy forces. On November 1–2, 1813, he landed artillery and rebuffed an attack by British gunboats at French Creek, New York. Continuing ahead, Brown next drove off a collection of Canadian militia at Hoople's Creek on November 10, 1813. He was thus absent during the debacle at Crysler's Farm, November 11, 1813, and escaped the disgrace heaped on superiors. Brown remained with his troops throughout their difficult winter at French Mills, New York, and worked closely with Dr. James Mann to ameliorate their suffering. Consequently, his good performance came to the attention of Secretary of War John Armstrong, who determined to empower younger, more capable leaders for the war effort. On January 24, 1814, Brown consequently gained promotion to major general and received command of the Left Division, 9th Military District. This small but potent formation ultimately consisted of two army brigades under generals Winfield Scott and Eleazar W. Ripley, and a volunteer brigade commanded by General Peter B. Porter. Brown was cognizant of Scott's abilities as a drillmaster and tasked him with running affairs at Buffalo, New York, while he returned to Sacketts Harbor that April. By the time he reappeared in June, Brown commanded the best-led, best disciplined American army raised in the War of 1812. He now received orders to cross the Niagara River and subdue the Niagara Peninsula as far as York (Toronto). Furthermore, he was led to believe that Commodore Chauncey's powerful squadron would assist him in reducing Fort George and other strong points he encountered along the lake shore. Perhaps Brown felt, in light of his victory at Sacketts Harbor, that the Navy was indebted to the military and would render assistance as needed.

Aggressive Brown crossed into Canada on July 3, 1814, and quickly subdued Fort Erie and its 120-man garrison. Marching northward, he bivouacked below Street's Creek where, on July 5, 1814, his camp was attacked by British forces commanded by Major General Phineas Riall across Chippawa Plain. The Americans, initially surprised, responded adroitly and Scott's brigade defeated Riall's forces in a stiff, standup encounter. Chippawa represented the first time American forces had engaged and bested their more experienced adversaries in an open field, and marks the birthplace of military professionalism in the U.S. Army. A few days later Brown resumed marching north, drove the British into the confines of the peninsula, and besieged Fort George. There he waited in vain for Chauncey to appear and bring him the necessary siege ordnance. Unfortunately, the commodore resented acting as handmaiden to the army so long as the Royal Navy was afoot on Lake Ontario, and refused to cooperate. A disappointed Brown fell back to Chippawa to shore up his lines of communication and possibly lure Riall out into the open to destroy him. Instead, Lieutenant General Gordon Drummond

Major General Jacob J. Brown. Library of Congress.

arrived with British reinforcements on July 25, 1814, and the two forces collided at Lundy's Lane. This proved to be the hardest-fought encounter of the entire war, waged mainly at night. The British battery was stormed and repeated counterattacks were driven off. However, both Brown and Scott were severely injured and General Ripley, who succeeded to command, refused to resume combat operations on the following day. Crestfallen, the Americans subsequently fell back to Fort Erie and entrenched while relations between Brown and Ripley, never cordial, were permanently estranged.

Distrusting Ripley, Brown summoned General Edmund P. Gaines from Sacketts Harbor and appointed him commander at Fort Erie. On August 15, 1814, Gaines bloodily repulsed Drummond's night attack, but a few days later he was seriously injured by a cannon shell and evacuated. Brown, still convalescing, refused to leave Ripley in charge so he hobbled back to personally take charge. Ignoring the pleas of subordinates to cross the army back to New York, he assembled a force of 3,000 militia, secretly ferried them over, and on September 17, 1814, launched a surprise sortie that heavily damaged British siege lines. These losses, combined with worsening weather, finally compelled Drummond to abandon Fort Erie and he drew north of Chippawa Creek and entrenched. Brown, meanwhile, was heartened to learn that General George Izard's Right Division was en route from Plattsburgh to join him. Izard, however, marched cautiously and did not arrive until October. Once at Niagara, Izard ignored Brown's exhortations to storm Drummond's fortifications across Chippawa Creek and the two men haggled over strategy. Brown then left the frontier in disgust and repaired back to Sacketts Harbor. His Niagara campaign proved of little consequence, strategically speaking, but did provide a major psychological boost to the nation, especially in the wake of the capital's destruction. Congress subsequently awarded Brown with a gold medal for his services and he gained renown as a national hero.

Brown remained in the postwar service as commander of the Northern Division, with headquarters at his home in Brownsville, New York. For seven years he capably administered his charge, toured northern fortifications, and helped formulate policies for increasing American security along the western frontier. In 1821, Congress mandated reductions in the military establishment and, following the resignation of General Andrew Jackson, he became senior officer under the title of commanding general of the army. In this capacity, Brown proved instrumental in helping to fashion and implement Secretary of War John C. Calhoun's reform measures. He also served as a military advisor to presidents James Monroe and John Quincy Adams, and labored incessantly to promote harmonious relations between Congress and the military. Despite small budgets and sometimes overt political hostilities towards the army, Brown's combination of tact and common sense usually prevailed. He remained a conspicuous public figure over the next seven years before dying in Washington, D.C., on February 24, 1828.

Brown was the most successful American leader of the War of 1812 in Canada, whose fearless and aggressive leadership earned him a sobriquet as "The Fighting Quaker." He was one of few senior commanders equally adept at leading militia or regulars — or both — in open combat. Ironically, Brown's 14 years as a senior military administrator have been vastly overshadowed by his two years of wartime service but these, long-term, proved equally as productive.

Next to Scott, he remains the most important military figure of the early republic.

Archival

2nd Brigade. Order book. Lilly Library. War of 1812 Papers; St. Lawrence, 1813.
RG94, Roll 38. Letters. National Archives. 1814–1815.
RG98, Item 19. Letters. National Archives. Letters to Daniel D. Tompkins, 1812–1814.
RG98, No. 394/277. Details. National Archives. 2nd Brigade, Aug.–Nov. 1813.
RG98, No. 456/355. Orderly book. National Archives. Insp. Gen., 9th Mil. Dist., 1814–1815.
RG98, No. 45/507. Misc. returns. National Archives. Left Division, 1813–1815.
RG98, No. 506/408. Orderly book. National Archives. 2nd Brigade, August–September, 1813.
RG98, No. 513/415. Register. National Archives. Men and officers detailed, June–Aug. 1814.
RG98, No. 556. Registers. National Archives. British prisoners, Fort Erie, 1814.
RG107. Letters. National Archives. Office of Secretary of War; 1813–1815.
Left Division. Order book. New York State. Charles K. Gardner Papers, 1814.

Manuscript

Brown, Jacob J. Letter, 1813. Boston Public Library. Ch.C.10.68; Sacketts Harbor.
Brown, Jacob J. Letters. Buffalo and Erie. B00-11, Niagara memoranda; 1814.
Brown, Jacob J. Letters. Buffalo and Erie. A00-64; to Peter B. Porter, 1814.
Brown, Jacob J. Letters. Buffalo and Erie. Peter B. Porter Papers; 1814–1815.
Brown, Jacob J. Papers. Clements Library. Jacob Brown Papers; Niagara, 1814–1815.
Brown, Jacob J. Letter, 1813. Gilder Lehrman. GLC002047; French Mills, possible attack.
Brown, Jacob J. Letter, 1814. Gilder Lehrman. GLC01469; Oswego, enemy fleet afoot.
Brown, Jacob J. Letters. Historical Society (Pa). Daniel Parker Papers; 1813–1815.
Brown, Jacob J. Letters. Historical Society (Pa). Simon Gratz Collection; 1813–1814.
Brown, Jacob J. Letter, 1814. Indiana Historical. M211, Box 3, Fld. 76; French Mills.
Brown, Jacob J. Papers. Library of Congress. 1812–1815; Niagara Memoranda, 1814.
Brown, Jacob J. Letters. Lilly Library. War of 1812 Coll.; 1812–1816.
Brown, Jacob J. Papers. Massachusetts Historical. Jacob Brown Papers; 1812–1815.
Brown, Jacob J. Letters. Massachusetts Historical. Henry Dearborn Papers; 1813.
Brown, Jacob J. Letters. New York Historical. Isaac Chauncey letter books; 1814.
Brown, Jacob J. Letters. New York Historical. Misc Mss B, Fort Erie; 1812–1815.
Brown, Jacob J. Letters. New York Public. Jacob Brown Miscellaneous Manuscripts.
Brown, Jacob J. Letters. New York Public. James Monroe Papers; 1814.
Brown, Jacob J. Letter, 1812. New York State. Mss. 1177, Ogdensburg, N.Y.
Brown, Jacob J. Letter, 1814. New York State. Mss. 7714; to Moss Kent, Sacketts Harbor.
Brown, Jacob J. Letters. New York State. KB12914; C. K. Gardner Papers; 1814.
Brown, Jacob J. Letters. New York State. Brown Family Papers; 1814.
Brown, Jacob J. Letters. Oneida Historical. Nathan Williams Papers; 1814.

Brown, Jacob J. Letters. Oneida Historical. Jacob Brown Papers; 1813–1815.
Brown, Jacob J. Letters. Owen D. Young. Brown-Kirby Family Papers; 1815.
Brown, Jacob J. Memoranda. Perkins Library. Jacob J. Brown Papers; 1814.

Printed Primary

Armstrong, John. *Notice of Mr. Adams's Eulogium on the Life and Character of James Monroe.* Washington, D.C.: N. P., 1832, 27–29. [Letter of November 28, 1814]
Brown, Jacob J. "Battle of the Falls." *Port Folio* 6 (September 1815): 219–230.
Cruikshank, Ernest A., ed. *Documents Relating to the Invasion of the Niagara Peninsula by the United States Army Commanded by General Jacob Brown in July and August, 1814.* Niagara-on-the-Lake, Ont.: Niagara Historical Society, 1920.
Hastings, Hugh, ed. *Public Papers of Daniel D. Tompkins, Governor of New York, 1807–1817.* 3 vols. Albany, N.Y.: J. B. Lyons, 1902.

Select Secondary

Barbuto, Richard V. *Niagara, 1814: America Invades Canada.* Lawrence: University Press of Kansas, 2000.
Fredriksen, John C. "Niagara, 1814: The United States Army Quest for Tactical Parity in the War of 1812 and Its Legacy." Unpublished Ph.D. dissertation, Providence College, 1993.
Graves, Donald E. *Where Right and Glory Lead! The Battle of Lundy's Lane, 1814.* Toronto: Robin Brass Studio, 1997.
Latimer, Jon. *Niagra, 1814: The Final Invasion.* Oxford: Osprey, 2009.
Morris, John P. *Sword of the Border: Major General Jacob Jennings Brown, 1775–1828.* Kent, Oh.: Kent State University Press, 2000.
Turner, Wesley B. *British Generals in the War of 1812: High Command in the Canadas.* Montreal: McGill-Queen's University Press, 1999, 113–140 [Gordon Drummond]
Whitehorne, Joseph. *While Washington Burned: The Battle for Fort Erie, 1814.* Baltimore: Nautical and Aviation Press, 1992.
Wilder, Patrick A. *The Battle of Sacketts Harbor, 1813.* Baltimore: Nautical and Aviation Publishing, 1994.

Henry Dearborn

Henry Dearborn was born in North Hampton, New Hampshire, on February 23, 1751, where he apprenticed as a physician. In 1775, he joined Colonel John Stark's militia regiment as a company commander and fought conspicuously at Bunker Hill. Dearborn subsequently accompanied Colonel Benedict Arnold's expedition, and was captured during the siege of Quebec. Paroled and exchanged, he next served as a major in Colonel Alexander Scammell's regiment and served with distinction during the Saratoga campaign of 1777. He also garnered praise for his conduct at Monmouth in 1778 and during General John

Sullivan's Indian expedition against the Iroquois in 1779; he ended the war on General George Washington's staff as an assistant quartermaster. After the war, Dearborn occupied numerous public offices at Kennebec, Maine, including major general of militia and U.S. Marshal, before gaining a Congressional seat in 1790. In this capacity, he came to the attention of fellow Democratic-Republican Thomas Jefferson, whom appointed him his Secretary of War in 1801. Jefferson, while not exactly anti-military, intended to slash government expenditures to pay off the national debt and Dearborn helped him pare down the size of the standing army and its Federalist-dominated officer corps. He also encouraged the foundation of the U.S. Military Academy at West Point, New York, where future military cadres could be imbued with republican principles. Finally, he abolished army officers' fancy breeches and buckled shoes as being inconsistent with the plainer attire more befitting republican soldiery. This emphasis on thrift notwithstanding, Dearborn toyed with numerous innovations, such as the mass-produced muskets of Eli Whitney, the Harper's Ferry Model 1803 rifle, and the first horse artillery company in American service. Dearborn resigned from office following the election of President James Madison in 1809, and was replaced by the equally fastidious Dr. William Eustis. He apparently received the post as collector of the port of Boston as a sinecure until January 27, 1812, when Madison appointed him the army's senior major general in anticipation of renewed conflict with Great Britain.

As the leading American commander, Dearborn presided over an area ranging from New England to the Niagara frontier. He helped formulate a three-pronged strategy for the conquest of Canada but, owing to the gross unpreparedness of all American forces, he failed to mount necessary diversions in support of other theaters. Consequently, the armies of General William Hull and Stephen Van Rensselaer came to grief at Detroit and Queenston Heights, in the summer and fall of 1812, respectively. Dearborn's own offensive against Montreal was delayed when Federalist governors of New England states refused to call out their militia to assist him. Deprived of an important source of trained manpower, the army scrounged for volunteers to augment its tiny core of untrained regulars. Dearborn finally got underway that October, yet his force proceeded no further than the Canadian border when the militia, acting upon Constitutional scruples, refused to cross. A spate of marching and countermarching ensued, at the end of which the general had little recourse but retrace his steps back. Thoroughly embarrassed, he tendered his resignation but President Madison, perhaps unwisely, refused to accept. Thereafter the tottering Dearborn was reviled in military circles as "Granny" on account of his physical slowness and indecision in the field.

In the spring of 1813, a new secretary of war, John Armstrong, ordered Dearborn to prepare an amphibious expedition for the reduction of Kingston

Major General Henry Dearborn. Portland Museum of Art.

on Lake Ontario. Capturing this strategic site would have facilitated the war effort but Dearborn, convinced that the place was too heavily defended, suggested a softer target farther west. This strategic shift culminated in the successful capture of York (Toronto) on April 1813, although Brigadier General Zebulon M. Pike was killed in an explosion. The following month Dearborn allowed Brigadier General John Parker Boyd to orchestrate the successful capture of Fort George, Upper Canada, on May 27, 1813, but he remained with the fleet and failed to counter General Morgan Lewis's disastrous decision to halt the pursuit of fleeing British forces. These rallied and counterattacked at Stoney Creek on June 6, 1813, capturing Brigadier Generals John Chandler and William H. Winder. Dearborn, ill and ineffectual, proved unable to influence the dismal course of events and, following the capture of an American column at Beaver Dams, a cry went up for his dismissal. On July 6, 1813, Dearborn yielded the palm to General James Wilkinson, ostensibly on the grounds of poor health, and supplanted General Thomas Humphrey Cushing as commander of the 1st Military District, headquartered at Boston. In one of the war's major ironies, he also presided over the court-martial of General Hull for the loss of Detroit, when many military and public officials felt he was equally culpable. Dearborn resigned from the army on June 15, 1815 and, when Madison's attempt to reappoint him as secretary of war engendered fierce opposition, he retired to private life in Roxbury, Massachusetts. He lived quietly there until 1822, when President James Monroe appointed him minister to Portugal. Dearborn died in Roxbury on June 6, 1829, an earnest public official, but too past his prime by 1812 to function effectively.

Archival

Mil. District No. 1. Order book. Boston Public. **C.33.15; Boston, 1812–1814.
Dearborn, Henry. Letter book. Burton Historical. 1st Military District; 1814.
Orderly book. Garrison Orders. Library of Congress. No. 109; Fort Independence, 1814.
Mil. District No. 1. Letter book. Massachusetts Historical. Ms. N-108; 1813–1815.
RG94. Letters. National Archives. Adjutant General's Office, 1812–1815.
RG98, No. 447/345. Orderly book. National Archives. Northern Dept., 1813–1813.
RG98, No. 466/365. Orderly book. National Archives. Adj. Gen., 3rd Mil. District, 1812–1815.
RG98, No. 449/347. Orderly book. National Archives. Adj. Gen., 3rd Mil. District, 1812–1815.
RG98, No.458/357. Orderly book. National Archives. Ins. Gen., 3rd Mil. Dist., 1813–1815.
RG98, No. 451/350. Orderly book. National Archives. Ins. Gen., 3rd Mil. Dist., 1813–1815.
RG98, Item 19. Letters. National Archives. Letters to Gov. Daniel D. Tompkins.
RG98, Item 57. List. National Archives. British prisoners, Fort George, 1813.
RG107. Letters. National Archives. Secretary of War's Office, 1812–1815.
Dearborn, Henry. Letter book. New York Historical. BV Sec D, June, 1812–December, 1813.

Manuscript

Dearborn, Henry. Letters. Buffalo and Erie. Peter B. Porter Papers; 1812–1813.
Dearborn, Henry. Letters. Chicago Historical. James Wilkinson Papers; 1813–1814.
Dearborn, Henry. Letter, 1814. Chicago Historical. Gunther Coll.; militia to Maine coast.

Dearborn, Henry. Letter, 1812. Chicago Historical. Dearborn Coll.; exchange of prisoners.
Dearborn, Henry. Letters. Chicago Historical. Dearborn Coll., orders; June–July, 1812.
Dearborn, Henry. Letters. Danvers Archival. PR/PO/C, Moses Porter Papers.
Dearborn, Henry. Letter, 1812. Gilder Lehrman. GLC00437; prisoner exchange.
Dearborn, Henry. Letters. Historical Society (Pa). Daniel Parker Papers; 1812–1815.
Dearborn, Henry. Letter, 1813. Historical Society (Pa). Gratz, Case 4, Box 33; loss of command.
Dearborn, Henry. Letter, 1814. Houghton Library. bMS AM 1250 (226); Boston affairs.
Dearborn, Henry. Papers. Library of Congress. Henry Dearborn Papers; 1812–1814.
Dearborn, Henry. Letters. Library of Congress. Miscellaneous Manuscript Collection.
Dearborn, Henry. Letters. Library of Congress. Anthony Lamb Papers, supply; 1812–1813.
Dearborn, Henry. Letters. Library of Congress. William Eustis Papers; 1812.
Dearborn, Henry. Letters. Library of Congress. James Madison Papers; 1812–1815.
Dearborn, Henry. Letters. Library of Congress. James Monroe Papers; 1814–1815.
Dearborn, Henry. Letters. Lilly Library. War of 1812 Coll., 1812–1813.
Dearborn, Henry. Letter, 1813. Lilly Library. John P. Boyd Mss., Niagara.
Dearborn, Henry. Papers. Maine Historical. Coll. 33; 1812–1815.
Dearborn, Henry. Letters. Maine Historical. Coll. 165, William King Papers; 1814.
Dearborn, Henry. Papers. Massachusetts Historical. H. Dearborn papers; 1811–1815.
Dearborn, Henry. Letter, 1814. Massachusetts Historical. C.E. French, Folder 12; Boston.
Dearborn, Henry. Letter, 1812. New England Historic. Autogs. 8D 13-2; to Eustis, supplies.
Dearborn, Henry. Papers. New Hampshire. Lake Champlain offensive; 1812.
Dearborn, Henry. Letters. New York Historical. Misc Mss D, to D. Tompkins, 1812–1813.
Dearborn, Henry. Letter, 1812. New York Historical. Misc Mss P, to William Plumer.
Dearborn, Henry. Letters. New York State. Correspondence, 1803–1818.
Dearborn, Henry. Voucher book. U.S. Military Academy. No. 103; 1812–1813, biographical sketches.
Dearborn, Henry. Letter, 1813. Virginia Historical. Mss1 Pg267 d 774–793; Black Rock, N. Y.
Dearborn, Henry. A. S. Manuscript. Maine Historical. Henry Dearborn biography, 7 vols.
Dearborn, Henry. A. S. Letters. Wisconsin Historical. Frontier Wars Papers, 22 U.

Printed Primary

American State Papers. Military Affairs. 7 vols. Washington, D.C.: Gales and Seaton, 1832–1861.
Dearborn, Henry. *Message from the President of the United States: Transmitting a Letter from the Secretary of War, Accompanied with Sundry Documents; in Obedience to*

a Resolution of the 31st of December Last Requesting Such Information as May Tend to Explain the Causes of the Failure of the Arms of the United States on the Northern Frontier. Washington, D.C.: A. & G. Way, printers, 1814.

Select Secondary

Crackel, Theodore J. *Mr. Jefferson's Army: Politics and Social Reform of the Military Establishment, 1801–1809*. New York: New York University Press, 1987.

Everest, Allen S. *The War of 1812 in the Champlain Valley*. Syracuse, N.Y.: Syracuse University Press, 1981.

Malcomson, Robert. *Capital in Flames: The American Attack on York, 1813*. Toronto: Robin Brass Studio, 2008.

Wade Hampton

Wade Hampton was born in Halifax County, Virginia, on May 3, 1754, and raised in Spartanburg County, South Carolina. In July 1776 his parents, a brother, and a nephew were all killed in a Cherokee ambush, but five brothers escaped to become officers in the Continental Army. Hampton, however, was slow to embrace the patriot cause, and he remained studiously neutral until September 1780. He then joined the guerilla band of General Thomas Sumter, the "Gamecock," and distinguished himself by leading cavalry at the battle of Eutaw Springs on September 3, 1781. After the war, Hampton displayed considerable enterprise by becoming one of the first purveyors of short staple cotton as a cash crop, and amassed a personal fortune. He also dabbled in politics by serving several terms in the South Carolina legislature. In 1787 he was present at Philadelphia during the Constitutional Convention as an Anti-Federalist, and voted against ratification. In 1795 Hampton won a seat in the U.S. Congress as a representative, serving there with little distinction until 1805. He next came out of retirement in the wake of the 1807 *Chesapeake-Leopard* Affair, whereupon President Thomas Jefferson appointed him colonel of the new Regiment of Light Dragoons. A competent soldier and administrator by contemporary standards, Hampton rose to brigadier general in February 1809 and succeeded James Wilkinson as commander of the New Orleans garrison. There he and his aide Winfield Scott gained Wilkinson's undying enmity by exposing the poor condition of the army during his tenure. Never one to neglect business matters, Hampton also put his lengthy tour of Mississippi to good use by acquiring several large sugar plantations, which he parleyed into considerable profit. In 1811 he also played a small role in suppressing a slave rebellion near New Orleans.

Hampton continued at New Orleans until May, 1812, when he was ordered to Norfolk, Virginia, to head up defenses there. He performed competently in that role until March 2, 1813, when he rose to major general commanding the Right Division, 9th Military District, at Plattsburgh, New York. This transfer came in anticipation of an eventual offensive into Lower Canada but, owing to the extreme rawness of his new recruits, he spent several months drilling his levies into shape. His partiality for punishment through caning led to the unsavory nickname of "Old Hickory." Regardless, this was one of the earliest attempts to impose systematic discipline on military recruits in a professional, if harsh, manner. Hampton also engaged in a heated diatribe with Governor Martin Chittenden, an antiwar Federalist, over his refusal to call out the militia to assist the military. Worse still, when Secretary of War John Armstrong finalized the invasion plan against Lower Canada, Hampton found himself subordinated under his archenemy Wilkinson. The general flatly refused to serve in this capacity and was eventually persuaded to accept orders directly from the War Department instead. It was under this awkward, divided command, that the United States embarked on its quixotic attempt to capture Montreal in the fall of 1813.

The American effort was doomed from the onset for many reasons, not the least of which was non-cooperative posturing by its two principal players. As Wilkinson's force departed Sacketts Harbor, New York, in a flotilla of small craft that transited the St. Lawrence River, Hampton was to march up the Champlain River Valley into Lower Canada and rendezvous with him. The two columns would then unite in a concerted drive against Montreal, an important British staging and supply center. Hampton's Right division, numbering 4,000 recruits, began advancing into densely wooded country on October 21, 1813, and slogged towards its objective. However, on October 26, 1813, they confronted a force of 1,800 Canadian militia under Lieutenant Colonel Charles de Salaberry, who were entrenched behind the Chateauguay River. Hampton subsequently decided to send General George Izard's brigade to attack the Canadians in front while his remaining brigade under Colonel Robert Purdy moved downstream to flank them. Unfortunately, Purdy became lost in the swampy morass and fell back. Hampton, greatly discouraged, recalled Izard and ordered a complete withdrawal back to Plattsburgh. Casualties on either side had been extremely light in this distressingly mishandled affair. Hampton subsequently disobeyed a direct order from Wilkinson to join him in Canada and, rather than face the consequences, tendered his resignation and fled to Washington, D.C., just ahead of an arrest warrant. The 1813 St. Lawrence Campaign, and Hampton's behavior in it, plunged the war effort to its lowest nadir. He finally mustered out on March 16, 1814, and saw no other action.

Major General Wade Hampton. Library of Congress.

Back in civilian life, Hampton returned to South Carolina, to concentrate on trading in cotton and slaves. At the time of his death in Columbia, on February 4, 1835, he was reputedly one of the South's wealthiest plantation owners. Ironically, his grandson, Wade Hampton III, enjoyed a reputation as one of the Confederacy's greatest cavalry leaders.

ARCHIVAL

Hampton, Wade. Orderly book. American Antiquarian. Mss #5F, Fort Norfolk, March–April, 1813.
King, William. General Orders. Minnesota Historical. M316 #846; Burlington, September 1813.
RG94. Letters. National Archives. Adjutant General's Office; 1812–1813.

RG98, No. 495/396. General Orders. National Archives. 5th/9th Mil. Dist., April–August, 1813.
RG98, No. 45/507. Misc returns. National Archives. HQ, Right Division, 1813–1815.
RG107. Letters. National Archives. Secretary of War's Office; 1812–1813.

Manuscript

Hampton, Wade. Letters. Chicago Historical. James Wilkinson Papers; 1813.
Hampton, Wade. Letters. Library of Virginia. 41557, James Barbour Papers; 1813.
Hampton, Wade. Letters. Lilly Library. War of 1812 Coll.; 1813.
Hampton, Wade. Letter, 1813. New York Historical. Misc Mss H, resents "blood suckers".

Printed Primary

American State Papers. Military Affairs. 7 vols. Washington, D.C.: Gales and Seaton, 1832–1861. Vol. 1.
Carter, Clarence E., ed. *The Territorial Papers of the United States: Vol. IX, The Territory of Orleans, 1803–1812.* Washington, D.C.: Government Printing Office, 1940.

Select Secondary

Bridwell, Ronald E. "The South's Wealthiest Planter: Wade Hampton I of South Carolina, 1754–1835." Unpublished Ph D. dissertation, University of South Carolina, 1980.
Campbell, Karen S. "Propaganda, Pestilence, and Prosperity: Burlington's Camptown Days During the War of 1812." *Vermont History* 64, no. 3 (1996): 133–158.
Cauthen, Charles E., ed. *Family Letters of the Three Wade Hamptons, 1782–1901.* Columbia: University of South Carolina Press, 1953.
Everest, Allen S. *The War of 1812 in the Champlain Valley.* Syracuse, N.Y.: Syracuse University Press, 1981.
Graves, Donald E. *Field of Glory: The Battle of Crysler's Farm, 1813.* Toronto: Robin Brass Studio, 1999.

William Henry Harrison

William Henry Harrison was born in Charles City County, Virginia, on February 22, 1773, son of Benjamin Harrison, a signer of the Declaration of Independence. In 1787 he attended Hampden-Sidney College to study medicine, and subsequently enrolled at the College of Physicians and Surgeons in Philadelphia, Pennsylvania. However, in August 1791, Harrison quit to become an ensign in the U.S. Army. He took readily to military life and was soon appointed aide-de-camp to General Anthony Wayne. In this capacity,

Major General William H. Harrison. National Portrait Gallery, Smithsonian Institution; gift of Mrs. Herbert Lee Pratt, Jr.

Harrison fought well at the August 20, 1794, battle of Fallen Timbers, which defeated a Shawnee-Miami coalition under Blue Jacket and restored peace to the Old Northwest. He then advanced to captain in command of Fort Washington, Ohio, but resigned his commission in June 1798 to pursue politics. Harrison proved equally adept in this avocation and, after serving as a territorial secretary and then delegate to Congress, he won appointment as governor of the Indiana Territory in May 1800. This was an enormous swath of land encompassing all of present-day Indiana, Illinois, Wisconsin, and western

Michigan; Harrison was only 27 years old at his time of appointment. His tenure was also marked by an aggressive policy of acquiring land from the Indians, and through the 1803 Treaty of Fort Wayne he added 1.1 million acres to the United States. However, such rapacity stoked Indian resistance in the form of Tecumseh and his mystic brother Tenskwatawa, who organized a confederation of tribes to oppose the Americans. In the fall of 1811 tensions exploded into violence when Harrison, determined to remove an illegal Indian community at Prophetstown, was attacked in his camp at Tippecanoe Creek on November 7, 1811. Harrison fought bravely, aided by the steadiness of the 4th U. S. Infantry under Colonel John Parker Boyd, and the Indians were driven off—although by the narrowest of margins. American losses totaled 62 dead and 126 wounded from a total force of 1,000 men, but Harrison's characterization of Tippecanoe as a decisive victory brought national recognition at a time when tensions were flaring along the western frontier.

After war with England commenced in June 1812, Harrison, sought out and received a high command in the West. Speaker of the U. S. House Henry Clay, a personal friend, arranged his promotion as a major general of Kentucky militia after President James Madison declined to offer him a regular army commission. Harrison then energetically organized American defenses following General William Hull's surrender in August and, after finally becoming an army brigadier general that month, he directed a relief column that lifted the siege of Fort Wayne. He next tried orchestrating Detroit's recapture but he was perpetually thwarted by supply shortages and an uncooperative Brigadier General James Winchester, his principal subordinate. After British forces destroyed Winchester's force at Frenchtown in January 1813, Harrison assumed a defensive posture, and constructed Fort Meigs, Ohio, to contain any counteroffensive. He also advanced to major general on March 2, 1813, and was appointed commander of the 8th Military District. Harrison successfully weathered a siege of Fort Meigs by British and Indian forces under General Henry Procter and Tecumseh and, on May 5, 1813, he conducted a successful sortie, although at the cost of General Green Clay's relief column. Procter, his Indian allies dissatisfied by the lack of progress, abandoned the siege. A second British attempt was also rebuffed on July 21–28, 1813, and, following an unsuccessful attack against Fort Stephenson that August, Procter boarded boats and returned to Upper Canada. Harrison, still beset by supply shortages, began marshaling his forces for offensive operations. These were unleashed in the wake of Commodore Oliver Hazard Perry's startling victory on Lake Erie, September 10, 1813, after which Harrison's army was conveyed by boat to Canada. His fast-moving column overtook Procter and Tecumseh at the Thames River on October 5, 1813, where a charge by mounted Kentucky volunteers under Colonel Richard M. Johnson carried the day. Tecumseh was slain and most of Procter's force was captured, but the threat of expiring enlistments forced Harrison's withdrawal back to Ohio. He served briefly in New York before simmering disagreements with Secretary of War John Armstrong convinced him to resign on May 31, 1814. Nevertheless, Harrison's stature as a national war hero was secure, and in 1818 Congress voted him a gold medal. Hardly a brilliant combat commander, his methodical approach to gathering supplies, training troops, and building forts and roads wrung the best possible performance from the volatile state levies comprising the majority of his soldiers.

Harrison returned to politics in 1816 by winning a seat in Congress, and in the 1830s his disenchantment with the Democrats induced him to join the new Whig Party. In 1840, campaigning under the slogan of "Tippecanoe and Tyler too," he was the first Whig candidate elected to the White House. He died only a month following his inauguration on April 4, 1841, becoming the first chief executive to die in office. Harrison was a capable leader of militia forces throughout the War of 1812, second only to Andrew Jackson, and his activity wielded dire consequences for Native Americans throughout the Northwest Territory.

Archival

RG94. Letters. National Archives. Adjutant General's Office; 1812–1814.
RG107. Letters. National Archives. Secretary of War's Office; 1812–1814.

Manuscript

Harrison, William H. Letter, 1812. Boston Public. Ch.C.8.80; to Return J. Meigs, Detroit.
Harrison, William H. Papers. Burton Historical.
Harrison, William H. Papers. Cincinnati Historical. Mss H323 RM; 1812–1815.
Harrison, William H. Battle orders. Filson Historical. A H521/6; October, 1813.
Harrison, William H. Letters. Historical Society (Pa). Daniel Parker Papers; 1812–1813.
Harrison, William H. Letters. Historical Society (Pa). Gratz Coll.; 1813–1814.
Harrison, William H. Letter, 1811. Houghton Library. Autograph File; Tippecanoe.
Harrison, William H. Letters. Huntington Library.
Harrison, William H. Letters. Indiana Historical. M364, Box 1–2; 1811–1814.
Harrison, William H. Letters. Kentucky Historical. 97SC209, Frenchtown; 1811–1814, 1824.
Harrison, William H. Papers. Library of Congress. 0506A, W. H. Harrison Papers; 1811–1815.
Harrison, William H. Letters. Library of Congress. 3825, Joseph Desha Papers; 1816, Thames.
Harrison, William H. Letters. Library of Congress. 2655; John Payne Papers.
Harrison, William H. Letters. Library of Congress. Henry Clay Family; 1811–1814.

Harrison, William H. Letter, 1811. Library of Congress. Martha E. Seely Collection.
Harrison, William H. Papers. Lilly Library. Harrison, W. H. Mss. II; 1812–1814.
Harrison, William H. Letters. Lilly Library. War of 182 Coll.; 1811–1813.
Harrison, William H. Letter, 1813. Minnesota Historical. M316 #692; to James Monroe.
Harrison, William H. Letter, 1813. Mudd Library. C1142, Andre de Coppet Collection.
Harrison, William H. Letters. New York Historical. Misc Mss H, sham battle, Vincennes.
Harrison, William H. Letters. New York Public. MssCol 17897 PM 188.1; to Isaac Shelby.
Harrison, William H. Letters. New York Public. George Croghan Papers; 1813.
Harrison, William H. Papers. Ohio Historical. MSS 331; 1813–1815.
Harrison, William H. Letter, 1813. Ohio Historical. VFM4951; to Return J, Meigs, movements.
Harrison, William H. Letters. Ohio Historical. Return J. Meigs Papers; 1812–1813.
Harrison, William H. Letters. Ohio Historical. Vol. 1232, Fort Fayette letter book, 1812.
Harrison, William H. Letters. Regenstein Library. John Payne Papers; 1813.
Harrison, William H. Letters. Ross County Historical. 1990.08, David Trimble Papers; 1813.
Harrison, William H. Letter, 1813. Rutherford B. Hayes. Fort Stephenson account.
Harrison, William H. Papers. Wisconsin Historical. Draper, 5X, William H. Harrison Papers.

Printed Primary

Carter, Clarence E., ed. *The Territorial Papers of the United States: Vol. VIII, The Territory of Indiana, 1810–1816.* Washington, D.C.: Government Printing Office, 1939.
Clanin, Douglas E., ed. "The Correspondence of William Henry Harrison and Oliver Hazard Perry, July 5, 1813–July 31, 1815." *Northwest Ohio Historical Quarterly* 60 (Autumn 1988): 153–180.
Clanin, Douglas E., and Ruth Dorrel, eds. *A Guide to the Papers of William Henry Harrison, 1800–1815.* 2nd ed. Indianapolis: Indiana Historical Society, 1999.
Esarey, Logan, ed. *Messages and letters of William Henry Harrison.* 2 vols. Indianapolis: Indiana Historical Society Commission, 1927. Vol. 2, 81–864.
Knopf, Richards C., ed. *William Henry Harrison and the War of 1812.* Columbus: Anthony Wayne Parkway Board, 1957.
"Papers Relating to the War of 1812." *Western Reserve Historical Society Tracts* No. 15 (April 1873): 1–3; No. 17 (November 1873): 1–5; No. 19 (November 1874): 1–4; No. 28 (October 1875): 1–4; No. 51 (December 1879): 115–123.

Select Secondary

Antal, Sandy. *A Wampum Denied: Procter's War of 1812.* Ottawa, Ont.: Carleton University Press, 1997.
Booraem, Hendrik V. "William Henry Harrison Comes to Cincinnati." *Queen City Heritage* 45 (Fall 1987): 3–22.

Gunderson, Robert G. "William Henry Harrison: Apprentice in Arms." *Northwest Ohio Quarterly* 65, no. 1 (1993): 3–29.
Millett, Alan R. "Caesar and the Conquest of the Northwest Territory: The First Harrison Campaign, 1811." *Timeline* 14, no. 4 (1997): 2–19.
Millett, Alan R. "Caesar and the Conquest of the Northwest Territory: The Second Harrison Campaign, 1813." *Timeline* no. 5 (1997): 2–21.
Nelson, Larry B. "Dudley's Defeat and the Relief of Fort Meigs during the War of 1812." *Register of the Kentucky Historical Society* 101, no. 1 (2006): 5–42.
Nelson, Michael B. "Les Habitants and William Henry Harrison's Frontier Campaigns in the Old Northwest." Unpublished master's thesis, Ohio State University, 2002.
Owens, Robert M. *Mr. Jefferson's Hammer: William Henry Harrison and the Origins of American Indian Policy.* Norman: University of Oklahoma Press, 2007.
Painter, Sue Ann. *William Henry Harrison: Father of the West.* Cincinnati: Jarndyce & Jarndyce Press, 2004.
St. Denis, Guy. *Tecumseh's Bones.* Ithaca, N.Y.: McGill-Queen's University Press, 2005.
Spencer, Rex L. "The Gibraltar of the Maumee: Fort Meigs in the War of 1812." Unpublished Ph.D. dissertation, Ball State University, 1988.
Sugden, John. *Tecumseh: A Life.* New York: Henry Holt, 1998.

George Izard

George Izard was born in London, England, on October 21, 1776, the son of U.S. Senator Ralph Izard. He was raised in Charleston, South Carolina, and in 1795 he enrolled at the prestigious Ecole du Genie at Metz, France. While in attendance, Izard was also commissioned a second lieutenant of engineers, U.S. Army, as of June 1794. Izard returned home during the Quasi-War with France and he helped construct Castle Pinckney in Charleston harbor. Promoted to captain, he subsequently served as aide-de-camp to General Alexander Hamilton and also commanded Fort Mifflin outside of Philadelphia, Pennsylvania, until international tensions subsided. He next transferred to West Point, New York, and clashed with his superior officer, the respected scientist and engineer Jonathan Williams, over the issue of using soldiers as waiters. In 1801, the Democratic-Republican administration of Thomas Jefferson took power and began culling the Federalist-dominated officer corps, and Izard resigned his commission in June 1803. He married and settled in Philadelphia to live the life of a wealthy young aristocrat and, possessing an intellectually bent, was active in the prestigious American Philosophical Society.

In light of anticipated hostilities with England, Izard reentered the army on March 12, 1812, as colonel of the new 2nd Regiment of Artillery. He reported back to Fort Mifflin to raise and instruct his charge, assisted by a very able lieutenant colonel, Winfield Scott. With two of the army's best drillmasters at their head, the 2nd Artillery quickly gained a reputation as one of its best-trained units. By dint of his good performance, Izard advanced to brigadier general in March 1813 and replaced the tottering Brevet brigadier General Henry Burbeck as commander of the 3rd Military District, headquartered at New York City. He again discharged his duties capably, and in August 1814 he transferred north to Plattsburgh, New York, as part of General Wade Hampton's Right Division. In this capacity Izard commanded a brigade at Chateauguay where, on October 26, 1813, he skillfully covered the American withdrawal during Hampton's ignominiously retreat. Izard, though desperately ill, elected to remain with his troops at Plattsburgh over the winter and fitfully saw to their needs. His superior performance caught the eye of Secretary of War John Armstrong, so on January 24, 1814, he was promoted to major general. Izard thus nominally outranked his more noted contemporaries Jacob Jennings Brown and Andrew Jackson, becoming, at the age of 38, the senior army commander along the Canadian frontier.

In May 1814, Izard returned to Plattsburgh, where he found the Right Division of the 9th Military District dispirited, poorly trained, and lacking supplies. He threw himself into militarily rehabilitating this mob and by late summer he had recruited, trained, and equipped a force of 5,500 men. It was an impressive achievement by War of 1812 standards and eclipses the smaller but more famous efforts by General Scott at Buffalo. By late summer Izard was preparing his base at Plattsburgh to receive a major British offensive led by Governor General Sir George Prevost. Secretary Armstrong, however, ordered him to proceed with the bulk of his division some 400 miles west and assist the General Brown at Niagara. Izard, aghast at these instructions, protested vigorously but to no avail. It was a fool's errand, but he dutifully marched with the brigades of Generals Thomas Adams Smith and Daniel Bissell, leaving Plattsburgh's fate in the hands of his remaining brigadier, Alexander Macomb. True to his prediction, the massive British invasion unfolded a few days following his departure. Izard was therefore concerned about marching overland to Sacketts Harbor, New York, where an enterprising enemy could catch his army strung out for miles; he consequently chose a lengthier but safer route to the south and west. After arriving, the squadron of Commodore Isaac Chauncey transported the bulk of his forces to Niagara where, after a long and fatiguing march of 29 days, the Right Division finally trudged into the Niagara frontier. From the onset Izard had difficult relations with the aggressive Brown, who sought to storm General Gordon Drummond's forces. The British were presently ensconced behind the 100-yard wide Chippawa Creek and Izard, cognizant that his was the sole intact division of

Major General George Izard. Courtesy Arkansas History Commission.

American regulars on the northern frontier, was wary of any operation with the potential of incurring enormous casualties. Brown interpreted this circumspection as timidity and angrily marched back to Sacketts Harbor in a huff. On October 28, 1814, Izard dispatched Bissell's brigade on an end run around Drummond's right flank, and he was expertly intercepted at the battle of Cook's Mills, October 28, 1814. Bissell prevailed but lacked the manpower to do much more, so he burned some stored grain and withdrew. Meanwhile, control of Lake Ontario also returned to the British following the launch of their enormous 102-gun warship HMS *St. Lawrence* and Izard, realizing that his line of communications were jeopardized should he advance, elected to quit Niagara altogether. In November he leveled the old American camp at Fort Erie and withdrew to winter quarters at Buffalo, New York. He was highly criticized in the press but his division remained intact. He also tendered his resignation to James Monroe, now acting secretary of war, who declined to accept, and Izard was allowed to honorably depart on June 15, 1815. Considering the resources he commanded, and the high expectations held for him, Izard's sojourn at Niagara was roundly viewed as an abject failure.

Izard resumed his civilian affairs back at Philadelphia until March 1825, when President John Quincy Adams appointed him governor of the Arkansas Territory. Here Izard functioned capably and honestly as a public bureaucrat and he peacefully oversaw the relocation of Quapaw and Choctaw Indians to reservations without incident. He died at Little Rock on November 22, 1828, the only American general officer of his generation possessing European military training. Routinely criticized by contemporaries and historians alike, Izard's patience, restraint, and professionalism mark him as one of the War of 1812's most capable commanders and one of the unluckiest.

Archival

Division of the North. Orderly book. Library of Congress. No. 108; Plattsburgh, Buffalo, 1814–1815.

RG94. Letters. National Archives. Adjutant General's Office, 1812–1815.

RG98, No. 466/365. Orderly book. National Archives. Adj. Gen., 3rd Mil. District, 1812–1815.

RG98, No. 449/347. Orderly book. National Archives. Adj. Gen, 3rd Mil. District, 1812–1815.

RG98, No. 458/357. Orderly book. National Archives. Ins. Gen., 3rd Mil. Dist., 1813–1815.

RG98, No. 451/350. Orderly book. National Archives. Ins. Gen., 3rd Mil. Dist., 1813–1815.

RG98, No. 405/289. Letters/Circulars. National Archives. HQ, 9th Mil. Dist., May 1814–June, 1815.

RG98, No. 406/290. Letters. National Archives. Ins. Gen., 9th Mil. Dist., 1814–1815.

RG98, No. 508/410. Orders. National Archives. Ins. Gen., 9th Mil. Dist., 1814.

RG98, No. 509/411. Orders. National Archives. Ins. Gen., 9th Mil. Dist., 1814.

RG98, No. 445/342. Orderly book. National Archives. Adj. Gen., 9th Mil. Dist, 1813–1815.

RG98, No. 442/339. Orderly book. National Archives. Adj. Gen., 9th Mil. Dist., 1813–1815.

RG98, No. 464/341. Orderly book. National Archives. Adj. Gen., 9th Mil. Dist, 1813–1815.
RG98, No. 465/364. Orderly book. National Archives. Adj. Gen., 9th Mil. Dist., 1813–1815.
RG98, No. 45/507. Misc returns. National Archives. Right Division, 1813–1815.
RG107. Letters. National Archives. Secretary of War's Office; 1812–1815.
Army of the North. Orderly book. New York State. Mss. 10015; Plattsburgh, August, 1814.

Manuscript

Izard, George. Letters. Buffalo and Erie. Peter B. Porter Papers; 1814.
Izard, George. Letters. Clements Library. War of 1812 Collection; 1814.
Izard, George. Letters. Clements Library. Thomas Brisbane Papers; 1814.
Izard, George. Letter, 1813. Hay Library. Drowne Papers, Box 10; New York City.
Izard, George. Letters. Historical Society (Pa). Daniel Parker Papers; 1813–1815.
Izard, George. Letters. Historical Society (Pa). Gratz Coll., 1812–1813.
Izard, George. Letter, 1813. Historical Society (Pa). Dreer Coll., to Aaron Ogden.
Izard, George. Letter, 1813. Historical Society (Pa). Rawle Collection; to Wilkinson.
Izard, George. Letters. Library of Congress. James Monroe Papers.
Izard, George. Letters. Lilly Library. Jonathan Williams Papers, 1812–1814.
Izard, George. Letters. Massachusetts Historical. Jacob J. Brown Papers; 1814.
Izard, George. Letters. Mudd Library. C0079, Richard Rush Papers, 1812–1813.
Izard, George. Memoranda New York Historical. Albert Gallatin Papers; artillery reforms.
Izard, George. Letters. New York Historical. Isaac Chauncey letter book; 1814.
Izard, George. Letters. New York Public. James Monroe Papers; 1812–1815.
Izard, George. Letter, 1813. New York State. 16185, improper salute at the Narrows.
Izard, George. Letter, 1814. New York State. 3652; to Peter Sailly.
Izard, George. Letter, 1814. New York State. 9828-47, to Melancton Smith.
Izard, George. Letters. Perkins Library. William D. Cheever Papers; 1813–1814.
Izard, George. Letter, 1813. Perkins Library. Louis Manigault Collection; to wife.
Izard, George. Letters. State Historical (Mo). Thomas Adams Smith Papers; 1814.

Printed Primary

Carter, Clarence E., ed. *The Territorial Papers of the United States: Vol. XX, The Territory of Arkansas, 1825–1829.* Washington, D.C.: Government Printing Office, 1954.
deSaussure, Charlton. "Memoirs of General George Izard, 1825." *South Carolina Historical Magazine* 78, no. 1 (1977): 43–55.
Fredriksen, John C., ed. "The War of 1812 in Northern New York: General George Izard's Journal of the Chateauguay Campaign." *New York History* 76 (April 1995): 173–200.
Izard, George. *Official Correspondence with the Department of War Relative to the Military Operations of the American Army under the Command of Major General Izard on the Northern Frontier in the years 1814 and 1815.* Philadelphia: Thomas Dobson, 1816.

Select Secondary

Barbuto, Richard V. *Niagara, 1814: American Invades Canada.* Lawrence: University Press of Kansas, 2000.

Everest, Allen. S. *The War of 1812 in the Champlain Valley.* Syracuse, N.Y.: Syracuse University Press, 1981.

Fredriksen, John C. "A Tempered Sword, Untested: The Military Career of General George Izard." *Journal of America's Military Past* 25, nos. 2–3, (Fall 1998): 5–18; (Winter 1999): 5–17.

Graves, Donald E. *Field of Glory: The Battle of Crysler's Farm, 1813.* Toronto: Robin Brass Studio, 1999.

Andrew Jackson

Andrew Jackson was born in Waxhaw, South Carolina, on March 15, 1767, the son of an Irish immigrant who died before he was born. He fought in the militia during American Revolution until being taken captive with his older brother in 1780. Both suffered badly in captivity; his brother died, and Jackson was slashed across the head with a sword for failing to polish a British officer's boots. Thereafter Jackson maintained an unquenchable, simmering hatred for everything English. Orphaned at 14, he was subsequently raised by relatives in Tennessee, where he studied law and opened a successful practice. Even at the onset of his public career he struck contemporaries by a gaunt, grim demeanor, which worked to his advantage in the political arena. He was successively elected a Congressman, a U.S. Senator, and finally a state supreme court justice. Jackson also evinced considerable interest in military affairs and in 1802 he served as a major general of militia. This experience held him in good stead when the War of 1812 broke out, and in December 1812 he was authorized by the War Department to conduct 1,500 militia from Nashville to Natchez in anticipation of invading Spanish West Florida. He was halfway towards his destination when General James Wilkinson, a personal enemy, convinced Secretary of War William Eustis to countermand his orders, and Jackson angrily slogged back to Tennessee. It was here that his men, in a combination of admiration and trepidation, nicknamed him "Old Hickory." Once home, Jackson also had an unfortunate altercation with Jesse and Thomas Hart Benton in the streets of Nashville, and was severely wounded in the shoulder by a bullet.

Jackson was still convalescing when word of the Fort Mims Massacre, August 30, 1813, arrived. This was the atrocity that ignited the bloody Creek War and, ignoring his injuries, Jackson cobbled together a militia force and marched directly down the Coosa River into the heart of Creek territory.

Severe retribution — Jackson style — was not long in coming. On November 3, 1813, he unleashed General John Coffee's mounted rifle brigade against the village of Tallusahatchee, wiping it out. Jackson and General William Carroll followed up this initial blow with a joint attack at Talladega, where another Creek settlement was annihilated on November 9, 1813. Between these two encounters, the Red Sticks, or hostile Creeks, lost nearly 500 warriors in exchange for 22 Americans killed and 130 wounded. Nevertheless, Jackson's battlefield success was compromised by unmitigated food and supply shortages, which drove his men to mutiny. Jackson, a no-nonsense martinet, resorted to his fabled temper to keep them in line. Nor had the Creek lost any of their militancy, and in the encounters of Emuckfau Creek and Enotachopco Creek on January 22 and 24, respectively, the Americans were placed on the defensive and nearly routed save for Jackson's personal intervention. He then withdrew to friendly territory to rest and refit is command.

Over the next two months Jackson carefully collected and built up supplies and, once augmented by the newly-recruited 39th Infantry, he conducted his final foray against the Creek. The Indians were finally cornered at Horseshoe Bend on the Tallapoosa River and had carefully barricaded themselves. On March 27, 1814, Jackson's 2,000 infantry, 700 cavalry, and 700 Cherokee allies surrounded the position on both sides of the river and attacked. The Creek responded with fanatical resistance, but were gradually crushed with a loss of 800 dead; American casualties totaled 50 killed and 150 wounded, including a very young Ensign Sam Houston. Shortly afterwards Chief Red Eagle (William Weatherford) surrendered to Jackson to plea for his people. He fully expected to be arrested and executed but Jackson, impressed by the chief's demeanor, released him. However, by the terms of the Treaty of Fort Jackson, all Creek, friendly and hostile alike, lost 23 million acres of land (present-day Alabama) to the United States. Jackson, meanwhile, was promoted to major general as of May 1, 1814, and he succeeded the querulous Thomas Flournoy as commanding general of the 7th Military District, headquartered at New Orleans. His elevation was tinged by controversy as Secretary of War John Armstrong, selecting him to fill the vacancy caused by William Henry Harrison's resignation, did so without consulting President Madison beforehand.

By this juncture, the locus of military events in the War of 1812 turned southward. The fall of Napoleon in April 1814 released thousands of crack British troops for service in America, and the strategic city of New Orleans, controlling the mouth of the Mississippi River, became the object of their attention. Its capture would place a stranglehold on the American economy and a large expedition was outfitted for that purpose. They began by occupying Spanish-held Pensacola, West Florida, as a staging area for aiding still-hostile

Indians. Jackson's response was immediate — and unauthorized. Gathering 2,800 regulars and militia, he rushed down from Mobile to Pensacola, seized the town in a single rush on November 7, 1814, and drove the British back to their ships. The general then divined that New Orleans was most likely their next object of their attention, so he hastened back to the city and awaited developments. On December 23, 1814, an advanced British force under General John Keane arrived at Villere's Plantation, seven miles below New Orleans, and encamped. Jackson responded vigorously as always by cobbling a scratch force of regulars and militia together and boldly attacking in a swirling night action, assisted by two schooners under Commodore Daniel T. Patterson. Though surprised, the British veterans — "Wellington's Invincibles" — rallied quickly and gradually drove the Americans off. Keane, however, fearing he was greatly outnumbered, declined to advance and awaited reinforcements.

Keane's hesitance granted Jackson a desperately-needed respite, whereby he established a fortified defensive line along the Rodriguez Canal. Here he commanded a polyglot assemblage of regulars, Tennessee and Kentucky riflemen, Haitian and French speaking militia companies, a contingent of African American slaves who had been promised freedom, and a colorful contingent of pirates under notorious smuggler Jean Lafitte. On January 1, 1815, the main British force paraded before them under Lieutenant General Edward Pakenham, the Duke of Wellington's brother-in-law, who launched several probes of Jackson's defenses over the next week. All were handily repulsed and, on January 8, 1815, Pakenham staked everything on a frontal assault, coupled with a flanking movement on the other bank of the Mississippi. The flanking attack succeeded brilliantly and drove off the Kentuckians of General David B. Morgan, but transpired too late to change the outcome of Pakenham's main attack. The crack British columns were mowed down by heavy cannon, rifle, and musket fire without seriously breaching Jackson's line. Pakenham died along with General Samuel Gibbs and 2,000 of his troops; Jackson circumspectly allowed the survivors to withdraw unmolested and kept within his lines. Incredibly, American losses amounted to six dead and seven wounded. More stunning yet was the revelation that the War of 1812 had been concluded with the Treaty of Ghent three weeks earlier (although ratification was pending), so the slaughter was unnecessary. Still, Jackson's lop-sided triumph instantly rendered him a national hero, and "Old Hickory" received the thanks of Congress, a gold medal, and the gratitude of an entire nation. Whatever his lack of professional military training, Jackson's indomitable will and singular ferocity to succeed proved infectious, inspired his citizen soldiers to fight, and proved capable of defeating Europe's finest soldiers.

Jackson was retained in the postwar military establishment as commander of the Southern Division, and in 1818, he conducted a retaliatory war against

Major General Andrew Jackson. Photograph by Glenn Castellano; courtesy of the Art Commission of the City of New York.

the Seminole of Florida. His arbitrariness in arresting and executing two British agents made him unpopular in Washington, D.C., and in 1821 Secretary of War John C. Calhoun, faced with Congressionally mandated reductions in army manpower, gave Jackson the choice of either reduction in rank or resignation. Jackson angrily chose the later, although President James Monroe allowed him to serve as the first governor of the newly-acquired Florida Territory. In 1828, Jackson parleyed his enormous popularity into politics by defeating John Quincy Adams for the presidency. He proved a popular incumbent, was easily reelected, and he lent his frontier populism to an entire period called "Age of Jackson." He died at his home in Tennessee on June 28, 1845, the personification of frontier energy and a national icon to generations of Americans. In terms of results, Jackson was much less a general than a force of nature, and also the most accomplished all-around military commander in the War of 1812.

Archival

RG94 Letters. National Archives. Adjutant General's Office; 1813–1815.
RG98, No. 407/291. Letters sent. National Archives. HQ, 1814–1815.
RG98, No. 391/275. Orderly book. National Archives. HQ, Adj. Gen., 1813–1815.
RG98, No. 454/353. Orderly book. National Archives. HQ, Adj. Gen., 1813–1815.
RG98, No. 62/212. Orderly book. National Archives. Adj. Gen., 1814–1815.
RG98, No. 433/330. Orderly book. National Archives. HQ, Adj. Gen., 1813–1814.
RG107. Letters. National Archives. Secretary of War's Office; 1813–1815.
Jackson, Andrew. Orderly Book. Wisconsin Historical. Frontier Wars Papers, 9 U; 1813.

Manuscript

Jackson, Andrew Papers. Alabama Department. SGO13377, Folder 10.
Jackson, Andrew. Papers. Alabama Department. SPR225; Pensacola.
Jackson, Andrew. Letters. Alabama Department. SPR368; Joseph Graham military records.
Jackson, Andrew. Letter, 1814. Boston Public. Mss. Acc.404; Pensacola/Mobile.
Jackson, Andrew. Papers. Chicago Historical. 1813–1815.
Jackson, Andrew. Letter, 1813. Gilder Lehrman. GLC07371; Tallaseehatchee battle.
Jackson, Andrew. Papers. Historic New Orleans. William C. Cook Collection; 1812–1815.
Jackson, Andrew. Letters. Historical Society (Pa). Daniel Parker Papers; 1812–1815.
Jackson, Andrew. Letters. Historical Society (Pa). Gratz Coll.; 1812–1813.
Jackson, Andrew. Letters. Houghton Library. Autograph file; 1813–1814.
Jackson, Andrew. Papers. Library of Congress. Andrew Jackson Papers; 1812–1815.
Jackson, Andrew. Letters. Library of Congress. James Monroe Papers; 1814–1815.
Jackson, Andrew. Letters. Library of Congress. 1081, David B. Morgan Papers; 1814–1815.
Jackson, Andrew. Letters. Lilly Library. Pensacola, New Orleans; 1813–1815.
Jackson, Andrew. Letters. Missouri Historical. A0818; 1812–1814.
Jackson, Andrew. Letters. Morristown National. Micro. Reel 26, 720–733; 1812–1814.
Jackson, Andrew. Letters. Mudd Library. CO280; 1813–1815.
Jackson, Andrew. Letters. New York Historical. Misc. Mss J; 1814–1815.
Jackson, Andrew. Letters. New York Public. James Monroe Papers; 1814.

Jackson, Andrew. Letter, 1814. Pace Library. West Florida.
Jackson, Andrew. Papers. Perkins Library. Dalton Collection; 1813–1814.
Jackson, Andrew. Letters. Perkins Library. Andrew Jackson Collection; 1814–1815.
Jackson, Andrew. Letter, 1815. Regenstein Library. Butler-Gunsaulus Collection; Fort Morgan.
Jackson, Andrew. Letters. Rosenbach Museum. To Rachel Jackson; Alabama events.
Jackson, Andrew. Letters. Southern Historical. M-1863, John Overton Papers; 1812–1814.
Jackson, Andrew. Letters. Tennessee Historical. Andrew Jackson Papers; 1812–1815.
Jackson, Andrew Papers. Tennessee State. Andrew Jackson Papers.
Jackson, Andrew. Letters. Thomas Gilcrease. Misc. Mss., 1813–1814.

Printed Primary

Craven, Avery O., ed. "Letters of Andrew Jackson." *Huntington Library Bulletin* 3 (February 1933): 109–134.
Moser, Harold D. et al., eds. *The Papers of Andrew Jackson*. 5 vols. Knoxville: University of Tennessee Press, 1980–.
Remini, Robert V., ed. "Andrew Jackson's Account of the Battle of New Orleans." *Tennessee History* 28 (Spring 1967): 23–42.
Rowland, Dunbar, ed. *Official Letter Books of W. C. C. Claiborne, 1801–1816*. Jackson, Miss.: State Department of History and Archives, 1917.
"Two Uncollected Letters by Andrew Jackson." *Florida Historical Quarterly* 15 (January 1937): 169–172.

Select Secondary

Brands, H.W. *Andrew Jackson, His Life and Times*. New York: Doubleday, 2005.
Buchanan, John. *Jackson's Way: Andrew Jackson and the People of the Western Waters*. New York: John Wiley, 2001.
Burns, Charles R. "The Devastation Before Horseshoe Bend: Jackson's Rampage to the Confluence of the Coosa and Tallapoosa." Unpublished master's thesis, Jacksonville State University, 2005.
Fleming, Thomas. "Old Hickory's Finest Hour." *MHQ* 13, no. 2 (2001): 6–17.
Groom, Winston. *Patriotic Fire: Andrew Jackson and Jean Lafitte at the Battle of New Orleans*. New York: Alfred A. Knopf, 2006.
Guice, John D. W. "Old Hickory and the Natchez Trace." *Journal of Mississippi History* 69, no. 2 (2007): 167–182.
Heidler, David S. *Old Hickory's War: Andrew Jackson and the Quest for Empire*. Baton Rouge: Louisiana State University Press, 2003.
Jones, Pam. "William Weatherford and the Road to the Holy Ground." *Alabama Heritage* No. 74 (2004): 24–32.
Kanon, Tom. "'Glories in the Field': John Cocke vs. Andrew Jackson During the War of 1812." *Journal of East Tennessee History* 71 (1999): 47–65.
Millett, Nathaniel. "Britain's 1814 Occupation of Pensacola and America's Response: An Episode in the War of 1812 on the Southeastern Borderlands." *Florida Historical Quarterly* 84, no. 2 (2005): 229–255.

Patterson, Benton R. *The Generals: Andrew Jackson, Sir Edward Pakenham, and the Road to the Battle of New Orleans.* New York: New York University Press, 2005.
Reid, John A. "Prelude to Horseshoe Bend: The Battles of Emuckfau and Entochopco, January, 1814." *Journal of the Indian Wars* 1 (No. 2 1999): 1–20.
Remini, Robert V. *Andrew Jackson.* New York: Palgrave Macmillan, 2008.
Rucker, Brian R. "Nixon's Raid and Other Precursors to Jackson's 1814 Invasion of Spanish West Florida." *Gulf South Historical Review* 14, no. 2 (1999): 33–50.
Turner, Jonathan S. "Horseshoe Bend: Epic Battle on the Southern Frontier." Unpublished master's thesis, Georgia Southern University, 1996.
Waselkov, Gregory A. *A Conquering Spirit: Fort Mims and the Redstick War of 1813–1814.* Tuscaloosa: University of Alabama Press, 2006.

Morgan Lewis

Morgan Lewis was born in New York City on October 16, 1754, the son of a prosperous merchant. He passed through the College of New Jersey (Princeton University) at the age of 19, and was studying law in the office of John Jay when the Revolutionary War commenced in 1775. Lewis joined a rifle company, proved adept at soldiering, and within two years served as colonel on the staff of General Horatio Gates at Saratoga. He subsequently received appointment as deputy quartermaster general and performed well during the final phases of the conflict in northern New York. During the war he also married into the influential Livingston family, which assured him a center stage in New York politics. Lewis commenced a successful law practice after the war and in November 1791 he rose to become state attorney general. The following year he was made chief justice of the state supreme court and functioned adequately, if without distinction, until 1804, when he defeated Aaron Burr in a race for the governorship. In this capacity Lewis proved an extremely partisan figure, promoting his own cronies and sacking those who disagreed with his policies. Having alienated the bulk of his own Republican party, he was defeated by Daniel D. Tompkins in 1807, although he used his connections to gain election to the state senate in 1810. On April 3, 1812, President James Madison, an old acquaintance, appointed him quartermaster general with a rank of brigadier. This was a position for which he possessed no formal training or experience. Moreover, Lewis was restricted in his authority to the Northern Department but, insomuch as quartermaster and supply functions were problematic anyway, he remained fully occupied simply trying to administer his charge. Lewis proved inept in this capacity, although departmental procedures were so flawed it is unlikely that others could have performed any better. Moreover, Lewis was studiously indifferent to critical matters like supply functions and he sought out a field

Major General Morgan Lewis. Photograph by Glenn Castellano; courtesy of the Art Commission of the City of New York.

command. Political connections again resulted in his appointment as a major general as of March 2, 1813, as part of Major General Henry Dearborn's army. His own position as quartermaster general was filled by the marginally better-qualified Robert Swartwout.

Lewis's performance as a military leader posted little improvement. He was technically in charge of the army during the May 27, 1813, capture of Fort George, Upper Canada, while Dearborn was ill, and he issued the fatal order halting General Winfield Scott's pursuit of defeated British forces. This allowed the latter to regroup and defeat a tardy American pursuit at Stoney Creek, June 6, 1813. In light of his mediocre reputation, he failed to succeed to command of the army after Dearborn was relieved, and was superseded by General James Wilkinson. Lewis played no significant role in the ill-fated St. Lawrence campaign of 1813, being largely ill, and failed to garner any distinction. In the spring of 1814 he was reassigned to the relatively quiet sector of New York City as head of the 3rd Military District. He commanded the city's defenses until the end of the war and finally mustered out on June 15, 1815. Lewis declined reentering politics in the postwar period, but he was extremely active in city matters, serving as president of the New York Historical Society, 1832–1836, a founder of New York University, and president of the Society of the Cincinnati from 1839 until his death. He died in New York City on April 7, 1844, a politically well-connected leader of marginal ability and less merit.

Archival

RG94. Letters. National Archives. Adjutant General's Office; 1812–1815.
RG107. Letters. National Archives. Secretary of War's Office; 1812–1815.

Manuscript

Lewis, Morgan. Letter, 1812. Historical Society (Pa). Daniel Parker Papers, financial matters.
Lewis, Morgan. Letter, 1812. Historical Society (Pa). Greer Coll., to John Armstrong.
Lewis, Morgan. Letter, 1813. Historical Society (Pa). Gratz Coll., To Henry Dearborn.
Lewis, Morgan. Letters. Library of Congress. Anthony Lamb Papers; 1812–1813.
Lewis, Morgan. Letters. Library of Congress. Van Deventer Papers; prisoners.
Lewis, Morgan. Letters. Lilly Library. War of 1812 Coll.; 1812–1813.
Lewis, Morgan. Letter, 1814. Manuscripts and Archives. Mss 554, Eli Whitney Papers.
Lewis, Morgan. Letters. Massachusetts Historical. Henry Dearborn Papers.
Lewis, Morgan. Papers New York Historical. Lewis Morgan Papers, Box 3; 1811–1815.
Lewis, Morgan. Letter New York Historical. Misc Mss L, vindication, Fort George.
Lewis, Morgan. Letters. New York Historical. Henry Dearborn letter book; 1812–1813.
Lewis, Morgan. Vindication. New York Public. U.S. Army Boxes, typed transcript, 1813.
Lewis, Morgan. Letter, 1812. New York State. Mss. 1215; to Anthony Lamb, supplies.
Lewis, Morgan. Letter, 1812. New York State. HA12015; Holland Family Papers.
Lewis, Morgan. Letter, 1813. New York State. (NIC) NYCE2IV-120-0003.
Lewis, Morgan. Letter, 1814. New York State. 13795, takes over District No. 3.

Printed Primary

Hastings, Hugh, ed. *Public Papers of Daniel D. Tompkins, Governor of New York, 1807–1817.* 3 vols. Albany, N.Y.: J. B. Lyons, 1902.

Select Secondary

Delafield, Julia. *Biographies of Francis Lewis and Morgan Lewis.* 2 vols. New York: A. D. F. Randolph, 1877. Vol. 2, 72–120.

Risch, Erna. *Quartermaster Support for the Army: A History of the Corps, 1775–1939.* Washington, D.C.: Office of the Quartermaster, 1962.

Thomas Pinckney

Thomas Pinckney was born in Charleston, South Carolina, on October 23, 1750, the scion of a wealthy aristocratic family. As such he was educated at Oxford University and also studied military science at the Royal Military Academy, Caen, France, before returning home to start a law practice in 1774. The Revolutionary War commenced a year later, so Pinckney joined the 1st South Carolina Regiment as a captain, and subsequently rose to major. He completed several uneventful years of garrison duty at Charleston and also served as a staff liaison during the Franco-American siege of Savannah in 1779, before joining the staff of General Horatio Gates. In this capacity he narrowly escaped capture at the fall of Charleston, but was wounded and taken at Camden on August 16, 1780. Pinckney was paroled and fulfilled his last round of military service at Yorktown as a staff officer. After the war he parlayed his wealth and political connections into politics, serving as governor of South Carolina from 1787 to 1789. In 1792 President George Washington appointed him Minister to Great Britain where he tried, and failed, to seek political accommodation concerning British forts in the Old Northwest and American fishing rights off Newfoundland. In 1794 Pinckney was appointed special envoy to Spain where he helped fashion the Treaty of San Lorenzo on October 27, 1795, his most important accomplishment abroad. This agreement granted the United States use of the port of New Orleans and also established a boundary between the American territory and West Florida. Back home, Pinckney ran for vice president as a Federalist and finished second behind Thomas Jefferson. He then served several terms in Congress before retiring back to his plantation to farm.

On March 27, 1812, President James Madison awarded Pinckney a major general's commission, much less on account of his military abilities than a pressing need to recruit high-visibility Federalists to support the war. He

Major General Thomas Pinckney. "General Thomas Pinckney" (1750–1828) by Charles Fraser (American, 1782–1860), watercolor on ivory, copyright Gibbes Museum of Art/Carolina Art Association, 1939.004.0002.

answered the call then assumed control of the far-flung 6th Military District, comprising North Carolina, South Carolina, and Georgia. Thus situated, Pinckney spent the bulk of his energies preparing forts and garrisons along a 600-mile strip of Southern coastline to thwart potential British assaults. He also conducted a careful balancing act with Spanish authorities in East Florida, attempted to secure their neutrality, and demanded that they refrain from arming hostile Indians. However, his biggest challenge came in August, 1813, when the Creek War erupted and Pinckney was forced to share slender resources with General Thomas Flournoy, commanding the 7th Military District at New Orleans. Because the Creek territory straddled both the districts, Pinckney had to carefully parcel out men and provisions while orchestrating his own three-pronged strategy for crushing the Indians. This involved arming, equipping, and dispatching columns from the Mississippi Territory, Georgia, and Tennessee, of which the later, under the steely leadership of General Andrew Jackson, proved the most successful. In this respect, Pinckney performed useful service by recruiting and dispatching the 39th Infantry to assist Jackson's force, which finally crushed the Creeks at Horseshoe Bend in March 1814. Pinckney next arrived at Fort Jackson, where he relieved Jackson and began negotiating a peace settlement with various Creek chiefs. Jackson, like many westerners, felt that Pinckney and Indian agent Benjamin Hawkins were too leniently disposed towards the Indians, and agitated for their removal. Within weeks Pinckney and Hawkins were reassigned back to the east coast, while Jackson became chief negotiator and imposed the harsh Treaty of Fort Jackson on the Creeks in August 1814. Pinckney resumed his administrative duties back at Charleston, at which he proved most adept, and finally mustered out from service on June 15, 1815. He retired back to private life on his farm and became noted for his innovative irrigation and breeding techniques. In 1825 Pinckney came out of seclusion to serve as president of the Society of the Cincinnati before dying in Charleston on November 2, 1828. Virtually unknown as a senior commander, he provided excellent staff work throughout his tenure in office.

Archival

RG94. Letters. National Archives. Adjutant General's Office; 1812–1815.
RG98, No. 677 General orders. National Archives. Charleston, S. C., June 1812–Feb. 1813.
RG98, No. 678. General orders. National Archives. Charleston, S. C., June 1812–Feb. 1813.
RG98, Nos. 679, 675. Letters sent. National Archives. 6th Mil. Dist, March, 1813–June 1815.
RG98, Nos. 681, 682. Orderly book. National Archives. Adj. Gen., 6th Mil. Dist., 1813–1815.
RG107. Letters. National Archives. Secretary of War's Office; 1812–1815.
6th Military District. Orderly Book. Southern Historical. Coll. 86; April 1813–May 1814.

Manuscript

Pinckney, Thomas. Letters. Alabama Department. SPR368; Joseph Graham military records.
Pinckney, Thomas. Letters. Clements Library. War of 1812 Collection; 1812.

Pinckney, Thomas. Letters. Historical Society (Pa). Daniel Parker Papers; 1814–1815.
Pinckney, Thomas. Letter, 1813. Historical Society (Pa). To Governor David B. Mitchell.
Pinckney, Thomas. Letters. Georgia Department. Georgia Military Affairs; 1812–1814.
Pinckney, Thomas. Letters. Library of Congress. Andrew Jackson Papers; 1813–1815.
Pinckney, Thomas. Letter, 1815. Lilly Library. War of 1812 Coll.; William H. Crawford.
Pinckney, Thomas. Letters. New York Historical. Thomas Pinckney Folder; 1814.
Pinckney, Thomas. Letters. New York Public. James Monroe Papers; 1812–1815.
Pinckney, Thomas. Letter, 1813. Perkins Library. James Iredell Mss; to William Hawkins.
Pinckney, Thomas. Letter, 1813. Perkins Library. Pinckney Papers; to William Hawkins.
Pinckney, Thomas. Letter, 1814. Perkins Library. Richard Singleton Papers.
Pinckney, Thomas. Letter book. South Carolina Historical. Pinckney Papers; 6th/7th Military Districts.
Pinckney, Thomas. Thomas. State Historical (Mo). Thomas Adams Smith Papers; 1812.

Printed Primary

Davis, T. Frederick, ed. "United States Troops in Spanish East Florida, 1812–1813." *Florida Historical Quarterly* 10 (July 1931): 24–34.
Moser, Harold D. et al., eds. *The Papers of Andrew Jackson*. 5 vols. Knoxville: University of Tennessee Press, 1980.
Rowland, Dunbar, ed. *Official Letter Books of W. C. C. Claiborne, 1801–1816*. 6 vols. Jackson, Miss.: State Department of History and Archives, 1917.

Select Secondary

Nicholas, Bruce F. "Postscript to a Career: Thomas Pinckney in the War of 1812." Unpublished master's thesis, Auburn University, 1975.
Owsley, Frank. *The Struggle for the Gulf Borderlands: The Creek War and the Battle of New Orleans, 1812–1815*. Gainesville: University of Florida Press, 1981.
Pinckney, Charles C. *Life of General Thomas Pinckney*. Boston: Houghton, Mifflin, 1895.
Williams, Frances L. *A Founding Family: The Pinckneys of South Carolina*. New York: Harcourt, Brace, Jovanovich, 1978.

James Wilkinson

James Wilkinson was born in Calvert County, Maryland, in 1757, where he studied medicine. He had barely opened his medical practice when the Revolutionary war erupted in 1775, and he joined Thompson's Pennsylvania

Regiment. Wilkinson was present during the siege of Boston and subsequently accompanied Colonel Benedict Arnold's arduous Quebec Expedition. By the fall of 1776 he was a captain and functioning as aide-de-camp to General Horatio Gates. Wilkinson performed capably over the next two years as a staff officer, becoming a brevet brigadier general at the age of 20, but also displayed an ingrained penchant for intrigue. This first manifested when, as a member of the Board of War, he joined the so-called Conway Cabal against General George Washington. The conspiracy was uncovered soon after, and Wilkinson resigned from the board to function as clothier general. He held that post until March 1781, when charges of fiscal impropriety required his departure. Wilkinson ended the war as a brigadier general in the Pennsylvania militia and a member of the state legislature. Soon after he relocated to Kentucky, where he labored to discredit George Rogers Clark and sought to manipulate the drive to statehood for his own advantage. When that failed, Wilkinson moved to New Orleans in 1787, to negotiate a lucrative trading monopoly on the Mississippi River with Spain. This arrangement carried a price, and thereafter Wilkinson operated as a spy for his benefactors. However, the deal collapsed when the Mississippi was opened to general trade, and he returned to Kentucky as a speculator until further intrigue was in the offing.

In 1792 Wilkinson rejoined the army as lieutenant colonel of the 2nd Infantry. In this capacity he fought with reasonable efficiency at the Battle of Fallen Timbers in 1794, although he despised General Anthony Wayne and worked to undermine his authority. When Wayne died of illness in 1796, Wilkinson became commanding general of the army with a rank of brigadier general, a post he occupied until 1812. In 1803 he accompanied Governor Charles C. C. Claiborne to New Orleans and claimed all the territory ceded to the United States through the Louisiana Purchase. He also found time to reforge ties with his Spanish paymasters and resuming spying for them. While at St. Louis as newly-appointed governor of the Missouri Territory, Wilkinson dispatched Lieutenant Zebulon M. Pike on his famous scouting exploration to the Southwest, while simultaneously alerting Spanish authorities to that same fact. Between 1802 and 1804, he also entertained a grandiose scheme with former vice president Aaron Burr to agitate a breakaway republic in the Southwest that would ally itself to Spain. Wilkinson remained a key player until his own interests were threatened, so in 1806 he alerted President Thomas Jefferson about Burr's intentions. Burr was brought to trial in 1807 and Wilkinson was the government's prime witness against him, but on the basis of his own testimony nearly indicted himself. He lost his governorship to explorer Meriwether Lewis and was reposted back to New Orleans as garrison commander. In 1809 Wilkinson's incompetence manifested in the disastrous Terre aux Boeufs expedition, whereby he encamped an army of 2,000

Major General James Wilkinson. National Portrait Gallery, Smithsonian Institution.

men in the middle of a swamp and watched it wither away. Subordinates like Colonel Wade Hampton and Lieutenant Winfield Scott railed against him, so in 1811 Wilkinson was court-martialed for military ineptitude and indifference. Unfortunately, his silver-tongued defense led to an acquittal, and he resumed command back at New Orleans just as hostilities with Great Britain commenced.

In time, Wilkinson's feckless and unscrupulous leadership proved his own undoing. As commander of the 7th Military District, he conspired with Secretary of War William Eustis to halt General Andrew Jackson's march from

Natchez, so as not to serve with him. He advanced to major general on March 2, 1813, and the following month advanced into Spanish West Florida and annexed Mobile on the pretext that it was being used by British agents. With that bloodlessly accomplished, he was summoned north by another Revolutionary War acquaintance, Secretary of War John Armstrong. Wilkinson was selected to head up the 9th Military District and lead an ambitious two-pronged strategy for conquering Montreal and, with it, Canada. In August 1813, Wilkinson established his headquarters at Sacketts Harbor, New York, and amassed an invasion force of 7,000 largely untrained soldiers. These he led down the St. Lawrence River in an armada of boats and small craft, while his arch-enemy, Hampton, marched 4,000 men up the Champlain River Valley. Both men were then to unite on a concerted drive against their objective. Unfortunately for the United States, neither Wilkinson nor Hampton proved cooperative, and coordination between the pincers proved impossible. Supplies delayed Wilkinson's main advance until November, when the weather was rainy and freezing cold, and he became ill. He was temporarily succeeded by Brigadier General John Parker Boyd, who ineptly bungled the Battle of Crysler's farm on November 11, 1813. It was subsequently learned that Hampton, too, had been bested at the battle of Chateauguay on October 28, and unceremoniously fell back to northern New York. At this juncture, the ailing general, somewhat delusional from doses of the opiate laudanum, cancelled his offensive, landed on the New York shore, then marched his men to winter encampments at French Mills. This proved an ordeal worthy of Valley Forge itself, for the soldiers were poorly victualed while lacking adequate heating, clothing, and shelter. Several weeks of deprivation ensued, then Wilkinson roused his freezing cohorts from their campfires and made for La Colle Mill, Lower Canada, to capture the British garrison there. On March 30, 1814, the 200 defenders, safe behind impenetrable stone walls, pluckily resisted and the Americans drew off with 180 casualties. This final debacle caused a public outcry and within weeks Wilkinson was relieved of command. He was court-martialed again in the fall of 1814, ably defended his actions, and was once more acquitted. Content to finally be rid of him, the government allowed Wilkinson to honorably resign from the army on June 15, 1815.

In 1816 Wilkinson published his *Memoirs of My Own Times*, a three-volume apologia which castigated others for disasters in the War of 1812 while minimizing his culpability for them. He retired to a sugar plantation in New Orleans until 1821, then ventured to Mexico City to obtain a land grant in Texas. Wilkinson died there on December 28, 1825, with the unique distinction of never having won a battle nor lost a court-martial. In every respect he embodied the very officer archetype that the Jeffersonian political establishment so dreaded from their own military.

Archival

Wilkinson, James. Orderly Book. Library of Congress. 7th Mil. District, 1812–1813.
Northern Army. Orderly book. Library of Congress. No. 108; St. Lawrence, 1813–1815.
RG94 Letters. National Archives. Adjutant General's Office; 1812–1814.
RG98, No. 369/236. Orderly book. National Archives. 1812–1813; New Orleans.
RG98, No. 45/507. Misc. returns. National Archives. HQ, Left Division, 1813–1815.
RG98, Item 19. Letters. National Archives. Letters to Gov. Daniel D. Tompkins.
RG107. Letters. National Archives. Secretary of War's Office; 1812–1814.

Manuscript

Wilkinson, James Letters. Buffalo and Erie. A. Conger Goodyear Collection.
Wilkinson, James. Letters. Buffalo and Erie. A00-489; Solomon Van Rensselaer, 1813.
Wilkinson, James. Papers. Chicago Historical. 1811–1815.
Wilkinson, James. Letter, 1812. Chicago Historical. Wilkinson Letter File; to David Holmes.
Wilkinson, James. Letters. Historical Society (Pa). Rawle Collection; 1812–1814.
Wilkinson, James. Letters. Historical Society (Pa). Daniel Parker Papers; 1813–1815.
Wilkinson, James. Letter, 1813. Historical Society (Pa). Dreer Coll., to John Armstrong.
Wilkinson, James. Letter, 1814. Huntington Library. HM22993; war events.
Wilkinson, James. Letter, 1814. Huntington Library. HM22982; war events.
Wilkinson, James. Letters. Library of Congress. James Madison Papers; 1812–1813.
Wilkinson, James. Papers. Library of Congress. 0837, James Wilkinson Papers; 1812–1815.
Wilkinson, James. Letters. Library of Congress. Andrew Jackson Papers; 1812–1813.
Wilkinson, James. Letter, 1813. Lilly Library. Jonathan Williams Papers.
Wilkinson, James. Letters. Lilly Library. War of 1812 Coll.; 1812–1815.
Wilkinson, James. Letters. Massachusetts Historical. Henry Dearborn Papers; 1813.
Wilkinson, James. Letters. Massachusetts Historical. Jacob J. Brown Papers; 1813–1814.
Wilkinson, James. Letter, 1813. Missouri Historical. Daniel Bisssell Papers; Champlain Valley.
Wilkinson, James. Letters. New York Historical. Isaac Chauncey letter books; 1813.
Wilkinson, James. Letters. New York Historical. Misc Mss W; 1812–1815.
Wilkinson, James. Letter, 1814. New York State. (N) 244; Royal Navy on Lake Champlain.
Wilkinson, James. Letter. Owen D. Young. Mss Coll. 132, St. Lawrence, 1813, 1815.
Wilkinson, James. Letters. Tennessee State. War of 1812 Collection.
Wilkinson, James. Letters. William T. Young. 55W30; court-martial matters, 1814–1815.

Printed Primary

American State Papers. Military Affairs. 2 vols. Washington, D.C.: Gales and Seaton, 1832–1861.
Carter, Clarence E., ed. *The Territorial Papers of the United States: Vol. IX, The Territory of Orleans, 1803–1812.* Washington, D.C.: Government Printing Office, 1940.

Rowland, Dunbar, ed. *Official Letter Books of W. C. C. Claiborne, 1801–1816*. 6 vols. Jackson, Miss.: State Department of History and Archives, 1917.

Wilkinson, James. "General Wilkinson to General Mooers." *North Country Notes* (September 1969).

Wilkinson, James. *Memoirs of My Own Times*. 4 vols. Philadelphia: Abraham Small, 1816.

Select Secondary

Crackel, Theodore J. *Mr. Jefferson's Army: Politics and Social Reform of the Military Establishment, 1801–1809*. New York: New York University Press, 1987.

Gosling, D. C. L. "The Battle of La Colle Mill, 1814." *Journal of the Society for Army Historical Research* 47 (1969): 169–174.

Graves, Donald E. *Field of Glory: The Battle of Crysler's Farm, 1813*. Toronto: Robin Brass Studio, 1999.

Montgomery, M. R. *Jefferson and the Gun-Men: How the West Was Almost Lost*. New York: Crown Publishers, 2000.

Porter, David O. "James Wilkinson: Spanish Agent or Double Agent." Unpublished PhD. dissertation, George Washington University, 2007.

Posey, John T. "Rascality Revisited: In Defense of General James Wilkinson." *Filson Club Quarterly* 74, no. 4 (2000): 309–351.

Rusche, Timothy M. "Treachery within the U. S. Army." *Pennsylvania History* 65, no. 4 (1998): 478–491.

Smith, Gene A. "'Our Flag was Display'd within Their Works': The Treaty of Ghent and the Conquest of Mobile." *Alabama Review* 52, no. 1 (1999): 3–20.

BRIGADIER GENERALS

Daniel Bissell

Daniel Bissell was born in Hartford, Connecticut, on August 15, 1769, and at the age of twelve he served in the American Revolution as a drummer boy. Military life appealed to him, so in 1788 he joined the nascent 1st U. S. Infantry as a private and began his long climb through the ranks. Bissell served as a sergeant at St. Clair's disastrous defeat in 1791, fought capably, and won a battlefield commission to ensign. Three years later he commanded an artillery detachment during the so-called Whiskey Rebellion in western Pennsylvania, being there commended by President George Washington. Bissell, by dint of good performance, advanced to lieutenant colonel in 1808, and proved instrumental in outfitting and training the first two companies of horse artillery in the U.S. Army. His peacetime career crested the following year with an appointment as commander of the Eighth Military District, headquartered at Fort Bellefontaine, which encompassed the vast Louisiana-Missouri Territories. In this capacity, Bissell oversaw the training and administration of scattered detachments under his jurisdiction and he handled his affairs with commendable efficiency.

The renewal of hostilities with Great Britain in June 1812 afforded Bissell additional opportunities for distinction. On August 15, 1812, he became colonel of the 5th Infantry and orchestrated defenses of the thinly-populated Missouri frontier against Indian attack. The following summer, 1813, he was succeeded by General Benjamin Howard and transferred to Fort George, Upper Canada, spending several weeks drilling his men in preparation for General James Wilkinson's St. Lawrence expedition. Bissell functioned with the advance guard under General Jacob J. Brown, acquitted himself well, and on March 9, 1814, he received a promotion to brigadier general. That month he also fought at La Colle Mill, Lower Canada, and subsequently joined General George Izard's Right Division at Plattsburgh, New York. There his men were exposed to the latter's thorough training regimen, but in August Bissell's

Brigadier General Daniel Bissell. Missouri History Museum.

brigade, along with that of General Thomas Adams Smith, accompanied Izard on his controversial march to the Niagara frontier.

After a summer of heavy fighting, American military activity at Niagara was at an impasse. Izard confronted a smaller British force under Lieutenant General Gordon Drummond, then was strongly posted behind Chippawa Creek. Knowing that frontal assaults against entrenched troops were potentially disastrous, Izard tried luring Drummond out of his trenches by dispatching

Bissell's brigade to attack a supply of grain stored along Lyon's Creek. There, on October 19, 1814, his 900 men were attacked by 750 British at Cook's Mills. The enemy drove in his pickets, but the Americans quickly rallied, and engaged them frontally while deploying to turn their left flank. Such adroit maneuvering induced the British to withdraw from the field of battle in good order. For a loss of 60 casualties, Bissell had prevailed in the final encounter between regular forces in Canada during the war. He then burned grain stores as ordered and returned to Fort Erie without incident. Izard publicly lauded him in his official dispatches. After the war, Bissell remained in service as colonel of the new 1st Infantry and part of General Andrew Jackson's Southern Division. He continued fulfilling a succession of important posts between St. Louis and New Orleans until 1821, when congressionally-mandated reductions in military spending forced his retirement. Bissell felt that his discharge was politically motivated and orchestrated by General Winfield Scott, so he enlisted the support of Missouri's influential Senator Thomas Hart Benton to regain his commission. Benton argued Bissell's case before Congress for over twelve years, but failed to get him reinstated. Bissell, meanwhile, had set himself up as a successful businessman and community leader. In April 1825 he chaired a committee supervising the arrival of the Marquis de Lafayette to St. Louis and personally welcomed that esteemed figure to Missouri. Bissell died at his St. Louis farm on December 14, 1833, a capable soldier and military administrator. In a career spanning 33 years, he covered every grade from drummer boy to brigadier general and his diligent, lifelong service also marks him as a significant contributor to the development of the early western frontier.

Archival

Bissell, Daniel. Letter book. Missouri Historical. Bissell Papers, Bellfontaine; 1812–1813.
RG94. Letters. National Archives. Adjutant General's Office; 1812–1815.
RG107. Letters. National Archives. Secretary of War's Office; 1812–1815.

Manuscript

Bissell, Daniel. Letters. Historical Society (Pa). Parker Papers, Box 14, 22; Belle Fontaine.
Bissell, Daniel. Letters. Historical Society (Pa). Gratz Coll., Box 32; postwar trials, 1816.
Bissell, Daniel. Letters. Library of Congress. Misc. Mss. Coll., postwar concerns.
Bissell, Daniel. Papers. Missouri Historical. Daniel Bissell Papers; 1812–1813.
Bissell, Daniel. Letters. Missouri Historical. Microfilm No. 56; originals filmed in 1959.
Bissell, Daniel. Letters. St. Louis Mercantile. M-9; 1812–1813.

PRINTED PRIMARY

Carter, Clarence E., ed. *The Territorial Papers of the United States: Vol. XIV, The Territory of Louisiana-Missouri, 1806–1814.* Washington, D.C.: Government Printing Office, 1949.

Ryan, Harold W. "Daniel Bissell — His Story." *Missouri Historical Society Bulletin* 12 (October 1955): 32–44.

SELECT SECONDARY

Kramer, Gerhard. "The Bissell House." *Missouri Historical Society Bulletin* 22, no. 4 (1966): 446–456.

Ryan, Harold W. "Daniel Bissell — Late General." *Missouri Historical Society Bulletin* 15 (October 1958): 20–28.

Zell, Carl J. "General Daniel Bissell." Unpublished Ph.D. dissertation, St. Louis University, 1971.

Joseph Bloomfield

Joseph Bloomfield was born in Woodbridge, New Jersey, on October 18, 1753, the son of a successful doctor. As part of the landed aristocracy, he was educated at private academies before studying law under the colonial attorney general of New Jersey. However, he sided with the Patriots once the Revolutionary War commenced and joined the 3rd New Jersey Regiment as a captain. Bloomfield handled himself well as a soldier, rose to major, and was wounded at Monmouth in 1778. His injuries necessitated an early retirement, but after the war he rejoined the militia as a brigadier general. In this capacity he commanded New Jersey troops during suppression of the Whiskey Rebellion of 1794. Bloomfield also acquired a taste for politics and, after functioning many years as a Federalist, he joined the Democratic-Republicans as a warm partisan of Thomas Jefferson. As such he became governor of New Jersey in 1801, lost his seat a year later, and was thereafter consecutively reelected to office over the next decade. His most notable act was signing a gradual emancipation law that reduced slavery in New Jersey to six percent of the population by 1860. Bloomfield was also a strong supporter of President James Madison's moves towards renewed war with Great Britain, and in 1812 he provided the state militia with a badly needed overhaul.

On March 27, 1812, Bloomfield's party ties culminated in his appointment as brigadier general in the U.S. Army, and commanding the 3rd Military District, headquartered at New York City. Here he energetically oversaw

Brigadier General Joseph Bloomfield. New Jersey State House Portrait Collection, administered by the New Jersey State Museum, SHPC42; photograph courtesy Frick Art Reference Library.

the recruitment and training of 8,000 soldiers at Plattsburgh until being superseded by General Henry Dearborn in the fall of 1812. At that time he also commanded the 1st Brigade, consisting of the 6th, 15th, and 16th Infantries. Bloomfield served briefly along the northern frontier until the spring of 1813, before transferring south to command 4th Military District (western New Jersey, Pennsylvania, and Delaware), headquartered at Philadelphia. Bloomfield never experienced combat in the War of 1812, but performed adequately as a military administrator. He mustered out of uniform on June 15, 1815, and resumed his political activities by gaining a seat in the U.S. Congress for several terms. Bloomfield, a cordial, old-style aristocrat, died from injuries received in a carriage accident on October 3, 1823.

Archival

Bloomfield, Joseph. Letter book. Clements Library. Plattsburgh; 1812.
Bloomfield, Joseph. Orderly book. Huntington Library. HM 672, 1st Brigade; 1812–1813.
Bloomfield, Joseph. Orderly book. Morristown National. Microfilm Reel No. 5, 608–951; 1812–1813.
RG94. Letters. National Archives. Adjutant General's Office; 1812–1815.
RG98, No. 393/276. Letters sent. National Archives. 4th Military District, 1813–1814.
RG98, No. 460/359. Orderly book. National Archives. 4th Military District, 1814–1815.
RG107. Letters. National Archives. Secretary of War's Office; 1812–1815.

Manuscript

Bloomfield, Joseph. Letters. Historical Society (Pa). Gratz Coll., Box 32; military; 1813–1814.
Bloomfield, Joseph. Letters. Historical Society (Pa). Daniel Parker Papers, Box 14, 23, 31.
Bloomfield, Joseph. Letter, 1814. Historical Society (Pa). Stauffier Coll., to Simon Snyder.
Bloomfield, Joseph. Letter, 1814. Historical Society (Pa). Cadwalader Coll., Box 32 T; 4th Mil. Dist.
Bloomfield, Joseph. Letters. Maine Historical. Coll. 33, Henry Dearborn Papers; 1812.
Bloomfield, Joseph. Letters. Manuscript and Archives. Mss 631, Box 85; 1813–1814.
Bloomfield, Joseph. Letter, 1813. New Jersey Historical. MG14; brigade strength, Burlington, Vt.
Bloomfield, Joseph. Letters. New York Historical. Allan McLane Papers.
Bloomfield, Joseph. Letters. New York Historical. Henry Dearborn letter books; 1813–1814.
Bloomfield, Joseph. Letters. Rutgers University. 3rd Military District; 1812–1813.

Printed Primary

Lender, Mark, and James Kirby, eds. *Citizen Soldier: The Revolutionary War Journal of Joseph Bloomfield*. Newark: New Jersey Historical Society, 1982.

Select Secondary

Stellhorn, Paul A., and Michael J. Birkner, eds. *The Governors of New Jersey*. Trenton: New Jersey Historical Commission, 1982.

John Parker Boyd

John Parker Boyd was born at Newburyport, Massachusetts, on December 21, 1764, and he enlisted in the U.S. Army as an ensign in 1786. Unfortunately, postwar retrenchment stifled his military ambitions, so in 1789 he ventured to Hindustan, India, and worked as a mercenary. Boyd tendered his services to the various feuding princes and at one point Nizam Ali Khad appointed him commander of the Madras garrison, numbering 10,000 men. He served in this capacity for two decades until 1806, when British consolidation of power in India made independent soldiering impractical. Boyd then returned to the United States and rejoined the army as colonel of the 4th Infantry on October 4, 1808. He appears to have functioned competently in this capacity and, in fact, took deliberate steps to enhance unit esprit d'corps by recruiting a military band and equipping his soldiers with fancy shakos and belly-style cartridge boxes. In 1811 he accompanied the regiment from Pittsburgh to the Indiana Territory, where it formed the nucleus of Governor William Henry Harrison's territorial army. Boyd fought bravely at the November 7, 1811, battle of Tippecanoe, where his regulars stood firmly in the face of a determined night attack on the American encampment. He received the thanks of the Indiana territorial legislature, but his impolitic remarks regarding the militia generated heated acrimony. Nevertheless, the War Department promoted him to brigadier general on August 26, 1812, to fill a vacancy created by the death of General Peter Gansevoort. Boyd was posted with the army of Major General Henry Dearborn in New York and fought well at the May 27, 1813, capture of Fort George, Upper Canada. Following the embarrassing capture of Generals John Chandler and William H. Winder at Stoney Creek on June 6, 1813, he functioned as the de facto regional commander at Niagara for several weeks. His principal activity was dispatching an unsupported column of troops under Lieutenant Colonel Charles G. Boerstler to seize British supplies, which came to grief at Beaver Dams on June 24, 1813. Boyd nevertheless remained at Fort George until the fall of 1813, when he transferred to command the 1st Brigade (5th, 12th, 13th Infantries) as part of General James Wilkinson's ambitious St. Lawrence expedition.

Due to supply shortages, Wilkinson was detained at Sacketts Harbor until late fall, in the middle of the rainy season. Inclement weather resulted in the commander's persistent illness and Boyd, senior brigadier present, assumed control of operations. The American flotilla continued sailing downstream, closely shadowed by British gunboats on the river and forces marching along the river bank. On November 11, 1813, Wilkinson ordered Boyd to land the troops and engage their pursuers. The ensuing battle of Crysler's Farm saw Boyd's 2,400 tired, wet, and ill-trained recruits square off against

800 British, Canadians, and Indians on an open field intersected by deep ravines. Numbers should have prevailed, but he grossly erred by committing his forces in piecemeal fashion, instead of a single, coordinated rush. Consequently, the gifted British commander, Lieutenant Colonel Joseph W. Morrison, adroitly shuffled his troops and repelled each thrust in detail. After General Leonard Covington fell critically wounded, the Americans quit the field in disarray and embarked en masse. Boyd's inept handling of affairs cost them over 300 casualties; British losses were one-third as much.

Charges of incompetence were leveled against Boyd, but no court-martial ever convened. Still, for the rest of the war, Boyd commanded the relatively quiet 3rd Military District (New York City and eastern New Jersey) until his final discharge on June 15, 1815. Thereafter he lived in obscurity in Boston, Massachusetts, until President Andrew Jackson appointed him naval agent shortly before his death on October 4, 1830. He also published a bombastic pamphlet in his own defense, which did little to redeem his reputation among critics. Winfield Scott, who served under Boyd at Niagara, considered him a sufficiently competent regimental commander, but "vacillating and imbecile beyond all endurance as a chief under high responsibility."

Archival

Boyd, John P. Orderly book. Burton Historical. 1811–1812.
Boyd, John P. Record book. Indiana Historical. BV95; 1808–1812.
RG94. Letters. National Archives. Adjutant General's Office; 1811–1815.
RG98, No. 466/365. Orderly book. National Archives. Adj. Gen., 3rd Mil. Dist., 1812–1815.
RG98, No. 449/347. Orderly book. National Archives. Adj. Gen., 3rd Mil. Dist., 1812–1815.
RG98, No. 458/357. Orderly book. National Archives. Ins. Gen., 3rd Mil. Dist., 1813–1815.
RG98, No. 451/350. Orderly book. National Archives. Ins. Gen., 3rd Mil. Dist., 1813–1815.
RG107. Letters. National Archives. Secretary of War's Office; 1811–1815.

Manuscript

Boyd, John P. Letters. Alderman Library. 10029-c, Cutts Papers; Crysler's Farm.
Boyd, John P. Letter, 1813. Boston Public. Ch.C.8.81; farewell to Henry Dearborn.
Boyd, John P. Letters. Buffalo and Erie. Peter B. Porter Papers; 1813.
Boyd, John P. Letter, 1811. Indiana Historical. M211, Box 3, Fld. 26; Tippecanoe.
Boyd, John P. Letter, 1811. Library of Congress. Miscellaneous Manuscripts Collection.
Boyd, John P. Papers. Lilly Library. 1811–1815.

Brigadier General John P. Boyd. Print Collection, Miriam and Ira D. Wallach Division of Art, Prints, and Photographs, The New York Public Library, Astor, Lenox, and Tilden Foundations.

Boyd, John P. Letters. Massachusetts Historical. Jacob J. Brown Papers.
Boyd, John P. Letters. New York State. 1812–1813.

Printed Primary

Boyd, John P. *Documents and Facts Relative to Military Events During the Late War.* Boston: N.p., 1816.
Boyd, John P. "Orderly Book of Colonel John P. Boyd and Extracts, 1811–1812, Fort Independence and Wabash." *Burton Historical Collection Bulletin* 1 (1914): 147–187.
Civis (Pseud). *Remarks on General Boyd's Pamphlet (From the New York Columbian).* N. p., 1816.

Select Secondary

Graves, Donald E. *Field of Glory: The Battle of Crysler's Field, 1813.* Toronto: Robin Brass Studio, 1999.
Patterson, William J. "A Forgotten Hero in A Forgotten War." *Journal of the Society of Army Historical Research* 68 (Spring 1990): 7–21.
Powell, E. Alexander. *Gentlemen Rovers.* New York: Charles Scribner's Sons, 1913.
Rosner, Ronald. "John Parker Boyd: The Yankee Mughal." *Asian Affairs* 34, no. 3 (2003): 297–309.

Henry Burbeck

Henry Burbeck was born in Boston, Massachusetts, on June 8, 1754, the son of a colonial militia officer. When the Revolutionary War broke out in 1775, Burbeck followed his father into service as an artillery officer, first as a lieutenant in Colonel Gridley's Artillery Regiment, and then its successor unit, Henry Knox's Continental Artillery Regiment. In these capacities he served actively in many northern battles such as Brandywine, Germantown, and Monmouth, gaining promotion to major before leaving the service in November 1783. Burbeck, however, rejoined the U.S. Army as a captain of the newly formed artillery battalion, and he spent many months garrisoning West Point, New York. While present, he agitated strongly for creation of a military academy at this very location, but the government proved disinterested. He subsequently fought under General Anthony Wayne during the Old Northwest Indian War, and helped to construct and garrison Fort Recovery, Ohio. Lieutenant William Henry Harrison, a future president, served under Burbeck and helped him collect and bury the remains of 200 victims from Arthur St. Clair's 1791 defeat. Burbeck's excellent service resulted in several consecutive promotions, and in 1802 he became colonel of the Regiment of Artillery. His most important service here was bringing to the attention of Secretary of War Henry Dearborn, a life-long acquaintance, his earlier recommendation for establishing a military academy at West Point to professionally train engineer and artillery officers. This plan finally came to fruition in 1802 as the U.S. Military Academy, for which Burbeck is entitled to some credit. In January 1811, he was also president of a board that denied Winfield Scott a majority in the Light Artillery Regiment owing to his recent suspension. Burbeck was serving as the army's senior ranking colonel when war with Great Britain recommenced in June 1812.

On July 10, 1812, Burbeck received a brevet promotion to brigadier general, while still technically in charge of what was now the 1st Regiment of

Brigadier General Henry Burbeck. Fraunces Tavern Museum, New York City.

Artillery, and he assumed command of the 3rd Military District, headquartered at New York City. There he founded the New York Arsenal on Governor's Island to which he assigned Lieutenant George Bomford as commanding officer. A year later Burbeck was succeeded by General George Izard and shunted next door to command the 2nd Military District, comprising Connecticut and Rhode Island. Military relations in these Federalist strongholds were frosty at best but Burbeck, himself a staunch Federalist, deferred to local authority and willingly submitted to militia Major General William Williams. However, after the Rhode Island militia refused to recognize the authority or wishes of the Federal government, Burbeck dismissed them from government employ and forced the state to assume all expenses for its own defense. This move wielded the desired effect and state authorities finally came to terms with federal authority. Burbeck nonetheless waxed critical of the war and the Madison administration, so in May 1814, the government ordered his transfer out of New London and replacement by General Thomas Humphrey Cushing. Burbeck remained active in Rhode Island until the end of hostilities and received his discharge on June 15, 1815. This act concluded a distinguished career stretching 38 years and he retired back to New London; he also functioned as president of the Society of the Cincinnati in the state of Massachusetts. Burbeck died in New London on October 2, 1848; for several decades he functioned as the army's senior artillerist.

Archival

Burbeck, Henry. Letter book. Burton Historical. 1st Military District, 1813–1815.
Burbeck, Henry. Orderly book. Fraunces Tavern. 2nd Military District; 1813.
Burbeck, Henry. Inspection book. Fraunces Tavern. Washington, Greenbush, Newport; 1812.
RG94. Letters. National Archives. Adjutant General's Office; 1812–1815.
RG98, No. 127. General Orders. National Archives. 2nd Military District, 1814–1815.
RG107. Letters. National Archives. Secretary of War's Office, 1812–1815.
3rd Military District. Orderly Book. New York Public Library. Case 9; July–September, 1812.
Burbeck, Henry. Letter book. Rhode Island Historical. Misc Mss BU; 2nd Mil. District, 1815.

Manuscript

Burbeck, Henry. Letters. Danvers Archival. PR/PO/C, Moses Porter Papers; 1812–1815.
Burbeck, Henry. Letters. Fraunces Tavern. 1812–1815.
Burbeck, Henry. Letter, 1812. Historical Society (Pa). Daniel Parker Papers, Box 3, troop report.
Burbeck, Henry. Papers. Library of Congress. Henry Burbeck Collection.
Burbeck, Henry. Letters. Lilly Library. Kingsbury Mss; 1812–1814.
Burbeck, Henry. Papers. New London Historical. Ms B891F; 1812–1815.
Burbeck, Henry. Letters. New York Public. Pers. Misc; 1812–1815.
Burbeck, Henry. Letters. Perkins Library. William D. Cheever Papers; 1813.
Burbeck, Henry. Papers. U.S. Military Academy. No. 65; prisoners.

Printed Primary

Harlow, Thompson R et al., eds. *John Cotton Smith Papers.* 7 vols. Hartford: Collections of the Connecticut Historical Society, 1940–1967.

Select Secondary

Gardner, Asa B. *Memoir of Brevet. Brig. Gen. Henry Burbeck, Founder of the U. S. Military Academy.* New York: A. S. Barnes, 1883.

Hickey, Donald R. "New England's Defense Problems and the Genesis of the Hartford Convention." *New England Quarterly* 50 (December 1977): 587–604.

Lewis Cass

Lewis Cass was born in Exeter, New Hampshire, on October 9, 1782, and he passed through the elite Phillips Exeter Academy as a classmate of

Brigadier General Lewis Cass. Courtesy of the Burton Historical Collection, Detroit Public Library.

Daniel Webster. He relocated to Ohio in 1800 to study law and two years later gained admittance to the state bar. By this time Cass developed an abiding interest in politics, so in 1806 he successfully stood for a seat in the state legislature. In this capacity he performed useful work by sponsoring a bill to grant the governor emergency powers to deal with Aaron Burr's secessionist schemes and, as a reward, President Thomas Jefferson appointed him a U.S. Marshal for Ohio. He held this position until the spring of 1812 when, being an ardent supporter of war with England, he became colonel of the 3rd Ohio regiment. Cass subsequently accompanied the army of General William Hull into Canada and won the first skirmish of the war on August 16, 1812, when he brushed aside a small British detail guarding the River Aux Canards bridge. Cass was not present with Hull when he surrendered Detroit later that month, but he was included in the surrender terms and had awaited his exchange before serving again. Appreciably, Cass entertained the most inveterate hatred for Hull and eagerly testified against him during his court-martial. It was not until February 20, 1813, that he resumed military service as colonel of the new 27th Infantry, which he promptly set about recruiting. Shortly after, on March 12, 1813, Cass gained promotion to brigadier general under General William Henry Harrison and part of the 8th Military District. He now commanded a brigade consisting of the 26th, 27th, and 28th Infantries, although most of his activities centered upon clerical and administrative work on Harrison's staff. Following Commodore Oliver Hazard Perry's victory of September 11, 1813, on Lake Erie, Cass supervised the embarkation of American forces into Canada, and helped orchestrate the pursuit of British general Henry Procter. He fought as a staff officer at the victory of the Thames on October 5, 1813, after which Harrison made him military administrator of Detroit and occupied portions of Upper Canada. On October 29, 1813, President James Madison also tendered him the governorship of Michigan Territory; he occupied the office for 18 years, longer than any other incumbent. Cass is also the first American military leader to administer captured enemy territory.

Cass, commanding only a handful of regular troops and surrounded by hostile Indians, capably managed his charge and did everything in his power to enhance frontier defenses. Foremost among his activities was conducting several parleys with various chiefs and securing their neutrality. Cass finally resigned his commission on May 1, 1814, to work full time in his civilian office. He performed useful work for the territory, both in obtaining various land cessions from neighboring tribes, and helping to found the University of Michigan. In 1831 he gained appointment as Secretary of War under President Andrew Jackson, where he enforced the policy of deporting Native Americans to new homes across the Mississippi River. He next served in the U.S. Senate, 1845–1848, ran for the presidency in 1848 and lost to War of

1812 veteran Zachary Taylor, then returned to the Senate, 1849–1857. Cass's most controversial service came as secretary of state under President James Buchanan, whereupon he resigned in 1860 to protest the latter's refusal to reinforce Fort Sumter. Cass died in Detroit on June 17, 1866, largely untried as a military figure, but an influential figure of the Antebellum period.

Archival

RG94. Letters. National Archives. Adjutant General's Office; 1813–1814.
RG107. Letters. National Archives. Secretary of War's Office; 1813–1814.

Manuscript

Cass, Lewis. Letters. Burton Historical.
Cass, Lewis. Letters. Clarke Library. 1812–1814.
Cass, Lewis. Papers. Clements Library. 1812–1814.
Cass, Lewis. Letters. Historical Society (Pa). Gratz Coll., Box 32; governor, 1814–1815.
Cass, Lewis. Letters. Historical Society (Pa). Parker Papers, 12, 20, 27, 31; 1813–1814.
Cass, Lewis. Letter, 1813. Library of Congress. William H. Harrison Papers; Michigan.
Cass, Lewis. Letters. New York Historical. Misc. Mss C; militia matters; 1813–1814.
Cass, Lewis. Letters. Ohio Historical. Thomas Worthington Papers; 1812–1815.
Cass, Lewis. Letter, 1812. Ohio Historical. VFM16, Indian affairs in Ohio.
Cass, Lewis. Letter, 1822. Providence Public. Mss 617, about Perry/Elliott row.

Printed Primary

Carter, Clarence E., ed. *The Territorial Papers of the United States: Volume X, The Territory of Michigan, 1805–1820*. Washington, D.C.: Government Printing Office, 1942.
"Documents Relating to Detroit and Vicinity, 1805–1813." *Michigan Historical Collections* 40 (1929): 25–754.
Emrich D., ed. "On Report. Gentlemen Army Officers, 1813." *American Heritage* 14 (August 1963): 112.
Miller, Albert. "Detroit in 1814." *Michigan Pioneer* 13 (1888): 503–507.

Select Secondary

Burns, Virginia. *Lewis Cass: Frontier Soldier*. Bath, MI: Enterprise Press, 1980.
"Detroit's Last Indian Massacre." *Totem Pole* 22 (December 16, 1948): 1–5.
Evelyn, George. "A Feather in the Cap? The Affair at River Carnard, 18th July, 1812." *Military Collector and Historian* 39 (Winter 1987): 169–171.
Klunder, Willard C. *Lewis Cass and the Politics of Moderation*. Kent, Oh.: Kent State University Press, 1996.

John Chandler

John Chandler was born in Epping, New Hampshire, on February 1, 1762, and in 1777 he enlisted in the militia and fought at the Battle of Saratoga. He was subsequently captured by the British but escaped and fulfilled another six months of military service. In 1784 he relocated to Monmouth, Maine, and established himself as a successful blacksmith and businessman. Chandler also served several terms in the Massachusetts legislature, which administered the Maine Territory, and in 1805 he gained election to Congress as a representative Four years later he was appointed sheriff of Kennebec County and continued his military service by serving as a militia officer. By the time war with England commenced in June 1812, Chandler was a major general commanding the 17th Division, although this was largely a symbolic office. Chandler used his political influence to obtain a brigadiership in the U.S. Army on July 8, 1812, notwithstanding his relative inexperience with high command. He next led an infantry brigade as part of Major General Henry Dearborn's army and accompanied the ill-fated advance into Lower Canada in the late fall of 1812. Several months later he was present at the capture of Fort George, Upper Canada, on May 27, 1813, but saw no combat. General Morgan Lewis, who was actually controlling the battle, gratuitously erred by halting an immediate pursuit of the defeated British and several days lapsed before Chandler and Brigadier General William Henry Winder finally took to the field. On the night of June 5, 1813, the two men had advanced as far as Stoney Creek, 46 miles from Fort George, and encamped carelessly, with inadequate sentinels. Chandler at the time commanded the 9th, 23rd, and 25th Infantries, along with a company of artillery and some riflemen, but his sloppy dispositions did not go unnoticed by enemy troops lurking nearby. On the morning of June 6, 1813, a picked force of 700 British troops under General John Vincent attacked the American camp and a wild melee erupted in the dark. The British, backlit by the American campfires, suffered serious losses but Winder and Chandler successively stumbled into their lines and became prisoners. The surviving senior American officer, Colonel James Burn of the 2nd Light Dragoons, was so nonplused that he immediately ordered a withdrawal back to Fort George over the protest of many subordinates. Thus, at a single stroke, British fortunes at Niagara were dramatically reversed and Upper Canada was saved.

Chandler, limping badly injured from a fall from his horse, spent nearly a year at Montreal before being exchanged in April 1814. That summer he was restored to command the 1st Military District (New Hampshire and Massachusetts) at Portland, Maine — a quiet sector — and spent several weeks organizing an intricate plan of harbor defense before orders abruptly transferred

Brigadier General John Chandler. Maine State Museum.

him to Portsmouth, New Hampshire. His military career concluded without further incident on June 15, 1815, and he returned to Maine to pursue business and politics. Chandler enjoyed a lengthy career as a public servant and was a driving force behind Maine's separation from Massachusetts in 1820. As an indication of his local popularity, he was appointed one of two U.S. Senators from the new state and held that position until 1829. That year President Andrew Jackson next appointed him to the lucrative post of customs collector at Portsmouth, where he remained until 1837, and he also functioned as a trustee of Bowdoin College. Chandler, who despite a brusque military bearing was infinitely more suited to politics than warfare, died in Augusta, Maine, on September 25, 1841. His tenure throughout the War of 1812 had been undistinguished or, when actually engaged, bordering on disastrous.

Archival

RG94. Letters. National Archives. Adjutant General's Office; 1813–1815.
RG107. Letters. National Archives. Secretary of War's Office; 1813–1815.

Manuscript

Chandler, John. Letters. Alderman Library. 10029-c; Richard Cutts Papers; 1812.
Chandler, John. Letter, 1813. Boston Public. **Ch.C.12.79; Stoney Creek.
Chandler, John. Letters. Historical Society (Pa). Gratz Coll., Box 32; military, 1813–1814.
Chandler, John. Letters. Lilly Library. War of 1812 Coll.; Maine, 1812, 1814.
Chandler, John. Letters. Massachusetts Historical. Ms. N-83; 1812–1814.
Chandler, John. Letter, 1813. Massachusetts Historical. Henry Dearborn Papers; Stoney Creek.
Chandler, John. Letter, 1814. New York Historical. Misc Mss C, British attack on Castine.

Printed Primary

Chandler, John. "Battle of Stoney Creek." *Niles Weekly Register* 2 (October 19, 1816): 116–119.
"General Chandler and the Affair at Stoney Creek." *Niles Weekly Register* 2 (January 4, 1817): 308–311.
Talbot, George F., ed. "Extracts from the Autobiography of General John Chandler." *Maine Historical Society Collections* 9 (1887): 178–205. [183–200]

Select Secondary

Elliott, James. *Strange Fatality: The Battle of Stoney Creek*. Montreal: Robin Brass Studio, 2009.
Stanley, George F. G. *Battle in the Dark: Stoney Creek, June 6, 1813*. Toronto: Balmuir, 1991.

Leonard Covington

Leonard Covington was born in Prince George's County, Maryland, on October 30, 1768, and in March 1792 he joined the U.S. Army as a cornet of cavalry. He rose to lieutenant in March 1793 while campaigning with General Anthony Wayne in Ohio against the Shawnee and Miami Indians. He received his baptism of fire while commanding a garrison of 50 light dragoons during the Battle of Fort Recovery, June 30, 1794, where his horse was shot from under him and he won commendation in Wayne's dispatches. Promotion to captain followed, and in August, Covington again distinguished himself

Brigadier General Leonard Covington. Library of Congress.

in fighting at Fallen Timbers. Here Wayne ordered the dragoons to turn the Indians' flank but, when his commanding officer was slain, Covington took over the troop and charged, killing two braves with his own sword. Wayne again praised him for his actions, but Covington subsequently resigned his commission on September 12, 1795, to pursue farming.

Back in Maryland, Covington developed a taste for politics and served several terms in the House of Delegates. In March 1805 he was also elected to the U.S. House of Representatives as a Democratic Republican, serving one term. However, British aggression in the *Chesapeake-Leopard* Affair of 1807 rekindled his interest in military affairs, so on January 9, 1809, President Thomas Jefferson appointed him lieutenant colonel of the new Regiment of Light Dragoons. He rose to full colonel a month late and galloped off to Fort Adams, Mississippi Territory, to assume command. Covington next orchestrated the American occupation of Baton Rouge on December 10, 1810, in concert with militia forces under Governor Charles C. C. Claiborne. Several months of garrison duty at Fort Stoddert and Pass Christian ensued before General James Wilkinson ordered his troopers to accompany his expedition to seize the Spanish town of Mobile, West Florida. On April 13, 1813, the Americans, backed by the gunboats under Commander John Shaw, occupied their objective without incident. The War of 1812 was then in full swing and Covington received orders transferring him north to participate.

Covington arrived at Sacketts Harbor, New York, in the summer of 1813, where promotion to brigadier general followed on August 1, 1813. He then assumed control of the 3rd Brigade, consisting of the 9th, 16th, and 25th Infantries, all part of General James Wilkinson's army. This force was preparing an ambitious foray down the St. Lawrence River to capture Montreal, but nagging supply shortages detained Wilkinson at Sacketts Harbor until late fall. A miserable, rain-soaked transit ensued before the Americans left their boats on November 11, 1813, to engage a British force shadowing them along the river bank. The ensuing battle of Crysler's Farm proved a debacle, for General John Parker Boyd committed his forces piecemeal into the fray where they were defeated in detail. At the height of battle, Boyd directed Covington's brigade to charge the enemy center during a snow-flecked storm. The Americans drove the British light troops back before stalling in the face of rippling musketry and artillery fire. It was during this critical juncture that Covington fell fatally wounded and was carried from the field. He was evacuated to the American shore, dying there on November 14, 1813. Covington thus became the second American general to die in combat that year after Zebulon M. Pike at York in April. His remains were initially buried at French Mills, New York, but were subsequently re-interred at Sacketts Harbor in August 1820. The towns of Fort Covington, New York, and Covington, Kentucky, were likewise named in his honor. Coming at the time it did, Covington's death was tragic in so much as it deprived the American army of a highly promising officer.

Archival

RG94. Letters. National Archives. Adjutant General's Office; 1812–1813.
RG107. Letters. National Archives. Secretary of War's Office; 1812–1813.

Manuscript

Covington, Leonard. Letters. McKeldin Library. Charles Lanman Papers.
Covington, Leonard. Papers. Mississippi Department. Covington-Wailes Families; 1812–1813.
Covington, Leonard. Letters. Mississippi Department. Winbourne M. Drake Papers; 1812–1813.

Printed Primary

Brandon, Nellie W., and W. W. Drake. *Memoir of Leonard Covington, edited by L. C. Wailes; Also Some of General Covington's Letters*. Natchez, Miss.: Natchez Printing, 1928.

Select Secondary

Adams, Charles. "General Leonard Covington, 1766–1813." *Christopher Gist Historical Society Papers* 1 (1949–1950): 104–112.
Drake, W. M. *Leonard Covington, 1768–1813*. Washington Cemetery Protection Agency, 1962. [Copy at the Mississippi Department of Archives and History]
Graves, Donald E. *Field of Glory: The Battle of Crysler's Farm, 1813*. Toronto: Robin Brass Studio, 1999.
Jamison, Leonard. *The Life and Times of General Covington*. Akron, Oh.: L. Jamison, 1987.

Thomas Humphrey Cushing

Thomas Humphrey Cushing was born at Pembroke, Massachusetts, on December 20, 1755, and in January 1776, he enlisted in the Continental Army as a sergeant. He served throughout the war with distinction, fought under Colonel Benedict Arnold at the Battle of Valcour Island in 1777, and was discharged in 1784 as a brevet captain. Cushing subsequently rejoined the U.S. Army as a captain of the 2nd Infantry in 1791, rose steadily through the ranks, and became lieutenant colonel in 1802. He was also active commanding troops along the Mississippi and Tombigbee Rivers near Natchez, and oversaw construction of Fort Stoddert. Cushing advanced to colonel in September 1805 and was ordered to Natchitoches by General James Wilkinson for the purpose of preventing Spanish violations of American territory east of the Sabine River. His negotiations with Spanish authorities amounted to little, but he had handled himself and his men commendably. Cushing next rose to brigadier general on July 2, 1812, and received command off the 1st Military District, headquartered at Boston, Massachusetts. Here he curried favor with

Brigadier General Thomas H. Cushing. Society of the Cincinnati, Washington, D.C.

the Federalist administration of Governor Caleb Strong by agreeing to keep army and militia troops under their own separate authorities. In June 1814, he was replaced by General Henry Dearborn and transferred to the 2nd Military District, headquartered at New London, Connecticut, where he displaced the outspoken General Henry Burbeck. Cushing again waxed cordial towards the Federalist regime of Governor John Cotton Smith until the latter appointed militia Major General Augustine Taylor to command all forces in the state. Cushing considered this a usurpation of his authority and warned militia leaders that disobedience of his orders was tantamount to mutiny and would be punished accordingly. He also paraded his handful of regular troops in front of General's Taylor's headquarters to underscore his determination. Taylor countered by assembling his far more numerous militia for "inspection," at which point Cushing had little recourse but to withdraw. He then angrily informed government agencies that the Connecticut militia had left federal service and ordered them to stop any payments or supplies accorded them. The impasse continued several more months until after the war and Cushing finally mustered out of service on June 15, 1815. He then settled in as customs collector of the port of New London, dying there on October 19, 1822; his war years were largely spent battling local militias, not the British.

Archival

Mil. District No. 1. Order book. Boston Public. **C.33.15; Boston, 1812–1814.
Mil. District No. 1. Letter book. Massachusetts Historical. Ms. N-108; 1813–1815.
RG94. Letters. National Archives. Adjutant General's Office; 1812–1815.
RG98, No. 127. General Orders. National Archives. 2nd Mil. District, 1814–1815.
RG98, Item 10. Records. National Archives. Orders, Fort Independence, 1812–1815.
RG107. Letters. National Archives. Secretary of War's Office; 1812–1815.

Manuscript

Cushing, Thomas H. Letters. Danvers Archival. PR/PO/C, Moses Porter Papers.
Cushing, Thomas H. Letter, 1812. Historical Society (Pa). Dreer Coll., to James Winchester.
Cushing, Thomas H. Letters. Historical Society (Pa). Gratz Coll., Box 32; military; 1813–1814.
Cushing, Thomas H. Letters. Historical Society (Pa). Daniel Parker Papers, Box 17, 18, 27.
Cushing, Thomas H. Letters. Lilly Library. Kingsbury Mss; 1812–1815.
Cushing, Thomas H. General Orders. Perkins Library. Campbell Family Papers; February 1813.

Printed Primary

Harlow, Thompson R., et al., eds. *John Cotton Smith Papers.* 7 vols. Hartford: Collections of the Connecticut Historical Society, 1940–1967. Vols. 1–5, 7.
Lee, W. *Trial of Col. Thomas H. Cushing before a General Court Martial Which Sat at Baton Rouge on Charges Preferred Against Him by Brig. General Wade Hampton.* Philadelphia: Moses, Thomas, 1812.

Select Secondary

Hickey, Donald R. "New England's Defense Problems and the Genesis of the Hartford Convention." *New England Quarterly* 50 (December 1977): 587–604.

Thomas Flournoy

Thomas Flournoy was born in North Carolina in 1775 and by the early 1800s he was practicing law in Augusta, Georgia. He was apparently a fastidious, touchy individual, and at one point a difference of opinion with Judge George Walton culminated in a duel with the judge's nephew. The extent of his political connections or militia experience are unknown but must have been considerable for, on July 18, 1812, Flournoy became a brigadier general in the U.S. Army and the following year he replaced General James Wilkinson as commander of the 7th Military District (Louisiana, Mississippi Territory, and Tennessee), headquartered at New Orleans. Flournoy initially spent several months recruiting and training militia forces to defend the lengthy Carolina and Georgia coastlines. He finally arrived at New Orleans just prior to the outbreak of the Creek War in August 1813, the conduct of which overlapped jurisdictions between his command and the 6th Military District under Major General Thomas Pinckney. Given the scanty resources available, and the fact that Secretary of War John Armstrong had assigned Pinckney overall command of the war effort against the Creeks, Flournoy responded with sullen indifference and non-cooperation bordering on insubordination. For example, when the 3rd Infantry of Colonel Gilbert C. Russell was ordered detached from Flournoy's district and sent to reinforce General Ferdinand L. Claiborne in the Mississippi Territory, he refused to provide them with supplies, declaring them no longer his responsibility. Flournoy also ruffled local sensibilities by dismissing the aristocratic Mississippi Dragoons of Major Thomas Hinds, pronouncing them untrained and unfit for service. He also clashed with the largely French-speaking legislature of Louisiana, openly berating them as unpatriotic and unwilling to serve in the militia. Fortunately, Pinckney insisted on his cooperation and ordered him to forward troops and supplies to General Andrew Jackson's forces invading Creek territory from the north. Flournoy fumed nonetheless and resented what he considered deliberate inroads upon his authority, especially after Jackson succeeded him as head of the 7th Military District on May 22, 1814, and he angrily resigned his commission the following September. Curiously, Secretary of War Armstrong had seriously entertained promoting Flournoy to a major general, but this scheme was discarded in favor of choosing Jacob Jennings

Brigadier General Thomas Flournoy. Print Collection, Miriam and Ira D. Wallach Division of Art, Prints, and Photographs, The New York Public Library, Astor, Lenox, and Tilden Foundations.

Brown to that rank. Flournoy's tenure at New Orleans was marginally competent but unproductive, largely on account of his condescension towards Louisianans, yet the equally touchy Jackson managed to inspire the inhabitants to fight willingly and valiantly for the United States during a very threatening British invasion. How they would have flocked to the colors had Flournoy continued at New Orleans is conjectural, but disaster seems the most predictable consequence. In any event, Flournoy resumed legal activities in Georgia after the war and in 1820 he became a commissioner to deal with the Creek. He died in Augusta on July 24, 1857, remembered less for War of 1812 activities than his recalcitrant, self-serving mien.

Archival

Flournoy, Thomas. Orderly Book. Library of Congress. 7th Mil. District, 1812–1814.
RG94. Letters. National Archives. Adjutant General's Office; 1812–1814.
RG98, No. 391/275. Orderly book. National Archives. Adj. Gen., 7th Mil Dist., 1813–1814.
RG98, No. 433/330. Orderly book. National Archives. Adj. Gen., 7th Mil Dist., 1813–1814.
RG107. Letters. National Archives. Secretary of War's Office; 1812–1814.

Manuscript

Flournoy, Thomas. Papers. Clements Library. 1812–1814.
Flournoy, Thomas. Letter, 1812. Gilder Lehrman. to Col. Thomas A. Smith in Florida.
Flournoy, Thomas. Letter, 1813. Historical Society (Pa). Daniel Parker Papers, Box 5; quartermaster.
Flournoy, Thomas. Letter. Historical Society (Pa). Gratz Coll., Box 33; 1814.
Flournoy, Thomas. Papers. Library of Congress. 1812–1814.
Flournoy, Thomas. Letters. Library of Congress. Andrew Jackson Papers; 1813–1814.
Flournoy, Thomas. Letter, 1813. Manuscript and Archives. Mss 397; deficient Georgia militia.
Flournoy, Thomas. Letters. Mississippi Department. J. F. H. Claiborne Coll., Book F, Group 3.
Flournoy, Thomas. Letters. Tennessee State Library. War of 1812 Collection.

Printed Primary

Carter, Clarence E., ed. *The Territorial Papers of the United States: Vol. VI, The Territory of Mississippi, 1809–1817.* Washington, D.C.: Government Printing Office, 1938.
Moser, Harold D. et al., eds. *The Papers of Andrew Jackson.* 5 vols. Knoxville: University of Tennessee Press, 1980–.
Rowland, Dunbar, ed. *Official Letter Books of W. C. C. Claiborne, 1801–1816.* 6 vols. Jackson:, Miss.: State Department of History and Archives, 1917.

SELECT SECONDARY

Owsley, Frank. *The Struggle for the Gulf Borderlands: The Creek War and the Battle of New Orleans, 1812–1815*. Gainesville: University of Florida Press, 1981.

Edmund Pendleton Gaines

Edmund Pendleton Gaines was born in Culpepper County, Virginia, on March 30, 1777, and raised along the Tennessee frontier. He joined the army in 1797 as an ensign in the 6th Infantry during the war scare with France. Gaines was retained after the reduction of 1801 and billeted at Fort Stoddert, Alabama Territory, in 1804 and, two years later, he also functioned as commanding officer and collector of the port of Mobile. However, it was as a first lieutenant of the 2nd Infantry in 1807 that he gained national attention for arresting the celebrated conspirator Aaron Burr. Gaines advanced to captain soon after and fulfilled a stint of routine garrison duties along the Southwestern frontier. In 1811 he took an extended leave of absence to study law and subsequently served as a judge in Pascagoula Parish, Mississippi. War with England commenced a year later, so Gaines rejoined as a lieutenant colonel of the 24th U. S. Infantry on July 6, 1812. Months of uneventful recruiting lapsed before he finally transferred to the staff of General William Henry Harrison as adjutant general. He then advanced to colonel, 25th Infantry, on March 12, 1813, and participated in General James Wilkinson's ill-fated St. Lawrence expedition. Gaines fought at Crysler's Farm, November 11, 1813, as adjutant under General Leonard Covington, and covered the American withdrawal so professionally that the British commander allegedly sent him his card with an invitation to get acquainted after the war. Gaines then accompanied the army throughout its freezing occupation of French Mills, New York, where promotion to brigadier general arrived on March 9, 1814. In spring he also gained a measure of notoriety in military circles by testily appearing before Congress, complaining about poor rations for the troops by civilian contractors, and insisting that they accounted for more American lives than enemy bullets.

By April 1814, Gaines was posted with the Left Division of General Jacob Jennings Brown and appointed garrison commander of strategic Sacketts Harbor, New York. In late July, Brown ordered him westward to command American defenses at Fort Erie, Upper Canada, then closely besieged by British forces under Lieutenant General Gordon Drummond. In the early morning of August 15, 1814, Gaines orchestrated an effective defense his post which bloodily repulsed a determined British attack, inflicting nearly 1,000 casualties for the loss of only 80 men. This represented the heaviest toll ever suffered by

Brigadier General Edmund P. Gaines. Courtesy of the Historical Society of Pennsylvania Collection, Atwater Kent Museum of Philadelphia.

the British in Canada, but Drummond continued tightening his grip on the fort and erecting new siege batteries. On August 28, 1814, an enemy shell struck Gaines's headquarters, wounding him severely. He was evacuated and spent several week convalescing before gaining reassignment as commander of the 4th Military District, headquartered at Baltimore. Shortly before the War of 1812 ended, he again transferred south to the staff of General Andrew Jackson at New Orleans and saw no further action. In light of his wartime service, Gaines received the Thanks of Congress, promotion to brevet major general, and a gold medal in addition to ceremonial swords voted him by the legislatures of Tennessee, Virginia, and New York.

After the war, Gaines embarked on a distinguished frontier career spanning over three decades. He fought in both Seminole conflicts in Florida, and supervised the construction of numerous forts and roads that facilitated western settlement and expansion. However, he is best known for engaging in a bitter and lengthy dispute with General Winfield Scott over the issue of seniority. Each refused to take orders from the other and their public feuding so embarrassed the government that in 1828, following the death of General Brown, both men were passed over as commanding general of the army by Alexander Macomb. In spite of his garrulous disposition, Gaines was nonetheless regarded as a far-sighted and imaginative officer, and in 1838 he penned a memorial to Congress outlining the need for fortifications, railroads, and steam batteries for harbor defense. Congress balked at the scheme owing to its expense, but Gaines's vision presaged by two decades the very measures that materialized during the Civil War. The elderly general had lost none of his ability to raise eyebrows when, in 1839, he married socialite Myra Clark, a woman half his age. Gaines then incurred further notoriety during the Mexican War of 1846–1848 when, as commander of New Orleans, he called out the militia of Louisiana, Alabama, Mississippi, and Missouri to support the army of General Zachary Taylor. He did so without governmental permission, and an angry President James K. Polk ordered him to rescind the mobilization immediately. Gaines was court-martialed and convicted of exceeding his authority, but he was such a military fixture that no punishments were leveled against him. The old soldier resumed his former billet at New Orleans in 1848, where he died of cholera on June 6, 1849. A capable War of 1812 commander, his memory is perpetuated by the city of Gainesville, Florida.

Archival

RG94. Letters. National Archives. Adjutant General's Office; 1812–1815.
RG98, No. 393/276. Letters sent. National Archives. 4th Mil. Dist., 1813–1814.
RG98, No. 462/359. Orderly book. National Archives. 4th Mil. Dist., 1814–1815.
RG98, No. 512/414. Orders. National Archives. 9th Mil. Dist., August, 1814.
RG98, No. 440/337. Orderly Book. National Archives. 9th Mil Dist., 1814–1815.
RG98, No. 446/343. Orderly book. National Archives. 9th Mil. Dist., 1814–1815.
RG98, No. 457/356. Orderly book. National Archives. 9th Mil. Dist., 1814–1815.
RG98, Item 78. Letters sent. National Archives. 9th Mil. Dist., Jan.–May, 1814.
RG107. Letters. National Archives. Secretary of War's Office; 1812–1815.
RG153, K-2. Court martial. National Archives. Edmund P. Gaines.

Manuscript

Gaines, Edmund P. Papers. Library of Congress. Miscellaneous Manuscripts; 1814.
Gaines, Edmund P. Letters. Historic New Orleans. Butler Family Papers; 1815.

Gaines, Edmund P.. Letters. Historical Society (Pa). Cadwalader Coll., Box 24 T, 4th Mil. Dist.
Gaines, Edmund P. Letters. Historical Society (Pa). Parker Papers, Box 4, 24, military texts.
Gaines, Edmund P. Letter, 1814. Historical Society (Pa). Simon Snyder Coll., defenses.
Gaines, Edmund P. Letters. Library of Congress. Jacob Brown Papers; 1814.
Gaines, Edmund P. Letters. McClung Historical. Howard Smith Collection; 1812–1814.
Gaines, Edmund P. Letter, 1813. Maryland Historical. Ms 1846; recruiting.
Gaines, Edmund P. Letters. Massachusetts Historical Jacob J. Brown Papers; 1814.
Gaines, Edmund P. Letters. New York State. KB12914, C. K. Gardner Papers; Fort Erie.
Gaines, Edmund P. Letter, 1815. Perkins Library. E.P. Gaines Papers, to George Bombford.
Gaines, Edmund P. Letters. Southern Historical. 1863, John Overton Papers; 1812–1814.
Gaines, Edmund P. Letters. Wisconsin Historical. William Henry Harrison Papers, 5 X.
Gaines, Edmund P. Letters. Tennessee State. War of 1812 Collection.
Gaines, Edmund P. Statement. Virginia Historical. Mss1 P9267 d 802–806; Fort Erie.

Printed Primary

Charges Against Major General Edmund P. Gaines of the United States Army. New York: E. Conrad, 1814.
"General Edmund P. Gaines's Official Report of the Battle of Fort Erie, August 15, 1814." *Pennsylvania Magazine of History and Biography* 21, no. 2 (1897): 263–266.

Select Secondary

Fredriksen, John C. "Niagara, 1814: The United States Army Quest for Tactical Parity in the War of 1812 and Its Legacy." Unpublished Ph. D. dissertation, Providence College, 1993.
Silver, James W. *Edmund P. Gaines, 1777–1849, Frontier General.* Baton Rouge: Louisiana State University Press, 1949.
Whitehorne, Joseph. *While Washington Burned: The Battle for Fort Erie, 1814.* Baltimore: Nautical and Aviation Press, 1992.

Benjamin Howard

Benjamin Howard is believed to have been born in Virginia around 1760, the son of a Revolutionary War veteran. As a young man he relocated to Boonesboro, Kentucky, joined the local militia, and participated in the Old Northwest Indian war under General Anthony Wayne. After 1795 he studied law, established a practice at Lexington, Kentucky, and served in the state legislature. In

Brigadier General Benjamin Howard. Missouri History Museum.

1807 he was elected to the U.S. House of Representatives, and advocated increases in military strength and dealing harshly with hostile Indians and British traders along the western frontier. Such bellicosity brought him to the attention of President James Madison, who, on April 18, 1810, appointed Howard governor of the District of Louisiana to replace the recently deceased explorer Meriwether Lewis. He reached St. Louis that fall and, while continually absent from the territory on business, still managed to overhaul the militia and strengthen frontier defenses. Howard also organized a company of mounted rangers to patrol threatened regions and intercept raiding war bands. On June 4, 1812, President Madison signed a law elevating the status of the region, which was renamed the Territory of Missouri, and Howard continued on as governor.

After the War of 1812 commenced, Howard pushed the government for offensive operations against hostile Indians in his territory, but to no avail. However, his agitation did stimulate recruitment of three additional ranger companies from Missouri. Madison also felt that military affairs would be better administered if Howard were to resign from office and accept a brigadier general's commission in the U.S. Army, which he did on March 12, 1813. As commander of the 8th Military District, he now oversaw the construction of numerous forts and blockhouses throughout his jurisdiction, and he also conducted occasional raids against Indian villages along the Missouri and Illinois rivers. Very little fighting resulted, but his activity did throw hostile tribes off balance and rendered them unable to attack settlements. Howard faced challenging prospects throughout his tenure as general, given the scanty military resources available in Missouri and Illinois, but he worked closely with Indian agent William Clark (the noted explorer) and somehow managed to secure the frontier. In January 1814 he received orders to join the army of General William Henry Harrison in Ohio, but political protests led to his reassignment back to Missouri. Howard died suddenly in St. Louis on September 18, 1814, a little-known but capable frontier leader. His popularity resulted in Howard County, Missouri, being posthumously designated in 1816.

Archival

RG94. Letters. National Archives. Adjutant General's Office; 1813–1814.
RG107. Letters. National Archives. Secretary of War's Office; 1813–1814.

Manuscript

Howard, Benjamin. Letter, 1812. Missouri Historical. Craighead Papers; Shawnee, Miami tribes.
Howard, Benjamin. Letters. Missouri Historical. Morrison Papers; 1813.
Howard, Benjamin. Letters. Missouri Historical. War of 1812 Papers; 1813.
Howard, Benjamin. Letters. Wisconsin Historical. Thomas Forsyth Papers, 1 T; 1813–1814.

Printed Primary

Carter, Clarence E., ed. *The Territorial Papers of the United States: Vol. XIV, The Territory of Louisiana-Missouri, 1806–1814.* Washington, D.C.: Government Printing Office, 1949.
Carter, Clarence E., ed. *The Territorial Papers of the United States: Vol. XVI, The Territory of Illinois, 1809–1814.* Washington, D.C.: Government Printing Office, 1948.

SELECT SECONDARY

Buckley, Jay H. *William Clark: Indian Diplomat*. Norman: University of Oklahoma Press, 2008.
Gregg, Kate. "The War of 1812 on the Missouri Frontier." *Missouri Historical Review* 33, no. 1 (October 1938): 3–22; 33, no. 2 (January 1939): 184–202; 33, no. 3 (April 1939): 326–348.

William Hull

William Hull was born in Derby, Connecticut, on June 24, 1753, and in 1772 he graduated with honors from Yale University. Hull pursued legal studies until the advent of war in 1775 induced him to seek a captain's commission in the militia. Over the next eight years, he fought with distinction at White Plains, Trenton, Princeton, Saratoga, and Monmouth, rising to major of the 8th Massachusetts Regiment in 1777. Two years later he spearheaded General Anthony Wayne's night assault against Stoney Point, New York, winning promotion to lieutenant colonel. At this juncture, General George Washington tendered Hull a position of his staff but he demurred, preferring instead to function as assistant inspector general under Baron Von Steuben. In this capacity he remained in the New York highlands region, making several successful forays against British outposts. By 1783 Hull had risen to full colonel and commanded the strategic American defenses at West Point. After the war, he was dispatched to Canada to confer with Governor General Haldimand about the transfer of several western posts to the United States. Hull finally returned to Massachusetts to practice law, but he also served as a major general of militia. In 1788 he took to the field while commanding the left wing of General Benjamin Lincoln's army, which crushed the rebellion of Daniel Shays in western Massachusetts. Hull then developed a taste for politics and served as a state senator and a judge. Strongly Democratic-Republican in outlook, he was next tapped by President Thomas Jefferson to become the first governor of the Michigan Territory in 1805.

Hull served as governor for seven years and his tenure, like that of Governor William Henry Harrison in the Indiana Territory, was marked by ongoing schemes to defraud local Indians of their lands. This behavior earned him the enmity of several tribal leaders, most notably Tecumseh, who increasingly turned to Great Britain for help. In the spring of 1812, a fearful Hull visited Washington, D.C., to secure additional government protection for frontier settlements; instead he received a brigadier general's commission dated April 8, 1812. Privately, Hull waxed pessimistic regarding American prospects in the

Northwest, insisting that control of Lake Erie, coupled with diversionary actions at various points of the Canadian border, were prerequisites for success. The government promised both yet he received neither, thanks to pervasive lethargy of Major General Henry Dearborn, commanding the northern front. Nevertheless, Hull did acquire the 4th Infantry, one of the crack prewar formations, to bolster his three Ohio militia regiments under colonels James Findlay, Lewis Cass, and Duncan McArthur. Hull's army, numbering perhaps 2,500 men, subsequently cut a 200-mile path through the Ohio swamps and woodlands to reach Detroit, and their path later became known as Hull's Trace. Unfortunately, his first indication that war had commenced occurred when the British seized his chief supply vessel, the *Cuyahoga*, as it passed Malden on the Detroit River. All his official papers and correspondence were thus captured and the exact strength and intention of his army was revealed. Hull then crossed into Canada and marched cautiously against Malden until word of Mackinac's untimely fall arrived. Fearing Indian assaults against civilians, he recrossed the straits and passively occupied Detroit to await developments. Such dithering undermined American morale and enabled General Sir Isaac Brock, an able and energetic leader, to rush reinforcements from the Niagara frontier. With parties of British and Indians harassing his supply lines, Hull half-heartedly dispatched the 4th infantry under Lieutenant Colonel James Miller to clear his communications to the south. Miller accomplished this handily at Maguaga on August 9, 1812, but was ordered back to Detroit just as General Brock prepared to cross and surround that settlement. Hull's gunners, manning 28 pieces of artillery, begged their general for permission to open fire on the enemy as they landed, but he refused. In fact, he seemed to be experiencing a complete mental breakdown and the garrison, which greatly outnumbered their antagonists, watched as their fortunes ebbed. The end came on August 16, 1812, when Hull, warned by Brock that he could not control warriors should fighting commence, surrendered rather than risk a massacre. Brock immediately paroled the militia but took the 700 regulars into captivity, where they languished many months in Quebec. News of Hull's disaster singularly stunned the nation, moreover, and it emboldened many heretofore reluctant Indian chiefs to take up the war hatchet Britain's behalf.

Hull was taken to Quebec as a prisoner, and paroled shortly afterwards. In April, 1814, his court-martial was presided over by General Dearborn, whose own inactivity was equally responsible for the disaster. In fairness, it must be reiterated that both Dearborn and Secretary of War William Eustis had left him in a strategic lurch from which escape was nearly impossible. Hull was nevertheless found guilty of treason and sentenced to be shot, but President James Madison commuted him in light of his Revolutionary War

Brigadier General William Hull. National Portrait Gallery, Smithsonian Institution.

service. Hull spent the rest of his life at Newton, Massachusetts, engaging in a furious and futile publishing campaign to exonerate himself. He died there in relative obscurity on November 29, 1825, the embodiment of ineptitude — and misfortune — from the War of 1812.

Archival

RG94. Letters. National Archives. Adjutant General's Office; 1812.
RG107. Letters. National Archives. Secretary of War's Office; 1812.

Manuscript

Hull, William. Biography. Boston Athenaeum. Mss .L109, by Mrs. R. E. Roberts, n.d.
Hull, William. Letters. Burton Historical. Otto G. Fisher Collection; 1812.
Hull, William. Papers. Burton Historical. C. M. Burton Papers; 1812.
Hull, William. Papers. Georgia Historical. various; 1814.
Hull, William. Letters. Historical Society (Pa). Gratz Coll., Box 32, 33, 34, surrender.
Hull, William. Letters. Historical Society (Pa). Daniel Parker Papers, Box 2, 7; 1812.
Hull, William. Letter, 1812. Historical Society (Pa). Dreer Collection, post-surrender.
Hull, William. Letters. Houghton Library. bMS Am 1569.6–7; 1812–1814.
Hull, William. Letters. Indiana Historical. M211, 1814.
Hull, William. Letters. Kentucky Historical.
Hull, William. Letters. Lilly Library. War of 1812 Collection; Detroit, 1812.
Hull, William. Letters. Massachusetts Historical. C.E. French; 1812–1814, Fort Wayne.
Hull, William. Letter, 1812. New York Historical. Misc Mss H, to Dearborn at Montreal.
Hull, William. Papers. Ohio Historical. VFM75; claims against government, 1826.
Hull, William. Letters. Vermont State. George Watson Papers, Detroit; 1812.

Printed Primary

Carter, Clarence E., ed. *The Territorial Papers of the United States: Vol. X, The Territory of Michigan, 1805–1820.* Washington, D.C.: Government Printing Office, 1942.
Cruikshank, Ernest A., ed. *Documents Relating to the Invasion of Canada and the Surrender of Detroit, 1812.* Ottawa: Government Printing Bureau, 1913.
"Documents Relating to Detroit and Vicinity, 1805–1813." *Michigan Historical Collections* 40 (1929): 25–754.
Forbes, James G. *The Trial of Brig. General William Hull.* New York: Eastburn, Kirk, and Co., 1814.
Hull, William. *Memoirs of the Campaign of the Northwestern Army of the United States, A. D. 1812.* Boston: True & Greene, 1824.

Select Secondary

Greer, David A. "Revolutionary, Federalist, Republican: The Early Life and Reputations of William Hull." Unpublished Ph.D. dissertation, Texas Christian University, 2007.
Rauch, Stephen. "The Eyes of the Country Were Upon Them: A Comparative Study of the Campaigns of the Northwestern Army Conducted by William Hull and William Henry Harrison." Unpublished master's thesis, Eastern Michigan University, 1992.
Sherer, T. M. "Governor Hull and the Michigan Indians." *Detroit Perspectives* 7 (Spring 1983): 33–45.
Turner, Wesley B. *British General in the War of 1812: High Command in the Canadas.* Montreal: McGill-Queen's University Press, 1999, 58–83. [Isaac Brock].

Duncan McArthur

Duncan McArthur was born in Dutchess County, New York, on January 14, 1772, where he received a rudimentary education. He worked many years with an Allegheny pack train before settling at Scioto, Ohio, to pursue surveying. He accumulated considerable wealth through land purchasing and speculation, and in 1805 he gained a seat in the state legislature. McArthur was also active in militia matters, rising to major general of militia in 1808. In the spring of 1812 he became one of three Ohio colonels that accompanied General William Hull to Detroit, and thence into Canada. Querulously disposed, McArthur argued with James Findlay and Lewis Cass as to who possessed more seniority, and openly criticized Hull's timorous leadership. He was not present at Detroit when Hull capitulated on August 16, 1812, but was included in the surrender terms and forced to capitulate in turn. McArthur returned to Ohio following his parole and won election to the U.S. House of Representatives, but he declined being seated in favor of an appointment as colonel of the 26th Infantry on February 20, 1813. The following month, on March 12, 1813, he rose to brigadier general in the U.S. Army and was posted with the Northwest Army of General William Henry Harrison. McArthur spent several months recruiting his regiments before he advanced to the relief of Harrison at Fort Meigs in May 1813. The following July he mustered the Second Division of Ohio militia and again marched for that beleaguered outpost during a second British siege, but saw no fighting. McArthur subsequently accompanied Harrison into Canada during the fall of 1813, but was assigned to command at Detroit. In concert with fellow brigadier Lewis Cass, he was responsible for defending several hundred square miles of American territory with the merest handful of regulars and territorial militia. However, McArthur succeeded Harrison to command of the Northwestern Army in May 1814, although he nearly resigned in August once apprised that Secretary of War John Armstrong had dispatched Lieutenant Colonel George Croghan and the bulk of his regulars on an expedition against Mackinac — without informing him. Armstrong quickly apologized and McArthur continued on in command.

By the fall of 1814, the frontier had slipped to the periphery of military matters and McArthur, eager for military distinction of some kind, determined to mount a diversion in western Canada to assist General George Izard at Niagara. On October 23 he led a column of 720 mounted Kentuckians, rangers, and Indians from Detroit and up the west side of Lake St. Clair, before crossing over to Canada on a 150-mile jaunt through British territory. Given the lax security of this region, he initially spread rumors that his real objective was hostile Indian settlements near Saginaw Bay. By November 6, McArthur's

Brigadier General Duncan McArthur. Ohio Historical Society.

force had galloped to the Grand River, where they learned that Izard had withdrawn back to the United States and British forces were concentrating on the peninsula to confront him. He then spurred his men south to Malcolm's Mills (Burford, Ontario) where they easily dispatched a large force of Canadian militia, killing 18 and taking 120 captives; American losses were one dead and six injured. This was also the last armed confrontation in Canada during the War of 1812. The raiders then burned several mills and flour stocks, loss of which imposed considerable hardship on British troops during the winter. McArthur's victorious little column finally clattered back into Detroit on November 17, 1814, having covered nearly 500 miles in only 27 days. This was one of the more successful American raids of the war and, although it pales in comparison to much larger mounted raids of the Civil War, it nonetheless helped secure Michigan's wafer-thin defenses from further attacks. McArthur himself mustered out of service on June 15, 1815, and resumed his successful political career in Ohio, eventually serving both as governor and a congressman. He died in Chillicothe on April 29, 1839, cantankerously disposed, but an accomplished citizen-soldier.

Archival

RG94. Letters. National Archives. Adjutant General's Office; 1813–1815.
RG107. Letters. National Archives. Secretary of War's Office; 1813–1814.

Manuscript

McArthur, Duncan. Papers. Burton Historical. Duncan McArthur Papers; 1813–1814.
McArthur, Duncan. Letters. Historical Society (Pa). D. Parker Papers, Box 12, 27; 1814–1815.
McArthur, Duncan. Papers. Library of Congress. Duncan McArthur Papers; 1812–1815.
McArthur, Duncan. Letters. Library of Congress. William H. Harrison Papers; 1813–1814.
McArthur, Duncan. Letters. Ohio Historical. 1812–1815.
McArthur, Duncan. Letter, 1813. Ohio Historical. VFM4954; quits Congress to fight in war.
McArthur, Duncan. Letters. Ohio State Library. Thomas Worthington Papers; 1812–1815.
McArthur, Duncan. Letters. Ross County Historical. 1943.59, Ohio; 1812–1813.
McArthur, Duncan. Letter, 1814. Western Reserve. Mss v.f. M; expedition into Canada.
McArthur, Duncan. Letters. Wisconsin Historical. Draper Coll., Frontier Wars Papers, 9 U.

Printed Primary

Carter, Clarence E., ed. *The Territorial Papers of the United States: Vol. X, The Michigan Territory, 1805–1820.* Washington, D.C.: Government Printing Office, 1942.
Knopf, Richard C., ed. *Thomas Worthington and the War of 1812.* Columbus: Anthony Wayne Parkway Board, 1957.

Select Secondary

Cramer, C. H. "Duncan McArthur: The Military Phase." *Ohio State Archaeological and Historical Quarterly* 46 (1937): 67–90.
Rammage, Stuart A. *The Militia Stood Alone: Malcolm's Mills, 6 November, 1814.* Summerland, B.C.: Valley Pubs., 2000.

Alexander Macomb

Alexander Macomb was born in Detroit, Michigan, on April 3, 1782, and raised in New York City. During the Quasi-War with France, 1798–1800, he served in the militia and was recommended by General Alexander Hamilton for a commission in the regular army. Macomb accordingly became a cornet of light dragoons in 1799, but was dismissed when the war scare ended. However, he rejoined the army as an infantry lieutenant in 1801, and completed several tours of the Southwest as part of General James Wilkinson's entourage. Macomb handled his responsibilities well, so in the fall of 1802 he became one of two officers scheduled to take courses at the new U.S. Military Academy, West Point. Although not a graduate, he was allowed to join the elite Corps of Engineers in 1805, and thereafter performed routine garrison duty along the Georgia and South Carolina coasts. He also published *A Treatise on Martial Law and Courts Martial* (1809), the first publication of its kind in army history. Macomb remained on station until the eve of the War of 1812, when he transferred to Washington, D.C., and became an adjutant general. However, once fighting began, he applied for a combat command and gained appointment as colonel of the newly raised 3rd Artillery on July 6, 1812.

Macomb spent the first months of the war honing his regiment to a fine edge, and it gained the reputation of an elite formation. Following a stint of garrison duty at Sacketts Harbor, New York, he led his men into combat at Fort George, Upper Canada, on May 27, 1813, and subsequently served with the advanced guard under General Jacob Jennings Brown during the St. Lawrence campaign in the fall. Macomb acquitted himself capably on both occasions, and on January 24, 1814, he advanced to brigadier general. In this capacity he fought at La Colle Mill the following March under Major General James Wilkinson, and briefly succeeded that officer to command the Right Division at Plattsburgh. He was eventually replaced by Major General George Izard, and spent the entire summer training and disciplining his brigade. In late August 1814, Secretary of War John Armstrong ordered Izard to transfer the bulk of his troops to Niagara, and he marched with the brigades of Thomas Adams Smith and Daniel Bissell. This left Plattsburgh defended by Macomb's force of 3,300 regulars and 1,500 militia, soon to face an army of 9,000 British veterans under Governor General Sir George Prevost. On September 6, 1814, Macomb deployed his advanced forces at Beekmantown Road, where they skirmished heavily with Prevost's advance guard. The British then occupied Plattsburgh and made preparations to storm the American position, which lay behind the Saranac River. The attack was finally mounted on September 11, 1814, and was just as quickly halted after the defeat of Commodore George

Brigadier General Alexander Macomb. Photograph by Glenn Castellano; courtesy of the Art Commission of the City of New York.

Downie's fleet on nearby Lake Champlain. The fate of General "Gentleman Johnny" Burgoyne casting a long shadow in this neck of the woods, Prevost behaved responsibly and retreated back to Lower Canada. Macomb, for his part in the victory, received the Thanks of Congress, a gold medal, and brevet promotion to major general.

After the war, Macomb commanded detachments in both New York and Detroit until 1821, when Congressional reductions forced him to accept demotion to colonel of engineers. He nonetheless continued working quietly and professionally until the death of General Brown, commanding general of the army, in 1828. Immediately, Generals Winfield Scott and Edmund Pendleton Gaines began a heated squabble over who should succeed him and so embarrassed the government that both were passed over in favor of Macomb. For the next 16 years he labored diligently and without fanfare, proving himself a far-sighted administrator. His primary concern was clarifying an ambiguous chain of command by bringing all staff branches and bureaus under his control, a move culminating with the court-martial of General Roger Jones in 1830. Macomb also penned several authoritative texts on military law, and also took a stab at drama by penning *Pontiac; or, the Siege of Detroit* in 1835. This capable and colorless military bureaucrat died in Washington, D.C., on June 25, 1841, with modern organization and administrative reforms his greatest legacy.

Archival

RG94. Letters. National Archives. Adjutant General's Office; 1812–1815.
RG98, No. 390/274. Orderly book. National Archives. 9th Mil. Dist, 1812–1813.
RG98, No. 447/345. Orderly book. National Archives. List of British deserters, Plattsburgh.
RG107. Letters. National Archives. Secretary of War's Office; 1812–1815.
Macomb, Alexander. Orderly book. Owen D. Young. Mss Coll. 132; February–September, 1814.

Manuscript

Macomb, Alexander. Letter, 1814. Boston Public. Ch.C.13.4; post–Plattsburgh.
Macomb, Alexander. Papers. Burton Historical. Macomb Family Papers.
Macomb, Alexander. Letter, 1814. Cecil County. Mitchell family File, Plattsburg.
Macomb, Alexander. Letters. Clements Library. Thomas Brisbane Papers; 1814.
Macomb, Alexander. Letters. Feinberg Library. Plattsburgh; 1814.
Macomb, Alexander. Letters. Historical Society (Pa). Gratz Coll., Box 34; Sacketts; 1813.
Macomb, Alexander. Letters. Historical Society (Pa). Parker Papers, Box 22, 24, 28; 1814–1815.
Macomb, Alexander. Letter, 1813. Library of Congress. Samuel Smith Papers; Sacketts Harbor.

Macomb, Alexander. Letter, 1812. Library of Congress. Misc. Mss Collection.
Macomb, Alexander. Letters. Lilly Library. Jonathan Williams Papers; 1812–1815.
Macomb, Alexander. Letter, 1813. New York Historical. Misc O'Connor; supplies, Sacketts Harbor.
Macomb, Alexander. Letter, 1813. New York Historical. Misc Mss M, to Dearborn, Sacketts Harbor.
Macomb, Alexander. Map, 1814. U.S. Military Academy. Jonathan Williams Papers; Plattsburgh.

Printed Primary

Macomb, Alexander. "The Battle of Plattsburg." *Journal of the Military Service Institute* 12 (January 1891): 76–79.

Select Secondary

Everest, Allan S. *The Military Career of Alexander Macomb and Alexander Macomb at Plattsburgh*. Plattsburgh, N.Y.: Clinton County Historical Association, 1989.
Fitz-End, David G. *The Final Invasion: Plattsburgh, the War of 1812's Most Decisive Battle*. New York: Cooper Square, 2001.
Skelton, William B. "The Commanding General and the Question of Civil Control in the Antebellum Army." *American Nineteenth Century History* 7, no. 2 (2006): 153–172.
Turner, Wesley B. *British Generals in the War of 1812: High Command in the Canadas*. Montreal: McGill-Queen's University Press, 1999, 24–57. [George Prevost].

James Miller

James Miller was born in Petersborough, New Hampshire, on April 25, 1776, and he attended Williams College, Massachusetts, to study law. Miller opened a successful practice after graduating, but he also developed an interest in military affairs and joined the local militia. He subsequently joined the army on July 8, 1808, as a major in the 4th Infantry and initially performed garrison duty at Fort Independence, Boston, for two years. He then advanced to lieutenant colonel 5th Infantry on November 30, 1810, and the following year accompanied Governor William Henry Harrison's expedition to the Wabash River. Miller missed the battle of Tippecanoe on account of illness, but he nonetheless performed valuable work at Fort Harrison by forwarding supplies. When the War of 1812 commenced, Miller's regiment formed the core of General William Hull's Northwestern Army at Dayton, Ohio, and he marched it to Detroit in a celebrated 200-mile trek through the wilderness. This force entered Canada in July 1812, but the inept and vacillating Hull soon recrossed back to Detroit and dispatched Miller southwest to restore his communications with the River Raisin. On August 9, 1812, his column, numbering 600 regulars and a handful of volunteers, encountered a mixed British/Indian force under Tecumseh and Maguaga, Michigan Territory, and came under heavy fire. With men falling fast around him, Miller ordered a bayonet charge that swept his strongly posted opponents from the field. This was the first American land victory of the war and Miller won a brevet promotion to colonel, but Hull recalled him back to Detroit where the rest of the army surrendered on August 16, 1812. Miller was sent to Montreal as a prisoner and ultimately exchanged for Captain James R. Dacres of HMS *Guerriere*. While a captive he was transferred to the 6th Infantry on September 14, 1812 as a lieutenant colonel.

In the spring of 1813, Miller joined General John Parker Boyd's brigade and he was present at the capture of Fort George on May 27, 1813. He next accompanied General James Wilkinson's ill-fated St. Lawrence expedition that fall and spent a harsh winter encamping at French Mills, New York. There, on March 9, 1814, Miller succeeded Eleazar Wheelock Ripley as colonel of the 21st Infantry, then regarded as among the best units in the army. He subsequently joined Ripley's brigade at Buffalo, New York, as part of General Jacob Jennings Brown's Left Division and fought in the famous 1814 Niagara campaign. Miller was present at the Battle of Chippewa, July 5, 1814, although ordered into action too late to achieve anything. Three weeks later at Lundy's Lane, July 25, 1814, Miller's 21st Infantry singularly distinguished itself. A powerful British battery had previously decimated General Winfield Scott's brigade and threatened to destroy the entire American army: General Brown hurriedly asked Miller if he could storm it. "I'll try, sir!" he famously replied—then expertly deployed his men in the darkness, stealthily approached his quarry, and seized his objective in the best-executed infantry attack of the entire war. British defenders were sent scampering down the slopes, at which point Miller deployed along the heights and withstood several determined counterattacks. Heavy losses, however, prompted the Americans to fall back to Fort Erie and entrench while Miller took a leave of absence. He returned a few weeks later, now a brevet brigadier general, and on September 17, 1814, fought conspicuously in Brown's desperate sortie from Fort Erie. Once the British entrenchments had been turned by militia under General Peter Buell Porter, Miller's column surged forward, pierced their line, and stormed two additional batteries. A sharp British counterattack prevented the Americans from seizing a third and final battery, and they quickly fell back to Fort Erie unscathed. For his War of 1812 services, Miller received a gold medal from Congress; he and George Croghan are the only regimental-grade officers of this war so honored.

Brigadier General James Miller. Peabody Essex Museum.

Miller was retained in the postwar military establishment as colonel of the new 5th Infantry and he served at various posts along the northwestern frontier. He resigned his commission in June 1819 after President James Monroe tendered him an appointment as the first governor of the Arkansas Territory. Among Miller's many achievements there were relocating the capital to present-day Little Rock, instituting a new legal code, and signing treaties with various Indian tribes. His health failing, Miller resigned from office in 1823 and was replaced by another War of 1812 veteran, George Izard. He then accepted appointment as collector of the port of Salem, Massachusetts, which he occupied for the next 24 years. Here Miller struck up cordial relations with noted writer Nathaniel Hawthorne, who dedicated the introductory chapter of *The Scarlet Letter* to him. Miller resigned after a stroke in 1849 and retired to his farm in Petersborough, New Hampshire. He died there on July 7, 1851, an accomplished officer from the War of 1812.

Archival

RG94. Letters. National Archives. Adjutant General's Office; 1812–1815.
RG107. Letters. National Archives. Secretary of War's Office; 1814–1815.

Manuscript

Miller, James. Letters. Clements Library. War of 1812 Papers; 1813–1818.
Miller, James. Letter, 1812. Historical Society (Pa). Parker Papers, Box 17; troop movements.
Miller, James. Letters. Lilly Library. War of 1812 Collection; 1811–815.
Miller, James. Letter, 1814. Gilder Lehrman. Fort Erie.
Miller, James. Letters. Massachusetts Historical. Jacob J. Brown Papers; 1814–1815.
Miller, James. Letters. U.S. Military Academy. James Miller Papers; 1811–1815.

Select Secondary

Holden, Robert J. "James Miller, Collector of the Port of Salem." *Essex Institute Collections* 104 (1968): 253–302.
Ledbetter, Carl. "General James Miller: Hawthorne's Hero in Arkansas." *Arkansas Historical Quarterly* 47 (Summer 1988): 99–115.

Thomas Parker

Thomas Alexander Parker was born in Westmoreland County, Virginia, on October 8, 1760, and he fought in the Revolutionary War with the 9th Virginia Regiment, rising to captain in 1778. He rejoined the army two decades later, becoming lieutenant colonel of the 8th Infantry as of January 8, 1799. Parker was discharged after the threat of war with France abated, but on March 12, 1812, he was reinstated as colonel of the 12th Infantry. Parker was known to have been on the Niagara frontier that fall, where he fought at Smyth's crossing. He then advanced to brigadier general on March 12, 1813, and was assigned to an infantry brigade at Burlington, Vermont, as part of General Wade Hampton's division. He did not accompany the Chateauguay campaign that fall, however, and his brigade was commanded by Colonel Robert Purdy for reasons which remain unclear. Shortly afterwards Parker repaired back to Virginia and succeeded General Robert Taylor as commander of the 5th Military District, headquartered at Norfolk, until being replaced by General Moses Porter. Parker then resigned his commission on March 1, 1814, although he was remained active in the state militia and witnessed the debacle at Bladensburg in August 1814. Parker died at his home in Clarke County, Virginia, on January 25, 1820, a minor player in a major conflict.

Archival

RG94. Letters. National Archives. 1813–1814.
RG107. Letters. National Archives. 1813–1814.

Manuscript

Parker, Thomas. Letter, 1812. Historical Society (Pa). David Parker Papers, Box 7, recruiting.
Parker, Thomas. Letter, 1814. Historical Society (Pa). Dreer Coll., to Charles F. Mercer.
Parker, Thomas. Letters. Perkins Library. Campbell Family Papers; 1812–1813.
Parker, Thomas. Letters. Virginia Historical. Mss1 C8835 a 331–353; Cropper Coll.
Parker, Thomas. Letters. Virginia Historical. Mss1 B2346 a 917–965; Barbour Family.

Printed Primary

[Parker, Thomas]. *A Narrative of the Battle of Bladensburg in a Letter to Henry Banning, Esq.* N.p., n.d.

Select Secondary

Foytik, Rodney L. "Aspects of Military Life of Troops Stationed Around Norfolk, 1812–1814." *Chesopiean* 22, no. 1 (Winter 1984): 12–20.

Zebulon Montgomery Pike

Zebulon Montgomery Pike was born near Trenton, New Jersey, on January 5, 1777, the son of a Revolutionary War veteran who was also an officer in the U.S. Army. Pike entered his father's company of the 2nd Infantry at the age of 15 and fought under General Anthony Wayne throughout the Northwest Indian War, 1790–1794. Pike proved himself a capable soldier and in March 1799 he acquired a second lieutenant's commission. For many months thereafter he performed routine garrison duty at various western posts. Beset by a meager education, Pike also instructed himself in Spanish, science, and mathematics in his spare time. He then came to the attention of General

James Wilkinson at Kaskaskia, Illinois Territory, who directed him to explore upper fringes of the newly-acquired Louisiana Territory for the government. On August 9, 1805, Pike set out with 20 men and a keel boat, venturing up the Mississippi River as far as present-day Minnesota. There he had several friendly exchanges with the Sioux and Sac Indians living there, and also purchased the land upon which Fort Snelling arose in 1819. Winter soon set in, so Pike grounded his boat and continued exploring the region on sleds. At length he encountered Leech Lake and incorrectly identified it as the source of the Mississippi. He also warned British traders that their presence violated the 1794 Jay Treaty and ordered them out. Pike successfully concluded his 5,000-mile foray by reaching St. Louis on April 30, 1806, and Wilkinson chose him for another important mission. That July Pike departed to explore the southwestern fringes of the Louisiana Purchase and possibly find the source of the Red River. Concurrently, he was to gather intelligence about Spanish military capabilities throughout that region. In November 1806 his team of 23 men had reached the Front Range of the Rocky Mountains, where Pike espied the 16,000-foot-high peak that carries his name. Pushing ahead, the expedition reached the Rio Grande River, which they followed as far as the Rio Conejos before being apprehended by Spanish cavalry in February 1807. Spanish authorities closely questioned Pike and confiscated his maps and charts, but he was released and returned to Natchitoches, Louisiana, in June 1807. He fully expected a hero's welcome, but instead was indicted as part of Aaron Burr's conspiracy to establish an independent republic in the Southwest. Fortunately, an inquiry headed by Secretary of War Henry Dearborn cleared him of any complicity and his career resumed.

Pike next rose to captain, having been promoted while he was out exploring. On July 6, 1812, just as the War of 1812 commenced, he rose to colonel of the newly raised 15th Infantry and assigned to the army of Major General Dearborn at Plattsburgh. He subsequently participated in Dearborn's farcical attempt to invade Lower Canada that fall, which collapsed once the militia, resting upon its constitutional scruples, refused to cross the border. He also concocted a bizarre experiment by equipping his regiment with long pikes and snow shoes for fighting in winter, a quixotic arrangement that was quickly abandoned. Pike, other than participating in a nighttime fire-fight with other American units, had handled himself capably and, on March 12, 1813, he advanced to brigadier general with concomitant responsibilities as Adjutant and Inspector General. He now led a brigade (6th, 15th, and 16th Infantries) at Sacketts Harbor, New York, and was slated to spearhead an amphibious assault against the Canadian capital at York (Toronto), Upper Canada. On April 27, 1813, covered by the cannon of Commodore Isaac Chauncey's Lake Ontario squadron, the aggressive general leapt in a boat, rowed ashore, and

Brigadier General Zebulon M. Pike. Independence National Historic Park.

directed the attack in person. The town fell after a stiff engagement and Pike was busily questioning prisoners when a magazine exploded, fatally injuring him and inflicting over 200 casualties — a conspicuous blot on an otherwise splendid operation. Pike then died on board Chauncey's flagship USS *Madison*, his head resting upon a captured British flag. His body was borne back to Sacketts Harbor and entombed beneath Fort Tompkins. Considering Pike's overall competence and aggressiveness, he might have figured prominently in military affairs and might have possibly risen to major general; as such his passing constituted a serious loss to the overall war effort. And, dying in the manner that he did, Pike also became one of the War of 1812's first military martyrs. Ironically, Captain James Lawrence, the naval martyr who perished in the frigate USS *Chesapeake*, also hailed from New Jersey.

Archival

Pike, Zebulon M. Letter book. Clements Library. 1812–1813.
RG94, Roll 1. Letters. National Archives. Zebulon M. Pike; 1812–1813.
RG107. Letters. National Archives. Secretary of War's Office; 1812–1813.

Manuscript

Pike, Zebulon M. Letters. Boston Public. Ms. 1463, to Capt. White Youngs; 1813.
Pike, Zebulon M. Letters. Brigham Young. Vault Mss 538; 1812–1813.
Pike, Zebulon M. Letter, 1813. Brigham Young. Vault Mss 132; to Melancthon T. Woolsey.
Pike, Zebulon M. Letter, 1813. Chicago Historical. Z. M. Pike file; generals, military affairs.
Pike, Zebulon M. Letter, 1812. Historical Society (Pa). Gratz, Box 84, about military career.
Pike, Zebulon M. Letter, 1813. Manuscripts and Archives. Mss 562, Series 1, fld. 6; Sacketts Harbor.
Pike, Zebulon M. Letter, 1813. Morristown National. Micro. Reel 45, 542; Sacketts Harbor.
Pike, Zebulon M. Letter, 1812. New York Historical. Gallatin Papers, 1812 #113, despises Hull.
Pike, Zebulon M. Letter, 1813. New York Historical. Misc Mss Pike, military affairs, chaos.
Pike, Zebulon M. Letter, 1813. Newberry Library. Ayer Manuscript Collection.
Pike, Zebulon M. Letter, 1813. Oberlin College. Orrin June Coll., seeks success at York.
Pike, Zebulon M. Letters. Oneida Historical. 1812–1813.
Pike, Zebulon M. Letters. Western Reserve. Miscellaneous Correspondence.

Select Secondary

Hutchins, John M. *General Zebulon M. Pike Reaches the Summit of Glory: The Battle for York, April 27, 1813.* Lakewood, Colo.: Avrooman-Apfelwald Press, 2006.
Malcomson, Robert. *Capital in Flames: The American Attack on York, 1813.* Montreal: Robin Brass Studio, 2008.
Malcomson, Robert. "The Battle for Little York." *MHQ* 21 (Autumn 2008): 40–49.
Montgomery, M. R. *Jefferson and the Gun-Men: How the West was Almost Lost.* New York: Crown Publishers, 2000.
Olson, Michael L. "Zebulon Pike and American Popular Culture, or, Has Pike Peaked?" *Kansas History* 29, no. 1 (2006): 48–59.
Turner, Wesley B. *British Generals in the War of 1812: High Command in the Canadas.* Montreal: McGill-Queen's University Press, 1999, 84–100. [Roger Hale Sheaffe].

Moses Porter

Moses Porter was born in Danvers, Massachusetts, on March 3, 1756. In May 1775, word of fighting between colonial militia and British troops at Lexington and Concord inspired him to march to nearby Marblehead and join Captain Samuel Trevett's artillery company as a corporal. Over the next 47 years, Porter was indelibly associated with that combat arm. He fought in the battle of Bunker Hill as part of Colonel Richard Gridley's artillery regiment, and helped save the only cannon rescued from capture. Porter was also present at such noticeable engagements as the siege of Boston, Long Island, Trenton and Princeton, and Newport before forming part of the garrison at strategic West Point, New York. By the time the Revolutionary War ended in 1783, Porter was a second lieutenant, and subsequently retained in the tiny postwar army. He commanded Fort Harmar, Ohio, for many years, and in 1791 he survived St. Clair's defeat at the hands of Miami chief Little Turtle. Promoted to captain, Porter next accompanied General Anthony Wayne during the decisive victory at Fallen Timbers in 1794. The following year the United States and Great Britain concluded the Jay Treaty, whereby the latter relinquished numerous posts in the Old Northwest. Consequently, in 1796 Porter arrived at Detroit, Michigan Territory, with a company of artillerists and raised the first American flag ever hoisted there. The following year he transferred to Fort Niagara, New York, where he remained until 1805. That year President Thomas Jefferson transferred him to newly acquired New Orleans, and he spent two years shoring up the city's defenses and promoting peaceful relations with neighboring Indians. In 1807 Porter ventured north again, where he prepared coastal defenses ranging from Boston to New York in anticipation of renewed warfare with Great Britain.

In March 1812, Porter gained promotion to colonel of the elite Regiment of Light Artillery, and that fall he proceeded to the Niagara frontier to succeed the disgraced General Alexander Smyth as regional commander. He functioned there until May 27, 1813, when he joined the army of General Henry Dearborn for an attack on Fort George, Upper Canada. Porter commanded all artillery units involved in the battle and also lost a race with youthful Lieutenant Colonel Winfield Scott to strike the British colors. Porter commanded Fort George until October 2, 1813, when he became chief of artillery during General James Wilkinson's St. Lawrence expedition and also received promotion to brevet brigadier general. On November 1, 1813, Porter landed several long 18-pounders from the flotilla at French Creek, New York, and drove off several British gunboats attempting to shadow them. It was not until the spring of 1814 that Porter received his most important wartime assignment, as commander of the Fifth Military District, headquartered at

Brigadier General Moses Porter. Peabody Institute Library.

Norfolk, Virginia. At the time, large British fleets were operating in Chesapeake Bay, and in July 1814 the Tenth Military District was organized for the defense of the Washington, D. C., area. Secretary of War John Armstrong intended to appoint Porter as commander, but President James Madison overruled him and nominated General William Henry Winder instead. In the wake of the Bladensburg disaster, Porter redoubled his efforts at defending Norfolk with new batteries and detachments of the 20th, 35th, and 38th

Infantries. The British apparently respected these endeavors enough to attack Baltimore, Maryland, instead. Porter then transferred north to sit on the court-martial of General Wilkinson shortly after peace returned.

In 1815 Porter reverted back to his nominal rank as colonel Light Artillery Regiment, and ventured to Philadelphia, Pennsylvania, as commander of the Fourth Military District. In 1818, he returned to Boston as president of a board of officers convened to establish a uniform system of artillery materiel for the army, a deficiency made painfully apparent by the recent war. In 1821, Congress consolidated both the Light artillery and the Corps of Artillery as a cost-cutting measure, and Porter became colonel of the newly created 1st Artillery. He was functioning in that capacity when he died at Watertown, Massachusetts, on April 14, 1822, a venerable witness to many significant events in American military history. Due to his penchant for profanity, the capable Porter was jocularly known throughout the army as "Old Blow Hard."

Archival

RG94. Letters. National Archives. Adjutant General's Office; 1812–1815.
RG98, No. 466/365. Orderly book. National Archives. Adj. Gen., 3rd Mil. District, 1812–1815.
RG98, No. 449/347. Orderly book. National Archives. Adj. Gen., 3rd Mil. District, 1812–1815.
RG98, No. 458/357. Orderly book. National Archives. Ins. Gen., 3rd Mil. Dist., 1813–1815.
RG98, No. 451/350. Orderly book. National Archives. Ins. Gen., 3rd Mil. Dist., 1813–1815.
RG107. Letters. National Archives. Secretary of War's Office; 1812–1815.

Manuscript

Porter, Moses. Papers. Burton Historical. Pre-war Detroit.
Porter, Moses. Papers. Danvers Archival. PR/PO/C; 1812–1815.
Porter, Moses. Letter, 1812. Historical Society (Pa). Gratz Coll., Box 3, iron guns to Boston.
Porter, Moses. Letters. Library of Congress. Mss5674; 1796–1806.
Porter, Moses. Letters. Library of Virginia. 41557, James Barbour Papers; 1814.
Porter, Moses. Letters. New York Historical. Henry Dearborn letter books; 1812–1813.

Select Secondary

Putnam, Alfred P. "General Moses Porter." *Historical Collections of the Danvers Historical Society* 15 (1927): 1–25.

Eleazar Wheelock Ripley

Eleazar Wheelock Ripley was born in Hanover, New Hampshire, on April 15, 1792, the son of a noted theologian and grandson of Eleazar Wheelock, who had founded Dartmouth College. He graduated from Dartmouth in 1800, studied law, and eventually established a law practice in Waterville, Maine Territory. There Ripley developed an interest in politics, and in 1807 he gained a seat in the Massachusetts House of Representatives. Politically adept, Ripley supplanted Joseph Story, a future Supreme Court justice, as speaker in 1811 and the following year he successfully stood for a seat in the state senate. However, the prospects of war with Great Britain were looming, so he resigned from office to become lieutenant colonel of the 21st Infantry on March 12, 1812. That June Major General Henry Dearborn ordered Ripley to command the coastal fortifications at Saco, Maine. In September he marched his men 400 miles overland to Plattsburgh to join General Joseph Bloomfield's brigade, and subsequently accompanied Dearborn's ill-fated invasion of Lower Canada. Ripley next wintered at Burlington, Vermont, where, in contrast with many contemporaries, he spent the entire period drilling and disciplining his troops. In the absence of a modern American manual, Ripley apparently drilled his men along British lines, transforming them into a model unit. On March 12, 1813, he rose to colonel and led the regiment to Sacketts Harbor as part of General Zebulon M. Pike's brigade. He formed the reserve during the successful capture of York, April 27, 1813, debarked ashore after Pike's death to restore order and prevent plundering. His regiment performed so capably in this role that the British subsequently released Lieutenant Peter Pelham, who was captured later that year, as a token of esteem. Ripley was next present during the May 27, 1813, capture of Fort George, Upper Canada, and he later accompanied the St. Lawrence expedition as part of General Robert Swartwout's 4th Brigade. His regiment was particularly active at Crysler's Farm, November 11, 1813, where it drove back numerous light troops and Indians, and Ripley was one of a handful of regimental officers to garner any distinction in combat. Consequently, he rose to brigadier general on April 15, 1814, and was posted to General Jacob Jennings Brown's Left Division at Buffalo, New York. Aged 32 years, Ripley was also the youngest brigadier in the army after Winfield Scott.

The Americans at this time were preparing for a major offensive operation into the Niagara Peninsula which Brown and Scott heartily endorsed but Ripley, upon further reflection, felt it would fail for want of manpower. To underscore his pessimism he rather undiplomatically tendered his resignation, which Brown refused to accept, but thereafter the two leaders were at cross purposes. The Left Division sortied across the Niagara River on July 3,

Brigadier General Eleazar W. Ripley. Hood Museum of Art, Dartmouth College, Hanover, New Hampshire; gift of Mrs. A. W. Roberts.

1814, quickly bagged the British garrison at Fort Erie, then two days later won an impressive victory over British forces at Chippawa. Ripley, though present, was ordered into battle too late and could not contribute. However, he was in the thick of fighting at Lundy's Lane on July 25, 1814, after the main British force under Lieutenant General Gordon Drummond had badly cut up Scott's brigade. Deploying in the darkness, he directed Colonel James Miller of the 21st Infantry to storm the British battery on the crest of the hill, which was brilliantly accomplished. Ripley then led up his remaining unit, the 23rd Infantry under Major George Mercer Brooke and helped rebuff Drummond's repeated counterattacks. Brown by this time was severely wounded and he mistakenly ordered the army back to Chippawa Creek to repose. Ripley complied but, at daybreak, seeing the emaciated condition of the army, he refused to renew combat with the British, now reoccupying their former strong position. The Americans subsequently fell back to Fort Erie and entrenched under his direction but Brown, thoroughly distrusting Ripley, ordered General Edmund Pendleton Gaines up from Sacketts Harbor to command while he convalesced. Drummond, meanwhile, had been reinforced and besieged Fort Erie closely. During the night of August 14, 1814, Ripley noticed that the incessant British bombardment suddenly stopped — which he interpreted as a sign of impending attack. He notified Gaines, who agreed and alerted the entire garrison in time to bloodily repel British columns in the morning hours of the 15th. A week later a British shell wounded Gaines and Brown, distrustful of Ripley as ever, hobbled back to assume command in person. On September 17, 1814, he planned a sortie against the British siege works and Ripley, who initially objected and declined to participate, changed his mind and accepted command of the reserve. The attack was highly successful, although Ripley was struck by a ball in the neck. In light of his Niagara services, he received brevet promotion to major general, along with the Thanks of Congress, a gold medal, and elaborate swords from the legislatures of New York and Georgia.

In 1815 a public furor developed over the laurels accorded Ripley when Brown, still angered by the latter's behavior, publicly questioned his moral courage. A spate of affidavits and anonymous publication ensued from both sides, until Ripley demanded and received a court of inquiry to clear his name. That body convened briefly at Albany, New York, when it was suddenly disbanded by order of President James Madison, apparently for political reasons. Ripley was the highest-ranking war hero from New England and the Democratic-Republicans, facing uncertain presidential prospects in 1816, did not want to alienate that valuable part of the electorate. This decision further enraged Brown, but Ripley emerged exonerated in most military circles. However, political enemies managed to delay presentation of his Congressional gold medal until 1834, two decades after it had been struck. In the fall of 1815, Ripley was also transferred to General Andrew Jackson's Division of the South, apparently to put as much distance as possible between himself and Brown. There he erected coastal fortifications until February 1, 1820, when old wounds forced his retirement from military service. Ripley resumed his legal practice in New Orleans and, in 1834, he was elected to Congress as a representative. Illness prevented him from seeking a third term and he died in West Felicia Parish on March 2, 1839. Ripley was an outstanding regimental commander in the War of 1812 and a talented defensive general. However, his circumspect approach to combat placed him at odds with aggressive leaders like Brown and Scott and at a time when the army could scarcely afford divisivness.

Archival

RG94. Letters. National Archives. Adjutant General's Office; 1812–1815.
RG107. Letters. National Archives. Secretary of War's Office; 1812–1815.

Manuscript

Ripley, Eleazar W. Letters. Clements Library. War of 1812 Collection; 1814–1815.
Ripley, Eleazar W. Letters. Historical Society (Pa). Dreer Coll., 1812–1815.
Ripley, Eleazar W. Letter, 1814. Historical Society (Pa). Gratz Coll., Box 4, Six Nations allies.
Ripley, Eleazar W. Letters. Lilly Library. War of 1812 Papers; 1814–1815.
Ripley, Eleazar W. Letters. Massachusetts Historical. Jacob Brown Papers; 1814–1815.
Ripley, Eleazar W. Letters. Massachusetts Historical. Ms. N-83; 1813–1814.
Ripley, Eleazar W. Letter, 1814. Massachusetts Historical. Ms.-L; eulogy to Eleazar D. Wood.
Ripley, Eleazar W. Letters. New York Historical. Henry Dearborn letter book; 1812–1813.
Ripley, Love A. Letters. Forbes Library. Allen Family Papers; 1812–1814.

Printed Primary

"Biographical Memoirs of Major General Ripley." *Port Folio* 5 (February 1815): 105–136.
Ripley, Eleazar W. *Facts Relative to the Campaign Upon the Niagara Frontier in 1814.* Boston: Patriot Office, 1815.

Select Secondary

Baylies, Nicholas. *Eleazar Wheelock Ripley and the War of 1812.* Des Moines, Ia.: Brewster, 1890.
Fredriksen, John C. "Niagara, 1814: The U. S. Army Quest for Tactical parity in the War of 1812 and Its Legacy." Unpublished Ph.D. dissertation, Providence College, 1993.
Graves, Donald E. *Where Right and Glory Lead! The Battle of Lundy's Lane, 1814.* Toronto: Robin Brass Studio, 1997.
Whitehorne, Joseph. *While Washington Burned: The Battle for Fort Erie, 1814.* Baltimore: Nautical and Aviation Press, 1992.

Winfield Scott

Winfield Scott was born near Petersburg, Virginia, on June 13, 1786, the son of a Revolutionary War officer. He briefly studied at William and Mary College in 1805 before dropping out to pursue law, but two years later, in the wake of the Royal Navy attack upon the American frigate *Chesapeake*, he joined a local cavalry unit which captured and detained a boatload of British sailors. Thereafter Scott was drawn towards a military career and he subsequently petitioned President Thomas Jefferson for a regular army commission. In 1808 he became a captain in the elite Regiment of Light Artillery and served several months with the garrison at New Orleans, observing first-hand the treacherous incompetence of General James Wilkinson. The lofty Scott, six-and-a half feet tall, was decidedly impolitic in denouncing his superior as a "traitor, liar, and a scoundrel," for which he was court-martialed for insubordination and suspended from active duty for a year. He put the period to good use by studying European military handbooks and by the time he rejoined the colors back at New Orleans in 1811, he was one of the most professionally-minded officers in service.

Shortly after the War of 1812 commenced, Scott became lieutenant colonel of the new 2nd Regiment of Artillery on July 6, 1812, and he initially served under Colonel George Izard at Philadelphia. These two officers were the outstanding drillmasters of the war, and through no coincidence their regiment gained a reputation as among the best-trained and best-led in the army. Scott, however, thirsted for glory on the battlefield and in the fall of 1812 he transferred to the brigade of General Alexander Smyth at Buffalo, New York. On October 13, 1812, Scott volunteered to fight at Queenston Heights, where he was captured and taken to Montreal. There he befriended a group of Irish deserters who had been captured while fighting for the Americans and now faced execution. Once exchanged, Scott promptly described their plight to President James Madison, who ordered a like number of British captives placed under close confinement and sentenced to death if the deserters were hung. Scott subsequently gained promotion to colonel on March 12, 1813, and joined the staff of General Henry Dearborn at Sackett's Harbor as his adjutant. In this capacity he helped plan and execute the successful attack upon Fort George, Upper Canada, on May 27, 1813, racing ahead of aged Colonel Moses Porter to strike the British colors by his own hand. He then vigorously pursued the defeated British under General John Vincent, and it took two direct orders from General Morgan Lewis before he relented. Scott remained idle at Fort George for several months, although in August 1813, he boarded Commodore Isaac Chauncey's fleet and led a brief amphibious raid against York, Upper Canada. That October Scott joined General Jacob Jennings Brown's advanced troops during the ill-fated St. Lawrence campaign, acquitting himself well. He thereupon returned to Washington, D. C., to report on the behavior of General Wilkinson and the state of the army in general. His candor and thoroughness so impressed Secretary of War John Armstrong that he received promotion to brigadier general as of March 9, 1814. Scott, a mere stripling of 28 years, was now the youngest field commander in the army.

Scott reported to Buffalo, New York, as part of General Brown's Left Division, whereupon he received command of the 1st Brigade. This consisted of the experienced but skeletal 9th, 11th, 22nd, and 25th Infantries, led by such regimental luminaries as Henry Leavenworth, John McNeil, Hugh Brady, and Thomas S. Jesup. Over the next 10 weeks Scott carefully supervised his men in a rigorous camp of instruction that utilized Smyth's 1812 translation of the famous French drill system. High standards of camp sanitation, dress, and military courtesy were also rigorously enforced. Any recruits trickling in were likewise trained alongside the others, and by summertime all ranks could march, maneuver, and fight with the precision of veterans. Scott's persistence paid handsome dividends on July 5, 1814, when 1,700 British troops under General Phineas Riall attacked the American camp near Chippawa Creek, Upper Canada, while he was in the act of drilling his brigade. Owing to a shortage of blue cloth, Scott's brigade had been outfitted in gray jackets, which gave the British an impression they initially opposed militia. Scott quickly outmaneuvered his adversary on an open plain, the first time an American army had deployed so adroitly, and drove them from the field. Victory here made Scott a national hero and gained him promotion to brevet major general. However, three weeks later he rashly attacked a larger British force at Lundy's Lane, July 25, 1814, while the latter enjoyed superior elevation and artillery. The 1st Brigade was cut to pieces in consequence, and Scott further depleted it with several headstrong counterattacks at night, all of which were repelled. He was seriously wounded in the shoulder and his fine command was decimated, but Scott's aplomb under fire resulted in a gold medal from Congress and a lustrous national reputation. Scott ended the war commanding the 10th Military District at Baltimore, where he directed the court of inquiry investigating General William Henry Winder's conduct at the battle of Bladensburg. He also oversaw a board which wrote the first drill manual adopted by the army since the Revolutionary War. In sum, Scott may have been rash under fire, but he helped lay the seeds of a professional military ethic that the army heretofore conspicuously lacked.

Scott's subsequent career as a preeminent battle captain is too well known to require further commentary here. Suffice to say that for half a century he remained a driving force behind greater professionalism in the army and, by dint of his conquest of Mexico City in 1847, also established himself as an

Brigadier General Winfield Scott. National Portrait Gallery, Smithsonian Institution.

outstanding strategist. No less an authority than the aged Duke of Wellington pronounced him the greatest living soldier of his day. Scott, whose towering ego and fastidiousness for decorum led to the moniker "Old Fuss and Feathers," made a final contribution to his country by promulgating the so-called "Anaconda Plan" through which the Confederacy was divided up and eventually defeated, 1861–1865. He then concluded five decades of conspicuous service by resigning in favor of General George B. McClellan in November 1861. Scott lived to see the republic preserved before dying at West Point, New York, on May 29, 1866, the military doyen of his age. A diamond in the rough initially, Scott, more than any other individual, institutionalized professionalism in the U.S. Army, and bequeathed to it outstanding traditions of thoroughness, preparation, and victory.

Archival

RG94, Roll 3. Letters. National Archives. Winfield Scott, 1812–1815.
RG98, No. 393/276. Letters sent. National Archives. 4th Mil. Dist., 1813–1814.
RG98, No. 460–359. Orderly book. National Archives. 4th Mil. Dist., 1814.
RG98, No. 452/351. Details. National Archives. Buffalo, May–July, 1814.
RG107. Letters. National Archives. Secretary of War's Office; 1814–1815.
Scott, Winfield. Brigade orders. New York State. Ms. 11225; Buffalo, April–July, 1814.
Taliaferro, Lawrence. Orderly Book. Minnesota Historical. M35; 1st Brigade, Fort George, 1813.

Manuscript

Scott, Winfield. Letter, 1813. Boston Public. Ch.D.7.11; supplies in New York.
Scott, Winfield. Letters. Buffalo and Erie. A64-286; 1812–1814.
Scott, Winfield. Letters. Buffalo and Erie. A71-47; pre–Niagara, 1814.
Scott, Winfield. Letters. Clements Library. Jacob Brown Papers; 1814–1815.
Scott, Winfield. Letters. Historical Society (Pa). Daniel Parker Papers.
Scott, Winfield. Letters. Library of Congress. Van Deventer Papers; prisoners.
Scott, Winfield. Letters. Library of Congress. Winfield Scott Papers; 1814.
Scott, Winfield. Letter, 1814. Library of Congress. Martin Van Buren Papers; Quebec by 1815.
Scott, Winfield. Letter, 1814. Lilly Library. Aid for British officers after Lundy's Lane.
Scott, Winfield. Letter, 1815. Manuscripts and Archives. Ms. 783, William Jackson Papers.
Scott, Winfield. Letter, 1812. Massachusetts Historical Endicott; prisoners in Montreal.
Scott, Winfield. Letters. Massachusetts Historical. Jacob J. Brown Papers; Niagara, 1814.
Scott, Winfield. Letter, 1814. New York Historical. Misc Mss S, to James Monroe.
Scott, Winfield. Letters. New York Public. Charles W. Elliott Collection; 1812–1815.
Scott, Winfield. Letters. New York State. KB12914, C. K. Gardner Papers; 1814.
Scott, Winfield. General Orders. Perkins Library. Chamberlayne Papers, November 1814.
Scott, Winfield. Letter, 1843. Pierpont Morgan. 131591; General Phineas Riall as prisoner.
Scott, Winfield. Letters. U.S. Military Academy. No. 292; Winfield Scott Papers; 1814–1815.
Scott, Winfield. Letters. University of Arizona. MS015; 1814.

Printed Primary

Scott, Winfield. *Memoirs of Lieutenant General Scott*. 2 vols. New York: Sheldon, 1864.
Scott, Winfield. "Strictures on General Brown's Report of the Battle of Lundy's Lane." *Historical Magazine* 10 (August 1866): 253–255.

Select Secondary

Daniels, James B. "The Battle of Chippewa." *American History* 42, no. 4 (October 2007): 46–53.
Eisenhower, John S. D. *Agent of Destiny: The Life and Times of General Winfield Scott.* New York: Free Press, 1997.
Graves, Donald E. *Where Right and Glory Lead! The Battle of Lundy's Lane, 1814.* Toronto: Robin Brass, 1997.
Graves, Donald E. *Red Coats & Grey Jackets: The Battle of Chippawa, 5 July, 1814.* Toronto: Dundurn Press, 1994.
Hallahan, John M. "No Doubt Blamable: The Transformation of Captain Winfield Scott." *Virginia Cavalcade* 40 (Spring 1991): 160–171.
Johnson, Timothy D. *Winfield Scott: The Quest for Glory.* Lawrence: University Press of Kansas, 1998.
Malcomson, Robert. *A Very Brilliant Affair: The Battle of Queenston Heights, 1812.* Toronto: Robin Brass Studio, 2003.
Meyer, J. A. "He is the Greatest Living Soldier." *Consortium on Revolutionary Europe, 1750–1850* (1998): 240–248.
Peskin, Allan. *Winfield Scott and the Profession of Arms.* Kent, Oh.: Kent University Press, 2003.
Phifer, Mike. "Slugfest at Lundy's Lane." *Military Heritage* 3, no. 6 (June 2002): 32–42.
Smith, Derek. "Disaster at Queenston Heights." *American History* 36, no. 5 (2001): 38–44.

Thomas Adams Smith

Thomas Adams Smith was born in Essex County, Virginia, on August 12, 1781, and raised in Georgia. In December 1803 he joined the army as a second lieutenant of artillery and served several months on the staff of General James Wilkinson throughout the Old Southwest. Smith rose to first lieutenant in December 1805, and two years later Wilkinson dispatched him to Washington, D.C., with information regarding the treasonable activities of Aaron Burr. As a reward, he was transferred from the artillery to the ranks of the newly established Regiment of Riflemen as a captain on May 3, 1808. He continued functioning capably on his own, although on July 31, 1812, Georgia Senator William H. Crawford helped arrange his promotion to lieutenant colonel over the heads of several more senior officers. Smith's first assignment commanding the elite riflemen was to march to the frontiers of Spanish East Florida and support the so-called Patriot War. This was a clandestine attempt by President James Madison to secure that region from Spain through a rebellion of American settlers there. However, in an attempt to keep

Brigadier General Thomas A. Smith. State Historical Society of Missouri, Columbia.

government involvement hidden, Smith only commanded two companies of riflemen and a handful of Georgia militia. This paucity of manpower effectively thwarted his stated objective, the capture of the fortified bastion of St. Augustine, and a lengthy impasse resulted. For several weeks into 1813, Smith loosely besieged the fort while his camp was continually harassed by Spanish gunboats which lobbed occasional cannonballs into his camp. When the Spanish managed to persuade nearby Seminole Indians to raid Smith's precarious supply lines, he abandoned the siege and fell back to the St. Johns River. By March 1813, Madison abandoned any hope of surreptitiously obtaining East Florida and ordered the "Patriot War" ended quietly. Smith, having succeeded Alexander Smyth as colonel of the Regiment of Riflemen, then proceeded north to partake of military events in Canada.

Throughout the summer of 1813, Smith performed recruiting duty at Nashville, Tennessee, before joining the army of General William Henry Harrison during its final phase of operations in the Old Northwest. On January 24, 1814, while functioning as garrison commander of strategic Sacketts Harbor, New York, he became one of six new brigadier generals in the army. Smith subsequently reported to Major General George Izard's Right Division at Plattsburgh, where he commanded a brigade of light troops. In light of his fine reputation, Izard granted Smith the honor of commanding an advance post at Champlain Village, 5 miles from the Canadian border, where heavy skirmishing was common. That August, however, the brigades of Smith and General Daniel Bissell accompanied Izard on his controversial march to the Niagara frontier, where they united with the Left Division of General Jacob Jennings Brown after several weeks of arduous marching. Little fighting materialized, so Smith left departed the winter cantonment at Buffalo to visit his family and conduct business in Tennessee.

After the war Smith reverted back to his lineal rank as colonel of riflemen and assumed command of the 9th Military District, headquartered at St. Louis. This constituted an enormous wilderness tract encompassing the Illinois and Missouri Territories, and largely unexplored. In the spring of 1816, Smith took several rifle companies and ascended the Mississippi River to confront potentially hostile Fox Indians. War was averted, but as a precaution he founded Fort Armstrong on Rock Island and Fort Edwards on the Des Moines River as a deterrent. Proceeding north, Smith next halted at Prairie du Chien, Wisconsin Territory, where he supervised construction of another valuable post, Fort Crawford. Turning southward, he also supervised military surveys of the Arkansas River region in concert with noted explorer Major Stephen H. Long before finally resigning his commission in November 1818. The following year Fort Smith, Arkansas, was named in his honor. Back in civilian life, Smith accepted President James Monroe's invitation to serve as receiver of public monies at Franklin, Missouri. He functioned there until 1826 before retiring to his plantation, which he named Experiment, in Saline County. For the last 14 years of his life, Smith was one of that state's wealthiest and most respected citizens before dying at home on June 25, 1844. While he never achieved the stature or recognition of such frontier contemporaries as Henry Atkinson or Henry Leavenworth, Smith nonetheless made valuable contributions to the early stages of western exploration and settlement.

Archival

RG94. Letters. National Archives. Adjutant General's Office; 1812–1815.
RG98, No. 439/336. Orderly book. National Archives. Rifle detachment, Aug.–Nov. 1813.
RG107. Letters. National Archives. Secretary of War's Office; 1812–1815.

Manuscript

Smith, Thomas A. Papers. State Historical (Mo). Florida, Plattsburgh; 1812–1814.

Printed Primary

Davis, T. Frederick, ed. "United States Troops in Spanish East Florida, 1812–1813." *Florida Historical Quarterly* 9 (Part I) (July 1930): 3–23; (Part II) 9 (October 1930): 96–116; (Part IV) 9 (April 1931): 259–278.

Select Secondary

Cusick, James. *The Other War of 1812: The Patriot War and the American Invasion of Spanish East Florida*. Athens: University of Georgia Press, 2003.
Fredriksen, John C. *Green Coats and Glory: The United States Regiment of Riflemen, 1808–1821*. Youngstown, N.Y.: Old Fort Niagara Association, 2000.
Napton, N. B. "General Thomas Adams Smith." In: *Past and Present of Saline County, Missouri*. Chicago: E. B. Bower, 1910, 318–324.

Alexander Smyth

Alexander Smyth was born on Rathlin Island, County Antrim, Ireland, on September 14, 1767, and he emigrated to Botetourt County, Virginia, at the age of ten. He studied law and was admitted to the state bar in 1789, and three years later gained a seat in the Virginia House of Delegates. Smyth proved himself a vigorous orator as well as an astute political operator, and by 1808 had won a seat in the state senate as a Democratic-Republican. President Thomas Jefferson was sufficiently impressed to appoint him colonel of the newly created Regiment of Riflemen on July 8, 1808. Smyth, however, lacked prior military training and possessed no relevant qualifications save for pristine political connections. Curiously, his lieutenant colonel was Philadelphia journalist William Duane, a bitter personal adversary, who did everything possible to undermine his authority. Over the next three years Smyth led his regiment in Louisiana, where it performed routine garrison duty and field work under General James Wilkinson. In 1811, Secretary of War William Eustis also authorized Smyth to compile a new system of military discipline to replace the outmoded *Blue Book* of Baron Von Steuben. Craving recognition, Smyth departed Louisiana for Washington, D.C., where he authored his *Regulations for the Field Exercises, Maneuvers, and Conduct of Infantry of the United States* (1812). This tract, essentially a rough abridgement of the famous French 1791 *Reglement*, was officially adopted by the army in March 1812, being the first new drill manual to appear since the Revolution. French drill techniques and tactics subsequently dominated American military thinking until after the Civil War. Ironically, Smyth's biggest critic remained his own lieutenant colonel, Duane, who disapproved of the manual and was anxious to sponsor a drill system of his own.

The renewal of hostilities with Great Britain in June 1812 granted Smyth additional venues to channel his ambition. By making the rounds in Washington, he secured from Eustis appointment as inspector general of the army with a rank of brigadier general, dated July 14, 1812. His official role was to oversee the training and organization of army troops from the nation's capital, a vitally important service. Smyth, however, looked upon paper work with disdain and sought glory on the battlefield. His machinations next landed him command of an infantry brigade stationed at Greenbush, New York, which he marched to the Niagara frontier. Unfortunately, no sooner did Smyth arrive than he quarreled with his designated superior, General Stephen Van Rensselaer, and refused to obey the orders of a militiaman. Consequently, when Van Rensselaer attempted crossing the Niagara River to Queenston Heights on October 13, 1812, Smyth's brigade of 1,600 regulars sat idly by. The invasion attempt was crushed for want of reinforcements, and when Van Rensselaer resigned in disgrace, Smyth was naturally on hand to succeed him as of October 24, 1812.

What followed proved farcical, even by War of 1812 standards. Smyth inherited a dispirited, poorly-trained force of 4,500 soldiers and militia, but he was determined to resume the offensive. For nearly a month he dallied at headquarters, issuing bombastic calls to glory with such regularity that his men dubbed him "Van Bladder." After several false starts, a crossing was finally attempted on November 28, 1812. Several companies made it across the Niagara River and seized a battery above Fort Erie, while Smyth made half-hearted attempts to reinforce them with the 14th Infantry of Colonel William Henry Winder. When this failed, the men were essentially abandoned and Smyth ascribed his defeat to the want of boats. Undeterred — and facing mounting disaffection from his troops — he mounted another attempt on December 1, 1812, with ludicrous results. No sooner had soldiers and militia taken to their craft in freezing weather than the operation was abruptly called off. Any pretense to morale and discipline then evaporated, and the men began firing their guns wildly into the air, with several shots directed at the com-

Brigadier General Alexander Smyth. Library of Congress.

mander's tent. Smyth fled the camp for his own safety and his army disbanded for the winter. Militia general Peter Buell Porter, who had witnessed the affair, publicly branded Smyth as a coward in a local newspaper and Smyth challenged him to a duel, which proved bloodless. He then repaired back to the capital to salvage what little military reputation remained, declaring his intent "to die, if Heaven wills it, in defense of my country." Congress responded by summarily striking Smyth's name from the army list on March 3,1813, removing the vital office of inspector general with it.

Smyth's political reputation survived his military disgrace and in 1816 he resumed politics in Wythe County, Virginia, by joining the Board of Public Works. The following year he was elected to Congress as a representative, where he sat over the next 13 years. Here Smyth functioned intermittently as chairman of the House Committee on Military Affairs and argued against the manpower reductions of 1821. He also experienced a religious conversion and authored numerous tracts dealing with the Apocalypse. Smyth died in Washington, D. C., on April 17, 1830, one of the most curious figures to besmirch American military history — and among the most disastrous.

Archival

RG94. Letters. National Archives. Adjutant General's Office; 1812.
RG107. Letters. National Archives. Secretary of War's Office; 1812.
RG159. Letters. National Archives. Inspector General's Office; 1812.

Manuscript

Smyth, Alexander. Letters. Buffalo and Erie. A00-424, Niagara; 1812.
Smyth, Alexander. Letters. Historical Society (Pa). Gratz Coll., Box 35, Buffalo, 1812.
Smyth, Alexander. Letters. Historical Society (Pa). Daniel Parker Papers, Box 17; 1812.
Smyth, Alexander. Letters. Library of Congress. Campbell–Preston–Floyd Papers.
Smyth, Alexander. Letters. Massachusetts Historical. Henry Dearborn Papers; 1812.
Smyth, Alexander. Letter, 1812. New York Historical. Gallatin LB2, 111–113, proclamation.
Smyth, Alexander. Letter, 1812. Perkins Library. William Eustis Papers.
Smyth, Alexander. Letter, 1812. Perkins Library. Campbell Family Papers, Niagara.
Smyth, Alexander. Papers. Virginia Historical. Mss2 Sm962 b; 1812.

Printed Primary

Hastings, Hugh, ed. *Public Papers of Daniel D. Tompkins, Governor of New York, 1807–1817.* 3 vols. Albany, N.Y.: J. B. Lyons, 1902.
Severance, Frank H., ed. "The Case of Brigadier General Alexander Smyth as Shown in His Writings." *Buffalo Historical Society Publications* 18 (1914): 213–235.

Select Secondary

Chitwood, W. R. "The Duels of General Alexander Smyth." *Wythe County Historical Review* 7 (July 1974): 7–15.
Clary, David A., and Joseph W. A. Whitehorne. *The Inspectors General of the United States Army, 1777–1903.* Washington, D.C.: Office of the Inspector General and Chief of Military History, 1987.
Fredriksen, John C. *Green Coats and Glory: The United States Regiment of Riflemen, 1808–1821.* Youngstown, N.Y.: Old Fort Niagara Association, 2000.
Graves, Donald E. "Dry Books of Tactics: U.S. Infantry Manuals of the War of 1812 and After." *Military Collector and Historian* 38 (Summer, Winter, 1986): 51–60, 173–177.
Malcomson, Robert. *A Very Brilliant Affair: The Battle of Queenston Heights, 1812.* Toronto: Robin Brass Studio, 2003.

Robert Swartwout

Robert Swartwout was born in Poughkeepsie, New York, in 1778, the son of a Revolutionary War veteran, and part of an old Dutch family that had migrated to the region in 1650. He trained as a merchant but also took an interest in military affairs, rising to colonel of militia at the start of the War of 1812. On March 21, 1813, Secretary of War and fellow New Yorker John Armstrong appointed him Quartermaster general of the army with the rank of brigadier general as of March 21, 1813. He succeeded the inept Morgan Lewis in this capacity, but not much could be expected given the slapdash nature of American supply and procurement arrangements. Also, Swartwout's authority did not extend beyond the 9th Military District, so, despite his rank, other quartermaster officers remained virtually independent

Brigadier General Robert Swartwout. Collection of the New-York Historical Society.

of his authority. His vaunted business acumen consequently did little to ameliorate the chaos attending military supply functions. That fall Swartwout also commanded the 4th Brigade (11th, 14th, and 21st Infantries) at Crysler's Farm, November 11, 1813, where he was closely engaged but achieved no real progress against the British. He seemed somewhat disillusioned by his position and offered to resign on April 1, 1814, but Secretary Armstrong refused to accept. Swartwout was retained in the postwar establishment as Quartermaster General until finally being discharged on June 5, 1816. He subsequently relocated to New York City where he served as a city alderman and died there on July 19, 1848. He ranks as another insignificant figure in high places during the war years.

Archival

RG94. Letters. National Archives. Adjutant General's Office; 1812–1815.
RG98, No. 452/351. Details. National Archives. 4th Brigade, October–December, 1813.
RG107. Letters. National Archives. Secretary of War's Office; 1813–1815.

Manuscript

Monroe, James. Letter, 1817. Gilder Lehrman. GLC01743.01; quartermaster activities.
Swartwout, Robert. Letter, 1814. Massachusetts Historical. Jacob J. Brown Collection.
Swartwout, Robert. Papers. New York Public. 1812–1814.

Select Secondary

Graves, Donald E. *Field of Glory: The Battle of Crysler's Farm, 1813.* Toronto: Robin Brass Studio, 1999.
Risch, Erna. *Quartermaster Support for the Army: A History of the Corps, 1775–1939.* Washington, D.C.: Office of the Quartermaster, 1962.
U. S. Congress. House. *A Bill for the Relief of General Robert Swartwout.* Washington, D.C., N.p., 1818.
Weise, A. J. *The Swartwout Chronicles, 1338–1899.* New York: Trow Directory, Printing, and Binding Co., 1899.

Joseph Gardner Swift

Joseph Gardner Swift was born on Nantucket island, Massachusetts, on December 31, 1783, the son of an army surgeon. In 1800 President John Adams appointed him a cadet in the Corps of Artillerists and Engineers, and he was instructed at Newport, Rhode Island, under veteran French officer Lieutenant

Brigadier General Joseph G. Swift. Photograph by Glenn Castellano; courtesy of the Art Commission of the City of New York.

Colonel Louis de Tousard. In October 1801 he transferred to West Point, New York, site of what was then a rather shoddy school of instruction. However, on March 16, 1802, Congress formally established the U.S. Military Academy at the urging of President Thomas Jefferson. Swift and one other student took engineering courses at the nascent institution, and graduated on October 12, 1802, as second lieutenants. Swift's name was listed first, so he is technically regarded as West Point's first graduate. Over the ensuing decade, Swift served at a variety of locales and rose steadily through the ranks. In 1804, he completed engineering duties along the Cape Fear River, North Carolina, and the following year he assumed command of Fort Johnson. He is thus the first engineering officer to command troops from other branches of the army. Swift became a major in 1807 and worked on the harbor defenses of Boston before returning for addition duty at Cape Fear. In 1811, he testified favorably at the court-martial of General James Wilkinson, who thereafter took him in as part of his personal coterie. Such favoritism did not stand well with the War Department, which was eager to rid itself of Wilkinson for his alleged spying for Spain and conspiracies with Aaron Burr. However, the exigencies of war prevailed, and in July 1812 he rose to become successively lieutenant colonel and chief engineer in General Thomas Pinckney's 6th Military District. Fate intervened when Chief Engineer Colonel Jonathan Williams resigned from the service in a huff; Swift was nominated to succeed him. Secretary of War William Eustis would have preferred inventor Robert Fulton, but Congress sought a military man for the post, and the 28-year old Swift was confirmed as chief engineer with a rank of colonel in December 1812. This assignment also carried responsibilities as superintendent of the military academy.

Swift's field assignments generally kept him away from West Point, and he appointed Major Alden Partridge to administer the school in his absence. After commanding the defenses on Staten Island, New York, he pressed for a combat assignment and in August 1813 he received permission to join the army of General Wilkinson at Sacketts Harbor. Swift participated as a staff officer during the ill-fated St. Lawrence expedition of that fall and he was present at the defeat of Crysler's Farm, November 11, 1813. Swift was subsequently summoned to Washington, D.C., to testify about Wilkinson's handling of the campaign. His favorable accounting of the general irritated Secretary of War John Armstrong, who nonetheless approved Swift's promotion to brevet brigadier general on February 19, 1814; he is the first West Point graduate to reach command status. Then Armstrong vindictively shunted him off to command the defenses of New York City, a relatively quiet sector, for the remainder of the war. Beginning in July 1814, after the Royal Navy began appearing in New York waters, the Committee of Defense appointed

Swift to take emergency measures to fortify the city. Accordingly, between August and September he orchestrated the energies of some 38,000 volunteer laborers and completely overhauled the city's harbor defenses to such good effect that the British never tested them. At war's end, the New York Common Council voted Swift "Benefactor of the City," and awarded him many gifts, including a full-length portrait by John Wesley Jarvis that remains on display in city hall.

The War of 1812 highlighted, among other things, the nation's weakness in terms of coastal defenses. Accordingly, President James Madison urged Congress to fund a comprehensive series of fortifications but the new secretary of war, William Harris Crawford, felt that only a European-trained engineer was qualified for the task. The officer he selected, Simon Bernard, was a French veteran of the Napoleonic wars, but his appointment caused bitter acrimony among the Corps of Engineers, which had performed well during the war and resented the nomination of a foreigner. Swift's repeated protests drew a banishment to West Point, where he was ordered to concern himself solely with academy affairs. In May 1817 he returned to Washington, D.C., to lodge additional complaints against Bernard, and it was during his absence that dissatisfaction with Major Alden Partridge's careless administration of West Point led to his removal and replacement with another Swift protégé, Sylvanus Thayer. This selection was provident for Thayer is regarded as one of the academy's finest superintendents. Nevertheless, Swift's continuing indignation over Bernard's appointment to the head of the Board of Fortification availed him nothing, and on November 12, 1818, he resigned from the army rather than submit to a foreigner. Swift nonetheless maintained his academy ties and served on its board of visitors in 1819, 1821, and 1823.

Over the next four decades, Swift cemented his reputation as one of the nation's leading and most productive civil engineers. He served many years as surveyor of the port of New York, then in 1829 President Andrew Jackson instructed him to supervise harbor improvements along the Great Lakes region. Swift remained preoccupied with this assignment for the next 16 years, and he gained additional distinction by helping to design railways in both New York and Louisiana. His work on the Pontchartrain Railroad was notable in that it overcame a previously impassable swamp and was the first system to utilize iron T-rails in the United States. Swift finally retired in 1845 and spent the rest of his life residing in Geneva, New York. He died there on July 23, 1865, proof of Thomas Jefferson's notion that military engineers could be of enormous help in the development of a nation.

Archival

RG77, M417. Letters. National Archives. Buell Collection, 1812–1815.
RG94, Roll 5. Letters. National Archives. Joseph G. Swift, 1812–1815.
RG107. Letters. National Archives. Secretary of War's Department, 1812–1815.
Swift, Joseph G. Letter book. U. S. Military Academy. No. 371, Extracts, 1812–1815.

Manuscript

Swift, Joseph G. Letters. Buffalo and Erie. A00-446, to Benson J. Lossing, 1860.
Swift, Joseph G. Letter, 1814. Historical Society (Pa). Dreer Coll., to John Armstrong.
Swift, Joseph G. Letters. Historical Society (Pa). D. Parker Papers, Box 22, 40; 1813–1814.
Swift, Joseph G. Letters. Library of Congress. Alden Partridge Paper; 1812–1815.
Swift, Joseph G. Letter, 1813. Manuscripts and Archives. Misc. Mss 271, Box 85, academy needs.
Swift, Joseph G. Letter, 1814. New York Historical. Misc Mss Swift, New York defenses.
Swift, Joseph G. Map. New York Historical. G3804.N4: 2M3S42 1814 .C7, New York.
Swift, Joseph G. Papers. New York Public. Postwar considerations.
Swift, Joseph G. Letter, 1815. Perkins Library. Alexander J. Dallas Papers.
Swift, Joseph G. Letter, 1815. Perkins Library. William H. Crawford Papers; to Monroe.
Swift, Joseph G. Papers. U.S. Military Academy. No. 313; 1812–1815; maps.

Printed Primary

Ellery, Harrison, ed. *The Memoirs of General Joseph Gardner Swift, LL. D., U. S. A.* Worcester, Mass.: Privately printed, 1890.

Select Secondary

Cullum, George W. *Biographical Sketch of Brigadier General Joseph G. Swift, Chief Engineer of the United States Army, July 31, 1812 to Nov. 12, 1818.* New York: C. A. Coffin, 1877.
Guernsey, Rocellus S. *Chronicles of Greater New York City During the War of 1812–15.* New York: A. S. Guernsey, 1911.
United States Army. Corps of Engineers. Office of History. *The U. S. Army Corps of Engineers: A History.* Alexandria, Va.: U. S. Army Corps of Engineers, 2007.

David Rogerson Williams

David Rogerson Williams was born in Robbin's Neck, South Carolina, the son of a planter. He attended Rhode Island College (Brown University)

Brigadier General David R. Williams. Courtesy of South Caroliniana Library, University of South Carolina.

to study law and was admitted to the state bar, but returned to South Carolina to inherit his father's plantation. Williams dabbled briefly in newspaper publishing before gaining election to the House of Representatives as a Democratic-Republican in 1805. Here he proved himself a staunch ally of Thomas Jefferson and the Embargo, despite the economic havoc it wreaked at home. As the War of 1812 drew nearer, Williams became identified with the influential "War Hawk" faction from his state, which included John C. Calhoun, Langdon Cheves, and William Lowndes. He was a particularly gifted speaker and acquired the moniker "Thunder and Lightning Williams" on account of his forceful delivery. After hostilities with England resumed in June, 1812, he functioned as chairman of the House Military Affairs Committee and took every possible measure to strengthen the army and prosecute the war. His outspoken loyalty to President James Madison culminated in an appointment as brigadier general in the army as of July 9, 1813. Williams arrived at Fort George, Upper Canada, shortly after and he commanded troops under General John Parker Boyd for several weeks. He was involved in outpost skirmishes but apparently grew disillusioned by the lackluster leadership at Niagara and requested a transfer south to fight in the Creek War. When this was not forthcoming, Williams resigned his commission on April 6, 1814, and returned to South Carolina. He found his state defenseless and in disarray, so he successfully stood for the governorship in December 1814 and spent the final weeks of the war revamping the militia and coastal defenses. Once his term ended in 1816, Williams basically withdrew from public life and turned to scientific farming and economic development of his region. He was a strong proponent of economic self-sufficiency for the South but staunchly opposed Calhoun on the issue of Nullification. The energetic Williams died on injuries received while supervising the construction of a bridge near his plantation on November 18, 1830, his military talents largely untested.

Archival

RG94. Letters. National Archives. Adjutant General's Office; 1813.
RG107. Letters. National Archives. Secretary of War's Office; 1813.

Manuscript

Williams, David R. Letter book. Library of Congress. Miscellaneous Manuscripts; 1814–1816.
Williams, David R. Letter, 1813. Perkins Library. John C. Calhoun Papers; to C. Irvine.
Williams, David R. Papers. South Caroliniana. 1812–1815.

Select Secondary

Cook, Harvey T. *The Life and Legacy of David Rogerson Williams.* New York: Country Life Press, 1916.

James Winchester

James Winchester was born in Carroll County, Maryland, on February 6, 1752, and when the Revolutionary War commenced in 1775 he joined the local militia. After being captured and exchanged on Staten Island, New York, he joined the 2nd Maryland Continentals as a lieutenant and was captured again at the fall of Charleston, South Carolina, in 1780. Paroled a second time, Winchester served capably in the army of General Nathaniel Greene until the war ended in 1783. Two years later he relocated to Tennessee, where he rejoined the militia and rose to brigadier general. After Tennessee became a state, Winchester proved his skill as a politician by winning seats in the legislature and cultivating particularly close ties with Democratic-Republicans at the national level. For this reason, President James Madison appointed Winchester a brigadier general in the army as of March 27, 1812, and, once hostilities commenced, he inherited several unruly Kentucky regiments at Cincinnati, Ohio. These rough-hewn frontiersmen resented their subordination to a regular army officer but, nonetheless, Winchester was appointed to command the Northwest Army following General William Hull's surrender of Detroit in August 1812. However, William Henry Harrison suddenly made his appearance as a major general of Kentucky militia and he commandeered Winchester's force for a relief expedition to Fort Wayne, Indiana Territory. A tug of war ensued between the two willful leaders and Winchester, resenting this usurpation, demanded and received written confirmation of his authority as commander, riding to Fort Wayne on September 18, 1812 to reclaim his men. There he discovered Harrison's recent promotion as major general of regulars along with a written order issued by President James Madison authorizing him to lead the Northwest Army. Harrison was intent upon recapturing Detroit and he ordered Winchester, commanding the left wing of the army, to encamp along the Maumee River (present-day Toledo). Winchester encountered no resistance from either the British or their Indian allies so he subsequently ordered an advance on the River Raisin (Monroe, Michigan) on January 18, 1813, to assist the settlers living there. A British blocking force was brushed aside after a sharp fight and Winchester slipped into comfortable winter quarters. Moreover, despite the potential proximity of enemy forces arriving from Detroit, defensive precautions remained minimal at best.

Unknown to the Americans, their arrival in Michigan prompted a sharp response by the main British army under Colonel Henry Procter. Winchester took no particular measures to enhance his security, so on January 22, 1813, his army was surprised in camp and routed with heavy loss. Winchester was taken prisoner mid-way through the encounter and he convinced the remainder of his hard fighting Kentuckians, who had repelled several British assaults, to capitulate. The Americans were then packed off for Detroit and captivity, while the Indians set upon 60 wounded Kentuckians left in their custody, scalping them. This massacre had an electrifying effect on Westerners

Brigadier General James Winchester. Courtesy Tennessee State Library and Archives.

and the vengeful cry, "Remember the Raisin!" was born. Winchester, meanwhile, was taken to Montreal as a prisoner and released the following year. In November 1814, he was next posted with the 7th Military District under General Andrew Jackson, and commanded the District of Mobile. The war proved uneventful in that quarter for several months but, in February 1815, the British expedition that had failed to take New Orleans now landed and invested Fort Bowyer. Lieutenant Colonel William Lawrence, who confronted thousands of Napoleonic veterans with a mere 200 men, called repeatedly to Winchester for assistance, but none was forthcoming. It was not until after Fort Bowyer capitulated that Winchester finally advanced any reinforcements, again too little and too late to help. He was strongly criticized for inactivity and resigned his commission on March 31, 1815. Winchester subsequently returned to Tennessee and resumed his political activities, which included founding the city of Memphis, and in 1819 he served on a commission that drew up the state boundary with Mississippi. He also engaged in a vigorous publishing effort to defend his actions in the recent war. Winchester, a military leader of minimal import and talents, died in Gallatin, Tennessee, on July 26, 1826.

Archival

Winchester, James. Dispatch book. Lilly Library. September–December, 1812.
RG94. Letters. National Archives. Adjutant General's Office; 1812–1813.
RG107. Letters. National Archives. Secretary of War's Office; 1812–1813.
Winchester, James. Logbook. William T. Young. 87M14, August–November, 1812.

Manuscript

Winchester, James. Papers. Burton Historical.
Winchester, James. Letter, 1812. Cincinnati Historical. Mss VF4203; purchases winter clothing.
Winchester, James. Letters. Historical Society (Pa). Dreer Coll., various military; 1812–1815.
Winchester, James. Letters. Historical Society (Pa). Gratz Coll., Box 35, military; 1812–1815.
Winchester, James. Letter, 1813. Historical Society (Pa). Society Collection, prisoners at Quebec.
Winchester, James. Letter, 1812. Kentucky Historical. 93SC19; construction of "water craft".
Winchester, James. Letters. Library of Congress. Andrew Jackson Papers; 1814–1815.
Winchester, James. Letters. Library of Congress. William H. Harrison Papers; 1812–1813.
Winchester, James. Letters. Library of Congress. James Winchester Papers, Misc. Mss. Coll.
Winchester, James. Orders, 1812. New York Historical. Misc Mss Winchester, Nashville.
Winchester, James. General Orders. Perkins Library. U.S. Army Orders Coll., February, 1815.
Winchester, James. Papers. Tennessee Historical. THS 27, Winchester Papers; 1812–1815.
Winchester, James. Papers. Tennessee Historical. THS 382, Winchester Additional Papers.

Winchester, James. Letters. Tennessee State. War of 1812 Collection; 1812–1815.
Winchester, James. Papers. Wisconsin Historical. Frontier Wars Papers, 6 U.

Printed Primary

Burton, Clarence M., ed. "Papers and Orderly Book of Brigadier General James Winchester." *Michigan Pioneer* 31 (1901): 252–313. [September 1812–January 1813]
"Papers Relating to the War of 1812." *Western Reserve Historical Society Tracts* No. 15 (April 1873): 1–3; No. 17 (November 1873): 1–5; No. 19 (November 1874): 1–4; No. 28 (October 1875): 1–4; No. 51 (December 1879): 115–123.
Winchester, James. *Historical Details Having Relation to the Campaigns of the Northwestern Army under General Harrison and Winchester During the Winter of 1812–1813.* Lexington: Worsley & Smith, 1818.

Select Secondary

Antal, Sandy. *A Waupum Denied: Procter's War of 1812.* Ottawa, Ont.: Carleton University Press, 1997.
Au, Dennis. *War on the Raisin.* Monroe, Mich.: Monroe County Historical Commission, 1981.
Durham, Walter T. "James Winchester." *Franklin County Historical Review* 20, no. 1 (1989): 6–14.
Durham, Walter T. *James Winchester: Tennessee Pioneer.* Gallatin, Tn.: Sumner County Library Board, 1979.
Rosentreter, Roger L. "Remember the River Raisin." *Michigan History Magazine* 82, no. 6 (1998): 40–48.

William Henry Winder

William Henry Winder was born in Somerset County, Maryland, on February 18, 1775, and he attended the University of Pennsylvania as a law student. He joined the Maryland state bar in 1802 and over the next decade established himself as one of that state's most respected attorneys. Winder was a Federalist by persuasion, but his antipathy for British harassment of American shipping led him to support the possibility of war with England. President James Madison, seeking broader political support for renewed conflict, accordingly tendered Winder a lieutenant colonel's commission in the 14th Infantry on March 16, 1812, despite of his complete lack of military training. He commenced recruiting activities in Baltimore and, once war was declared, he rose to full colonel in July and was dispatched along with his regiment to the Niagara frontier. Winder served as part of General Alexander Smyth's brigade and saw no part of the Queenston Heights disaster that fall, but bore

Brigadier General William H. Winder. Courtesy Maryland Historical Society.

a full measure of the latter's farcical attempt to cross the Niagara River on November 28, 1812. His efforts to reinforce a body of American soldiers that had successfully captured a battery above Fort Erie was blasted back by British fire, and Smyth ultimately abandoned the attempt. Winder was not held accountable for the debacle and he advanced to brigadier general on March 12, 1813. He subsequently commanded a brigade as part of General Henry Dearborn's amphibious assault on Fort George, Upper Canada, May 27, 1813, whereby the Americans triumphed but failed to pursue and the defenders escaped intact. It was not until June 5, 1813, that Winder's brigade, consisting of the 5th, 13th, 14th, and 16th Infantries, accompanied by General John Chandler's force, carelessly encamped at Stoney Creek for the evening. This brought on a swift British riposte from General John Vincent, who in the ensuing nighttime fracas captured both American leaders. Winder was imprisoned at Quebec until the spring of 1814, although he lingered there several weeks longer to negotiate future prisoner exchanges. On May 9, 1814, he also received an appointment as Adjutant and Inspector General of the army.

In July 1814, President Madison arranged Winder to serve as commander of the new 10th Military District to defend Washington, D.C., from a possible British invasion. This was over the objections of Secretary of War John Armstrong, who sought the seasoned General Moses Porter for the post. Winder basically owed his new command to nepotism, being the nephew of Governor Levin Winder of Maryland, who would provide the bulk of militia forces should an attack materialize. Over the ensuing six weeks, Winder made no moves to fortify his charge nor concoct a plan for its defense. On August 19, 1814, a force of 4,000 British soldiers and sailors landed at the Patuxent River and advanced on the capital. Winder, commanding 7,000 ill-trained levies, attempted to make a stand at Bladensburg, Maryland, but his troops had been placed in three unsupported lines through the interference of Secretary of State James Monroe. It being too late to redeploy, Winder was subsequently routed by this smaller force on August 24, 1814, resulting in such a stampede to the rear that detractors labeled it the "Bladensburg Races." British forces under Admiral George Cockburn and General Robert Ross then occupied Washington, torched the public buildings, and withdrew unmolested to their fleet. Winder, who was not asked to resign, tried asserting his authority at Baltimore but troops there refused to serve under him. He then asked for and received a court of inquiry for the Bladensburg disaster, which exonerated him, and he finally left the military on June 15, 1815. Afterwards, Winder resumed his legal career in Baltimore with little interruption and also won election to the state legislature. He died there on May 24, 1824, a leader whose marginal leadership abilities held grave implications for the nation he served.

Archival

RG94. Letters. National Archives. Adjutant General's Office; 1812–1814.
RG98, No. 511/413. Details. National Archives. 10th Mil. Dist., Oct.–Nov. 1814.
RG107. Letters. National Archives. Secretary of War's Office; 1812–1814.

Manuscript

Winder, William H. Letter, 1813. Library of Congress. Miscellaneous. Manuscript Collection.

Winder, William H. Papers. Library of Congress. Peter Force Papers, Coll. 7E, Entry 161.

Winder, William H. Letters. Library of Congress. Samuel Smith Papers, Box 6 & 7; 1814.

Winder, William H. Papers. Maryland Historical. Ms 918; 1814.

Winder, William H. Letter book. Maryland Historical. Ms 919; 1814.

Printed Primary

American State Papers. Military Affairs. 2 vols. Washington, D.C.: Gales and Seaton, 1832–1861.

Winder, William H. "General Winder and the Capture of Washington." *Historical Magazine* 5 (August 1861): 227–229.

Select Secondary

Elliott, James. *Strange Fatality: The Battle of Stoney Creek*. Montreal: Robin Brass Studio, 2009.

"General William H. Winder." *Genealogical Magazine and Historical Chronicle* 21 (1919): 217–219.

George, Christopher T. *Terror on the Chesapeake: The War of 1812 on the Bay*. Shippensburg, Pa.: Whitemane Books, 2000.

Pitch, Anthony. *The Burning of Washington: The British Invasion*. Annapolis, Md.: Naval Institute Press, 1998.

Smith, Eric M. "Leaders Who Lost: Case Studies of Command Under Stress." *Military Review* 61 (1981): 41–45.

Stanley, George F. *Battle in the Dark: Stoney Creek, June 6, 1813*. Toronto: Balmuir, 1991.

Taylor, Blaine. "Shaky Stand at Bladensburg." *Military Heritage* 6, no. 5 (2005): 66–73, 81.

Whitehorne, Joseph W. A. *The Battle for Baltimore, 1814*. Baltimore, Md.: Nautical & Aviation Press, 1997.

Williams, Glenn F. "The Bladensburg Races." *MHQ* 12, no. 1 (1999): 58–65.

Various Departments

Adjutant General

Archival

RG94. Letters. National Archives. Adjutant General's Office, 1812–1815.
RG98, No. 396/279. Details. National Archives. French Mills, Nov. 1813–Feb. 1814.
RG98, No. 389/273. Orderly book. National Archives. Adj. Gen., 3rd Mil. Dist., 1812–1815.
RG98, No. 466/365. Orderly book. National Archives. Adj. Gen., 3rd Mil. Dist., 1812–1815.
RG98, No. 449/347. Orderly book. National Archives. Adj. Gen., 3rd Mil. Dist., 1812–1815.
RG98, No. 453/352. General orders. National Archives. Adj. Gen., 4th Mil. Dist, Jan.–Feb. 1815.
RG98, No. 391/275. Orderly book. National Archives. Adj. Gen., 7th Mil. Dist., 1813–1815.
RG98, No. 454/353. Orderly book. National Archives. Adj. Gen., 7th Mil. Dist., 1813–1815.
RG98, No. 433/330. Orderly book. National Archives. Adj. Gen., 7th Mil. Dist., 1813–1814.
RG98, No. 445/342. Orderly book. National Archives. 9th Mil. Dist., Right Wing, 1813–1815.
RG98, No. 442/339. Orderly. book. National Archives. 9th Mil. Dist., Right Wing, 1813–1815.
RG98, No. 464/341. Orderly book. National Archives. 9th Mil. Dist., Right Wing, 1813–1815.
RG98, No. 465/364. Orderly book. National Archives. 9th Mil. Dist., Right Wing, 1813–1815.
RG98, No. 508/410. Details. National Archives. 9th Mil Dist., Right Wing, Mar.–Dec. 1814.
RG98, No. 509/411. Details. National Archives. 9th Mil Dist., Right Wing, Mar.–Dec. 1814.
RG98, No. 390/274. Orderly book. National Archives. 9th Mil. Dist., Sacketts Harbor, 1812–1813.

RG98, No. 440/337. Orderly Book. National Archives. 9th Mil. Dist., Sacketts Harbor, 1814–1815.
RG98, No. 446/343. Orderly book. National Archives. 9th Mil. Dist., Sacketts Harbor, 1814–1815.
RG98, No. 457/356. Orderly book. National Archives. 9th Mil. Dist., Sacketts Harbor, 1814–1815.
RG98, No. 507/409. Details. National Archives. 9th Mil. Dist., Sacketts Harbor, 1813.

Manuscript

Bankhead, James. Letters. Library of Virginia. 41557, James Barbour Papers; 1812–1814.
Clarke, Newman S. Letter, 1814. Lilly Library. War of 1812 Papers; Lundy's Lane.
Duane, William. Letter, 1814. Hay Library. Russell Papers; military events.
Duane, William. Letters. Historical Society (Pa). Daniel Parker Papers; 1812–1815.
Duane, William. Letters. Library of Congress. Thomas Jefferson Papers; 1812–1815.
Duane, William. Letters. New York Historical. Allan McLane Papers; 1813–1814.
Duane, William. Letters. New York State. 792, 4611, to Callender Irvine, 1813.
Duane, William. Letters. New York State. Charles K. Gardner Papers, Box 2, 19813.
Duane, William. Letter, 1813. Oberlin College. No. 41, Orrin June Coll., unruly recruits.
Gardner, Charles K. Papers. New York State. KB12914, C. K. Gardner Papers.
Hite, Robert G. Letters. Massachusetts Historical. Thomas Jefferson Papers; 1813.
Nourse, Charles J. Papers. U.S. Army Military. 1814–1815.
Parker, Daniel. Papers. Historical Society (Pa). 1812–1815.
Parker, Daniel. Letter, 1812. Massachusetts Historical. C.E. French; Washington's defenses.

Printed Primary

Duane, William. "Selections from the William Duane Papers." *Historical Magazine* 4 (August 1868): 60–75.
Ford, Worthington C., ed. "Letters of William Duane." *Massachusetts Historical Society Proceedings* 20 (May 1906): 247–394. [349–376]

Select Secondary

Damiani, Brian P. "William Duane, the Philadelphia War Hawk." Unpublished master's thesis, University of Delaware, 1966.
Vigman, Fred K. "William Duane's American Military Library." *Military Affairs* 8 (Winter 1944): 321–326.

Inspector General

Archival

RG98, No. 447/345. Orderly book. National Archives. Northern Dept., Sept. 1812–Feb. 1813.
RG98, No. 458/357. Orderly book. National Archives. 3rd Mil. Dist., 1813–1815.
RG98, No. 451/350. Orderly book. National Archives. 3rd Mil. Dist., 1813–1815.
RG98, No. 357/416. Returns. National Archives. 3rd Mil. Dist., companies, Jan.–Dec. 1814.
RG98, No. 453/352. General orders. National Archives. 4th Mil. Dist., January–February 1815.
RG98, No. 358/418. Reports. National Archives. 4th Mil. Dist., January–April 1815.
RG98, No. 681. Orderly book. National Archives. 6th Mil Dist., March 1813–August 1814.
RG98, No. 682. Orderly book. National Archives. 6th Mil. Dist., February–June 1815.
RG98, No. 406/290. Letters. National Archives. 9th Mil. Dist., Right Wing, 1814–1815.
RG98, No. 508/410. Details. National Archives. 9th Mil Dist., Right Wing, Mar.–Dec. 1814.
RG98, No. 509/411. Details. National Archives. 9th Mil Dist., Right Wing, Mar.–Dec. 1814.
RG98, No. 456/355. Orderly book. National Archives. 9th Mil. Dist., Left Wing, 1814–1815.
RG159. Letters. National Archives. Inspector General's Office, 1812–1815.

Manuscript

Nicoll, Abimael Y. Letter book. Georgia Historical. Ms 587, 1812.
Walbach, John B. Orders. Chicago Historical. Uniforms, recruiting; 1814.
Walbach, John B. Letters. Danvers Archival. PR/PO/C, Moses Porter Papers.
Walbach, John B. Letter, 1814. Indiana Historical. M211, Box 3, Fld. 25; Portsmouth, N. H.
Walbach, John B. Letter, 1814. Lilly Library. War of 1812 Coll.
Walbach, John B. Letter, 1813. Regenstein Library. Mss. C.1; his activities at Crysler's Farm.

Select Secondary

Clary, David A., and Joseph W. A. Whitehorne. *The Inspectors General of the United States Army, 1777–1903*. Washington, D.C.: Office of the Inspector General and Center of Military History, 1998.

Medical Department

Archival

RG94. Letters. National Archives. Adjutant General's Office; 1812–1815.
RG98, No. 566. Lists. National Archives. Deaths at various hospitals, 1813–1816.
RG98, Item 56. Registers. National Archives. Patients at Williamsville, NY, 1814–1815.
RG98, No. 680. Registers. National Archives. Patients at Williamsville, NY, 1814–1815.
RG98, No. 683. Registers. National Archives. Patients at Williamsville, NY, 1814–1815.
RG107. Letters. National Archives. Secretary of War's Office; 1812–1815.

Manuscript

Anonymous. Diary. Huntington Library. BR17; Pass Christian; 1812.
Archer, Robert. Memoranda. Virginia Historical. Mss5:5 Ar245:1; 1814–1815; Norfolk.
Bates, James M. Papers. Yarmouth Historical. Coll. 26; surgeon's mate.
Bull, Ezekiel W. Letters. New York Historical. William Thomas Papers; 1812–1813.
Horner, William E. Letter, 1814. Van Pelt Library. Misc. Mss 1.1/a; Buffalo, to James Tilton.
Mann, James. Letter, 1815. Lilly Library. War of 1812 Collection; York, 1813.
Thomas, William. Letters. New York Historical. 1812–1815; surgeon's mate.
Tilton, James. Letter, 1814. Darling Biomedical. James Mease Papers, Series 3, Box 1.
Waterhouse, Benjamin. Letter, 1814. Boston Public. Ms. 474; supplies and procedures.
Waterhouse, Benjamin. Letter, 1816. Pierpont Morgan. 136829; wartime service.
Whitridge, Joshua B. Letters. South Carolina Historical. 1114.00; Niagara, 1813.

Printed Primary

Horner, W. E. "Surgical Sketches: A Military Hospital at Buffalo, New York, in the Year 1814." *Medical Examiner and Record of Medical Service* 16 (December 1852): 753–774; 17 (January 1853): 1–25.
Mann, James. *Medical Sketches of the Campaigns of 1812, 1813, and 1814.* Dedham, Mass.: H. Mann, 1816.
Tilton, James. *Economical Observations on Military Hospitals and the Prevention and Cure of Diseases Incident to an Army.* Wilmington, Del.: J. Wilson, 1813.

Select Secondary

Gillett, Mary C. *The Army Medical Department, 1775–1818.* Washington, D.C.: Army Center of Military History, 1981.

Commissary of Ordnance

Archival

RG94, Roll 17. Letters. National Archives. Abram R. Wooley, 1812.
RG156. Letters. National Archives. Chief of Ordnance; Decius Wadsworth.

Manuscript

Hathaway, Joshua. Papers. New York State. SC13762; U.S. Arsenal, Rome, New York.
McKay, Aeneas. Journal. Wisconsin Historical. SC328, useful observations; 1812–1814.
Wadsworth, Decius. Letters. Beinecke Library. Eli Whitney Papers; 1812–1815.
Wadsworth, Decius. Letters. Danvers Archival. PR/PO/C, Moses Porter Papers.
Wadsworth, Decius. Letters. U.S. Military Academy. Jonathan Williams Papers.

Select Secondary

Reed, C. Wingate. "Decius Wadsworth, First Chief of Ordnance, U. S. Army, 1812–1821." *Army Ordnance* 24 (May–June, 1943): 113–116.
Rosecrans, George A., and Bill Turner. "Decius Wadsworth — An Enigma." *Ordnance* 3 (1985): 2–6.

Judge Advocate General's Department

Archival

RG98, No.461/360. General Orders. National Archives. 3rd Mil. Dist., Proceedings, 1814–1815.
RG98, No. 455/354. General Orders. National Archives. 9th Mil. Dist., Right Wing, July–Sept. 1814.

Quartermaster Department/Supply Services

Archival

RG92. Letters. National Archives. Quartermaster General's Records.

Manuscript

Anderson, Elbert. Account book. New York Historical. Elbert Anderson Papers; 1812.
Barton, Benjamin. Letter book. Buffalo and Erie. A64–87, Niagara, 1812–1814.
Brady, Josiah. Papers. Burton Historical. Northwestern Army; 1812–1813.

Brown, Henry. Letters. Cincinnati Historical. Mss QB878, Piqua, Ohio; Fort Wayne.
Brown, Henry. Papers. Dayton/Montgomery. Robert Patterson Collection; 1812–1815.
Camp, John G. Letters. Buffalo and Erie. B00-15, War of 1812 Papers; Niagara.
Camp, John G. Papers. Olin Library. No. 891; Niagara; 1814.
Cheever, William D. Order book. Owen D. Young. War of 1812 Collection; supplies, stores.
Cheever, William D. Papers. Perkins Library. Supplies, New York; 1813–1814.
Cox, Tench. Letter. Historical Society (Pa). Coxe Papers, clothier; 1812–1815.
Eubank, James T. Papers. Kentucky Historical. 88SC08, Kentucky, Ohio; 1813–1814.
Fort Fayette. Letter book. Ohio Historical. Supplies in Ohio; 1811–1812.
Hathaway, Joshua. Papers. New York State. 13762; family papers.
Hegins, Charles. Papers. Western Reserve. Ms. 3402; food purchases, Ohio, Michigan.
Irvine, Callender. Letters. Hagley Museum. U.S. Army Miscellany; 1812.
Irvine, Callender. Letters. Historical Society (Pa). Daniel Parker Papers.
Irvine, Callender. Letters. Historical Society (Pa). Irvine Family Papers; 1812–1815.
Irvine, Callender. Letters. Manuscripts and Archives. Ms. 554, Eli Whitney Papers; 1813.
Irvine, Callender. Letter, 1812. New York State. 4518; army clothing.
Irvine, Callender. Letters. U. S. Military Academy. Jonathan Williams Papers.
Johnson, N. Letter book. Ohio Historical. Vol. 1232; Fort Fayette, 1811–1812.
Kerr, Joseph. Account book. Ohio Historical. Joseph Kerr Papers, Sandusky; 1812.
Lamb, Anthony. Letters. Library of Congress. Anthony Lamb Papers; 1812–1814.
Lamb, Anthony. Papers. New York Historical. Lamb Papers, Philadelphia; 1812–1813.
Northern Army. Letters. New York Historical. Supplies, New York; 1813–1815.
Northwestern Army. Letters. Lilly Library. Harrison, W. H. Mss., II; 1812–1814.
Piatt, John H. Letter book. Library of Congress. Misc. Mss Coll.; Ohio, 1812–1814.
Pinder, Joseph W. Papers. Georgia Historical. Military records, Georgia and South.
Quartermaster's Dept. Order book. Library of Congress. Misc. Mss; issues and returns; 1812–1814.
Quartermaster general. Letters. New York State. 13133; 9th Mil. Dist.; 1813–1815.
Swearingen, James S. Letters. Ross County Historical. N/A103, receipts; 1812–1814.
Taylor, James. Papers. Burton Historical. James Taylor Papers; 1812–1814.
Taylor, James. Papers. Cincinnati Historical. Micro. No. 46; settles with U. S. Treasury.
Taylor, James. Statement. Cincinnati Historical. Mss VF1210; claims to Congress; 1834.
Taylor, James. Papers. Filson Historical. A T243; 1812–1815; payments and claims.
Taylor, James. Letters. Indiana Historical. Arthur G. Mitten Collection; 8th Mil. Dist.
Taylor, James. Papers. Kentucky Historical. 84M05; 1812–1815.
Thorne, James. Papers. New York Historical. provisions, northern New York; 1812–1814.
Townsend, Isaiah. Letter, 1813. Buffalo and Erie. A00-452; supplying beef and pork.
Townsend, Isaiah. Papers. New York Public. Company records, Albany; 1812–1815.
Townsend, Isaiah. Papers. New York State. DC10441; Albany, 1812–1815.
Townsend, Isaiah. Letters. Perkins Library. James W. Thorne Papers; 1813–1815.

Townsend, John. Letter, 1814. New York State. 13315; supplies at Utica and Watertown.
Tracy, Elisha. Letter book. New London Historical. MsBd.T6741812; 1812–1813.
Tracy, Elisha. Letter book. New London Historical. MsBd.T6741813; 1813–1814.
U.S. War Department. Records. Library of Congress. Oversize 0114J; Frankfort Arsenal, Pa.
Wheaton, Joseph. Papers. Manuscripts and Archives. Joseph Wheaton Papers; 1812–1815.

Printed Primary

Thomas, James. *A Brief Statement of the Transactions and Accounts of Qr. M. Gen. James Thomas, attached to the Army on the Niagara Frontier, in the year 1812–13*. N. P., 1815.
Wheaton, Joseph. *Appeal of Joseph Wheaton, Late Deputy Quarter Master General and Major of Cavalry, to the Senate and House of representatives of the United States of America*. Washington, D.C.: N.p., 1820.

Select Secondary

Risch, Erna. *Quartermaster Support of the Army: A History of the Corps, 1775–1939*. Washington, D.C.: Office of the Quartermaster, 1962.
Vitz, Robert C. "James Taylor, the War Department, and the War of 1812." *Old Northwest* 2, no. 2 (1976): 107–130.

U. S. Military Academy

Archival

RG94, M91. Letters. National Archives. Military Academy correspondence.
Partridge, Alden. Letter book. U.S. Military Academy. No. 371, Extracts; 1812–1815.

Manuscript

Partridge, Alden. Papers. Library of Congress. 3085, Alden Partridge Papers; 1812–1815.
Partridge, Alden. Papers. U.S. Military Academy. No. 261; 1812–1815.

Select Secondary

Aimone, Alan. "West Point's Contribution to the War of 1812." *Journal of America's Military Past* 25, no. 2 (Fall 1998): 37–48.
Crackle, Theodore J. *West Point: A Bicentennial History*. Lawrence: University Press of Kansas, 2004, 53–81.
Cullum, George W. *Biographical Register of the Officers and Graduates of the U. S. Mil-*

itary Academy 9 vols. West Point, N.Y.: Association of Graduates, U. S. Military Academy, 1868. Vol. 1, 51–130.

McDonald, Robert M. S., ed. *Thomas Jefferson's Military Academy: Founding West Point.* Charlottesville: University of Virginia Press, 2004.

Shrunk, William A. "Services of Graduates in the War of 1812." In: *United States Military Academy. Centennial of the United States Military Academy at West Point, New York, 1802–1902.* Washington, D.C.: Government Printing Office, 1904, 586–601.

Webb, Lester A. *Captain Alden Partridge and the United States Military Academy, 1806–1833.* Northport, Ala.: American Southern, 1965.

Drill and Tactics

Bonura, Michael A. "French Thought and the American Military Mind: A History of French Influence on the American Way of Warfare from 1814 through 1941." Unpublished Ph.D. dissertation, Florida State University, 2008.

Graves, Donald E. "Dry Books of Tactics: U.S. Infantry Manuals of the War of 1812 and After." *Military Collector and Historian* 38, no. 2 (Summer 1986): 50–61; 38, no. 4 (Winter 1986): 173–177.

Kretchik, Walter E. "Peering through the Mist: Doctrine as a Guide for United States Army Operations, 1775–2000." Unpublished Ph.D. dissertation, University of Kansas, 2001.

Personnel

Skelton, William B. "High Army Leadership in the War of 1812: The Making and Remaking of the Officer Corps." *William and Mary Quarterly* 52, no. 2 (1994): 253–274.

Smith, Christopher. 'American Rebels': Soldiers' Protests in the Early American Military, 1754–1815." Unpublished Ph.D. dissertation, University of Houston, 2007.

Stagg, J.C.A. "'Enlisted Men in the United States Army, 1812–1815: A Preliminary Survey." *William and Mary Quarterly* 43, no. 4 (1986): 615–645.

Stagg, J.C.A. "Soldiers in Peace and War: Comparative Perspectives on the Recruitment of the United States Army, 1802–1815." *William and Mary Quarterly* 57, no. 1 (2000): 79–120.

Watkins, Eugene D. "'Cousin Jonathan': The Common United States Soldier in the War of 1812." Unpublished Ph.D. dissertation, University of Toledo, 2007.

Uniforms

Chartrand, Rene. *Uniforms and Equipment of the United States Force in the War of 1812.* Youngstown, N.Y.: Old Fort Niagara Association, 1992.

Elting, John R., ed. *Military Uniforms in America.* 3 vols. San Rafael, Calif.: Presidio Press, 1974–1982. Vol. 2.

Kochan, James L. *The United States Army, 1812–1815.* Oxford, U.K.: Osprey, 2000.

Artillery

Regiment of Artillerists/
1st Regiment of Artillery

Raised: March 16, 1802
Recruited: one battalion, Maine and New Hampshire; one battalion, Rhode Island and Connecticut; one battalion, North Carolina, South Carolina, Georgia

Battle Honors

1812: Mackinac (det.); Maguaga (det.); Detroit (det.); Queenston Heights (det.); Fort Niagara (det.)
1813: Fort Meigs (det.); Sacketts Harbor; Fort Niagara (det.)

Prior to 1812, the Regiment of Artillerists was the senior artillery unit of the U.S. Army until it was redesignated the 1st Regiment of Artillery that year. Each of its five battalions consisted of four companies and were distributed along the eastern seaboard and western frontier as fortress garrisons. The regiment also enjoys the melancholy distinction of losing the War of 1812's first "engagement" on July 17, 1812, when the 57-man detachment of Lieutenant Porter Hanks, uniformed by the government that hostilities had begun, was surprised by superior British forces at Michilimackinac and surrendered without a fight. The detachment was paroled and sent to join the main American force at Detroit, where it fought in the Battle of Maguaga on August 9, 1812, and subsequently fell captive again when General William Hull surrendered on August 16, 1812. Lieutenant Hanks had previously died during the British bombardment of that settlement. Another detachment of the 1st Regiment was apparently present at Queenston Heights on October 13, 1812, although details of its involvement are not known. A month later Captain Nathaniel Leonard's company, stationed at Fort Niagara, participated in the bombardment of Fort George on November 21–22, 1812. The gunners managed to sink a schooner at its wharf across the Niagara River while losing two killed and three wounded.

The regiment next saw action during the siege of Fort Meigs, Ohio, and April–May 1813. One gunner was wounded during the proceedings although the detachment commander, Major Amos Stoddard, sustained injuries and died of tetanus. On May 5 another detachment accompanying General Green Clay's militia column was captured during the ill-fated sortie. That same month part of the 1st Regiment under Lieutenant Ketcham fought at Sacketts Harbor on May 29, 1813. They occupied Fort Tompkins and manned a pivot-mounted 32-pounder throughout the fighting, showering the British advance with grapeshot. The regiment then experienced a second humiliation when Captain Leonard's entire company was captured during the surprise attack upon Fort Niagara on December 19, 1813. The remaining companies continued conducting their usual round of quiet garrison duty until May 12, 1814, when they were amalgamated into the new Corps of Artillery. The 1st Regiment of Artillery was never deployed in any unit larger than a company, hence it spent the bulk of the war defending forts and harbors.

Promotions

Captain John B. Walbach, brevet major. November 11, 1813. Gallant conduct — Battle of Crysler's Farm.

Archival

Freeman, Constant. Order book. Library of Congress. No. 106; Fort Nelson, Va., 1812–1814.
RG94, Roll 32. Letters. National Archives. James S. Swearingen, 1813–1814.
RG98, No. 184/18. Company book. National Archives Capt. Thomas Bennett, 1810–1815.
RG98, No. 194/26. Company book. National Archives. Capt. Julius Heilman, 1813–1815.
RG98, No. 187/21. Company book. National Archives. Capt. James Reed, 1812–1815.
1st Military District. Order book. U.S. Military Academy. No. 333, 1813–1816.

Manuscript

Dalliba, James. Diary. Wisconsin Historical.
Hanks, Porter. Muster roll. Wisconsin Historical. Michilimackinac; 1811–1812.
Sands, Abraham L. Letter book. Nassau County Historical. Mobile, Fort Bowyer; 1813–1815.
Van Deventer, Chris. Letters. Clements Library. Prisoner correspondence; 1813–1815.
Van Deventer, Chris. Letters. Library of Congress. Prisoner correspondence; 1813–1815.

Printed Primary

Dalliba, James. *Narrative of the Battle of Brownstown, August 7, 1812*. New York: D. Longsworth, 1816.

Select Secondary

Dastrup, Boyd L. *King of Battle: A Branch History of the U. S. Army's Field Artillery*. Fort Monroe, Va.: Office of the Command Historical, U. S. Army Training and Doctrine Command, 1992. [35–60]

"Early Systems of Artillery." *U. S. Ordnance Notes* 25 (May 1874): 137–167.

Haskin, William L. *The History of the First Artillery, From Its Organization in 1821 to January 1, 1876*. Portland, Me.: B. Thurston, 1879.

Kohler, C. Douglas, and Douglas De Croix. "At the Point of a Bayonet! The British Capture of Fort Niagara." *Western New York Heritage* 9, no. 4 (2007): 48–56.

2nd Regiment of Artillery

Raised: January 11, 1812

Recruited: one battalion, Pennsylvania and Delaware; one and one-half battalions, Maryland and Virginia; one and one-half battalions in Kentucky, Ohio, Missouri Territory, Michigan Territory, Illinois Territory, and Indiana Territory.

Battle Honors

1812: capture of British ships *Detroit* and *Caledonia* (det.); Queenston Heights (det.)

1813: Fort Meigs (det.); Fort George; Stoney Creek

The 2nd Regiment of Artillery was organized into two ten-company battalions, and was fortunate in possessing two of the army's best drill masters, George Izard and Winfield Scott, as colonel and lieutenant-colonel, respectively. It consequently emerged as one of the army's premier outfits and invariably rendered distinguished service in combat. In the fall of 1812 several companies deployed along the Niagara frontier where, on October 10, 1812, a detachment of 50 men under Captain Nathan Towson, assisted by bluejackets under Captain Jesse D. Elliott, cut out the British brigs *Detroit* and *Caledonia* lying anchored beneath the guns of Fort Erie. Towson's and Barker's companies subsequently participated in heavy fighting at Queenston Heights on October 13, 1812, suffering heavy losses. These were soon after supplemented by the company of Captain Samuel B. Archer,

Nathan Towson, 2nd Artillery. Courtesy Maryland Historical Society.

who wintered at Williamsburg, New York, until campaigning resumed that spring.

The garrison of Fort Meigs, Ohio, was also augmented by a company of the 2nd Regiment under Captain Daniel Cushing, who led it during the siege of April–May 1813, before he died of illness. Meanwhile, Winfield Scott, now colonel, led several companies during the amphibious attack upon Fort George, May 27, 1813, where they were equipped and fought as light infantry. The 2nd Regiment spearheaded the landing with Captain Jacob Hindman becoming the first American to leap ashore. Several detachments also garrisoned Fort Niagara across the river where they assisted in the bombardment of Fort George. Casualties this day amounted to nine dead and 20 wounded. Several companies, serving both as light infantry and artillery, subsequently accompanied the belated pursuit of British forces into the Niagara Peninsula, which came to grief at Stoney Creek on June 6, 1813. Previously, Hindman commanded the advance guard with Captain Thomas Biddle and Captain Nicholas's companies. A surprise attack that evening nearly overran the American picket guard and also captured several cannon and tumbrils belonging to Towson's company, although Towson himself managed to escape. Losses to the regiment on this occasion amounted to three killed and six wounded, with an unknown number of prisoners thrown in the mix. The rest of 1813 proved anticlimactic as the bulk of the regiment remained garrisoned at Fort George until they ventured down the St. Lawrence River as part of General James Wilkinson' army. One company under Captain Spotswood Henry was slightly engaged in these proceedings, and the entire force spent an uncomfortable winter at French Mills, New York. Another company is known to have been garrisoned Detroit at this time. Several veteran companies under Captains Thomas Biddle, Nathan Towson, Alexander J. Williams, and John Ritchie eventually transferred back to Buffalo as part of the Left Division where, in May 1814, they were reconstituted as part of the new Corps of Artillery under recently promoted Major Hindman.

Promotions

Captain Nathan Towson, brevet major. October 8, 1812. Capture of the enemy brig *Caledonia* off Fort Erie.
Captain Samuel B. Archer, brevet major. May 27, 1813. Meritorious services in bombarding Fort George.

Archival

RG94, Roll 6. Letters. National Archives. Samuel B. Archer, 1812–1814.
RG94, Roll 3. Letters. National Archives. Winfield S. Scott, 1812–1813.
RG98, No. 178/12B. Company book. National Archives. Capt. James N. Barker, 1812–1815.
RG98, No. 189/12A. Company book. National Archives. Capt. James N. Barker, 1812–1815.
RG98, No. 186/20. Company book. National Archives. John Ritchie/A. C. Fanning, 1812–1814.
RG98, No. 175/9. Clothing book. National Archives. John Ritchie/A. C. Fanning, 1812–1815.
RG98, No. 183/17. Company book. National Archives. Capt. Moses Swett, 1812–1815.
RG98, No. 182/16. Company book. National Archives. Capt. Alexander J. Williams, 1813–1815.
2nd Artillery Report. New Windsor. Staten Island, September, 1813.

Manuscript

Cushing, Daniel. Letter, 1813. Ohio Historical. VFM2018, Fort Meigs siege.
Larwill, Joseph H. Journal. Burton Historical. 1813–1815.
Larwill, Joseph H. Letters. Ohio Historical. MSS154; Larwill Family Papers.
Williams, Alexander J. Letters. Lilly Library. Jonathan Williams Papers; 1812–1814.

Printed Primary

Archer, Mary R., ed. "Military Journal of the War of 1812." *Pennsylvania Magazine of History and Biography* 17, nos. 2–3 (1893): 129–158, 281–315. [Lieutenant Isaac Roach]
Fredriksen, John C., ed. "The Memoirs of Jonathan Kearsley: A Michigan Hero from the War of 1812." *Indiana Military History Journal* 10 (May 1985): 4–16.
Howe, Henry. *Historical Collections of Ohio.* 2 vols. Cincinnati: Robert Clarke, 1888. Vol. 2, 865–868. [Lieutenant Joseph H. Larwill memoir]
Lindley, Harlow, ed. *Captain Cushing in the War of 1812.* Columbus: Ohio State Archaeological and Historical Society, 1944.
Livingston, John. *Portraits of Eminent Americans.* New York: R. Craighead, 1854, 390–392. [Captain Nathan Towson letter, May 7, 1842]
O'Reilly, Isabelle M., ed. "A Hero of Fort Erie." *Buffalo Historical Society Publications* 5 (1902): 63–93. [Lieutenant Patrick McDonough letters]
Quaife, Milo M., ed. "A Narrative of the Northwest Campaign of 1813." *Mississippi Valley Historical Review* 15 (March 1929): 519–529. [Captain Stanton Sholes memoir]
Rainwater, P. C., ed. "The Siege of Fort Meigs." *Mississippi Valley Historical Review* 19 (September 1932): 261–264. [Captain Daniel L. Cushing letter]
Scott, Winfield. *Memoirs of Lieut-Gen. Scott, LL.D. Written by Himself.* 2 vols. New York: Sheldon, 1864.
Sholes, Stanton. "A Narrative of the Northwest Campaign of 1813." *Mississippi Valley Historical Review* 15 (March 1929): 519–525.
Towson, Nathan. *Correspondence, etc., in Relation to the Capture of the British Ships Detroit and Caledonia on the Night of October 8, 1812.* Washington, D. C.: N.p., 1835.

Select Secondary

Morell, Michael N. "The Artillery at Fort Meigs, 1813." *Military Collector and Historian* 38 (Summer 1986): 78–79.

3rd Regiment of Artillery

Raised: January 11, 1812
Recruited: two battalions, New York and New Jersey; two battalions northern New York and Vermont.

Battle Honors

1812: Queenston Heights, Fort Niagara
1813: York (det.); Fort George (det.); Sacketts Harbor (det.)
1814: La Colle Mill, Oswego

Unlike the 1st Regiment of Artillery, which was 13 companies strong, the new 3rd Regiment of Artillery consisted of two 10-company battalions. A

George Armistead, 3rd Artillery. Courtesy Maryland Historical Society.

small detachment under Lieut. Bayley was present at Queenston Heights on October 13, 1812, where it lost one dead, one wounded, and fifteen captured. During the bombardment of Fort George on November 21, 1812, it further sustained an additional one killed and one wounded when a 12-pounder cannon in the southeast battery burst. The balance of the regiment remained at Greenbush Cantonment, New York, under Colonel Alexander Macomb, who trained them to a fine edge. The following spring several companies marched overland to Sacketts Harbor, where they boarded ships and assisted in the capture of York on April 27, 1813, losing three dead and 16 wounded. Macomb subsequently led several companies ashore during the amphibious attack upon Fort George, May 27, 1813, fighting as infantry and losing five dead and seven wounded. Major George Armistead, of Fort McHenry fame, also commanded several cannon at Fort Niagara during this engagement. A detachment under Major Samuel Nye left behind at Sacketts Harbor manned at battery at Fort Volunteer and fought conspicuously during the British attack there on May 29, 1813.

Macomb joined them soon after with the balance of the regiment and several companies accompanied him down the St. Lawrence River as part of the reserve. They fought in several skirmishes, particularly at French Creek on 1–2 November 1813 against British gunboats, and subsequently wintered at French Mills, New York. The following spring several companies accompanied Lieutenant Colonel George E. Mitchell back to Sacketts Harbor, although two companies remained to fight at the abortive attack upon La Colle Mill, March 30, 1814; eight soldiers fell wounded.

In late spring Mitchell was ordered to take four companies of the 3rd Regiment to Buffalo, New York, to reinforce the Left Division gathering there. En route, he was diverted to the important entrepôt of Oswego, New York, where, on May 5–6, 1814, the companies of Captains James H. Boyle, James S. Romayne, Rufus McIntire, and Benjamin K. Pierce fought desperately against a larger British raiding party under Lieutenant General Sir Gordon Drummond and Commodore Sir James Lucas Yeo. The Americans were gradually forced back in severe fighting that cost the 3rd Regiment six killed and 38 wounded. British casualties were considerably heavier, and they also failed to seize a large shipment of heavy cannon intended for the American Lake Ontario squadron. These had been laboriously evacuated beforehand by men of the 3rd Regiment and shortly after the entire unit was incorporated into the new Corps of Artillery.

Promotions

Captain Ichabod B. Crane, brevet major. November 13, 1813. Meritorious services.

Lieutenant Colonel George E. Mitchell, brevet colonel. May 5, 1814. Gallant conduct — Battle of Oswego.

Captain James H. Boyle, brevet major. May 5, 1814. Gallant conduct — Battle of Oswego.

ARCHIVAL

VanDeursen, William. Records. Connecticut Historical. 93845, Fort Trumbull; 1812–1815.
Stockton, Thomas. Returns. Indiana Historical. M211, Box 3, Fld. 25; Fort George, 1813.
RG94, Roll 94. Letters. National Archives. George Armistead, 1812–1814.
RG94, Roll 17. Letters. National Archives. John Watts, 1812–1813.
RG98, No. 397/280. Orderly book. National Archives. December, 1813.
RG98, No. 197/29. Company book. National Archives. Capt. Ichabod B. Crane, 1812–1815.
RG98, No. 190/23A. Company book. National Archives. Capt. A. C. W. Fanning, 1812–1815.
RG98, No. 191/23B. Clothing book. National Archives. A. C. Fanning/ Roger Jones, 1812–1815.
RG98, No. 192/24. Company book. National Archives. Capt. Rufus McIntire, 1812–1815.
RG98, No. 188/22. Company book. National Archives. Capt. Benjamin K. Pierce, 1813–1815.
RG98, No. 179/13. Company book. National Archives. Capt. James B. Romayne, 1812–1815.
RG98, No. 176/10. Company book. National Archives. Capt. Horace H. Watson, 1812–1815.
RG98, No. 181/15. Company book. National Archives. Capt William VanDeursen, 1812–1814.
Macomb, Alexander. Orderly book. New York State. BD 9962; Sacketts Harbor, 1812–1813.
House, James. Letter book. Rhode Island Historical. Mss 9001-H; Fort Columbus, 1812–1813.
Huger, Francis. Orderly Book. Southern Historical. Coll. 86; 6th Military District, 1813–1814.

MANUSCRIPT

Jones, Roger. Letter, 1814. Virginia Historical. Mss2 J7247 a 1; Sacketts Harbor.
Macomb, Alexander. Papers. Burton Historical.
Macomb, Alexander. Letter, 1812. Cecil County. Mitchell family File, Sacketts Harbor.
Macomb, Alexander. Papers. New York State.
O'Connor, John M. Papers. Clements Library. War of 1812 Collection; 1814–1815.
O'Connor, John M. Letters. Massachusetts Historical. Thomas Jefferson Papers; 1813.

O'Connor, John M. Papers. New York Historical. 1813–1815.
Stockton, Thomas. Papers. Library of Congress. Misc. Mss. 2057; 1812–1814.
Watts, John. Letters. Rare Books. Surgeon; 1812–1813.

Printed Primary

Churchill, Frank H. *Sketch of the Life of Bvt. Brig. General Sylvester Churchill, Inspector General, United States Army.* New York: Willis McDonald, 1888.
Fredriksen, John C., ed. "Reynold M. Kirby and His Race to Join the Regiment: A Connecticut Officer in the War of 1812." *Connecticut History* 32 (November 1991): 51–82.
Fredriksen, John C., ed. "The War of 1812 in Northern New York: The Observations of Captain Rufus McIntire." *New York History* 68 (July 1987): 297–324.
McIntire, Philip W. "Presentation of the Sword of Rufus McIntire." *Maine Historical Society Collections* 1 (1904): 187–190.
O'Connell, Barry. *On Our Ground: The Complete Writings of William Apess, A Pequot.* Amherst: University of Massachusetts Press, 1992.

Select Secondary

Archer, George W. "George Edward Mitchell." *Military Surgeon* 88 (June 1941): 670–673.
Barbuto, Richard V. "The U.S. Third Artillery: A War of 1812 Regiment." *Military Collector & Historian* 60, no. 1 (Spring 2008): 11–25.
Johnson, George. "George Edward Mitchell." In: *History of Cecil County, Maryland.* Elkton, Md.: The Author, 1881, 497–507.
Sheads, Scott. *Guardian of the Star Spangled Banner: Lt. Colonel George Armistead and the Fort McHenry Flag.* Baltimore: Toomey Press, 1999.
Malcomson, Robert. "War on Lake Ontario: A Costly Victory at Oswego, 1814." *Beaver* 75, no. 2 (1995): 4–13.

Corps of Artillery

Raised: March 30, 1814
Recruited: all states, New York City and Pittsburgh being the principal rendezvous areas.

Battle Honors

1814: Chippawa, Lundy's Lane, Fort Erie, Mackinac, Plattsburgh, Fort McHenry, Chippawa River, Villere's Plantation
1815: New Orleans, Fort St. Phillip

By the time the Corps of Artillery arose from the 1st, 2nd, and 3rd Regiments of Artillery, it incorporated largely veteran soldiers and experienced officers from, arguably, the three best units in the army. Little wonder, then, why it accrued more brevet promotions than any other unit during the final year of the war. The new formation consisted of twelve battalions of four companies each. The most famous of these was commanded by Major Jacob Hindman, whose four-company detachment under Captains Nathan Towson. Thomas Biddle, John Ritchie, and Alexander J. Williams constituted the artillery train of General Jacob Brown's Left Division at Buffalo, New York. Fort Erie was captured on July 3, 1814, and promptly garrisoned by Williams's company. On July 5, 1814, Towson's company distinguished itself in combat at Chippawa, losing 4 killed and 16 wounded. Three weeks later at Lundy's Lane, July 25, 1814, Hindman's entire force was closely engaged, losing 10 killed (including Captain Ritchie) and 35 wounded. Afterwards, Hindman's gunners formed the core of American defenses at Fort Erie where, on August 15, 1814, they pulverized attacking British columns at a cost of four killed (including Captain Williams) and four wounded. Captain Towson's company occupied the American left flank on a position called Snake Hill, and so rapidly did his guns lash out in the darkness that the battery was dubbed "Towson's lighthouse." A further 10 artillerists were killed and 24 were wounded throughout the prolonged British bombardment, which finally ended on September 17, 1814. Shortly afterwards, General George Izard's Right Division arrived at Niagara, and on October 15, 1814, the companies of Towson and Captain Samuel B. Archer bombarded British positions across Chippawa Creek, losing two dead and one injured. A detachment also accompanied the aborted attack against Mackinac on August 4, 1814, sustaining three wounded. The Corps of Artillery was represented at Plattsburgh, September 6–11, 1814, by several companies including Captain Alexander Brooks's command, which occupied Fort Brown and lost three dead and one injured.

During this same time frame, Captain Frederick Evan's company garrisoned Fort McHenry, Baltimore harbor, during the British attack, and withstood a fierce bombardment by the Royal Navy. Overall command of this vital position devolved upon Major George Armistead, who lost a total of 27 wounded. British operations then shifted southward to the Gulf of Mexico where gunners partook of the wild nighttime engagement at Villere's Plantation, Louisiana, on December 23, 1814. Here a detachment under Lieutenant Samuel Spotts suffered one killed; his two-gun detachment was nearly overrun by British troops after supporting Marines Corps elements gave way but, once rallied and assisted by the 7th U. S. Infantry, the guns were rescued from imminent capture. Two weeks later several batteries figured prominently in General Andrew Jackson's position at New Orleans where, on January 8,

Jacob Hindman, Corps of Artillery. Courtesy Maryland Historical Society.

1815, their concentrated fire inflicted the majority of the 2,000 casualties suffered by the British. Captain Enoch Humphrey's battery (No. 1), planted only 70 feet from the banks of the Mississippi River, did particular execution on forces attempting to storm a nearby redoubt. Further down the line, Battery No. 5, consisting of two six pounders under Lieutenant Ker, and Battery No. 7, seven long 18 pounders and a single six pounder under Lieutenant Spotts, were also heavily engaged. During this same interval, three companies under Captains Charles Wollenstonecraft, Michael Walsh, and Thomas Murray withstood a prolonged bombardment by Royal Navy vessels at Fort St. Phillip, January 9–18, 1815, suffering only two killed and four wounded. The Corps of Artillery was retained intact during the peacetime establishment, having accrued a wartime record comparable to contemporary European formations.

Promotions

Captain Roger Jones, brevet major. July 5, 1814. Distinguished services in the Battle of Chippawa.

Brevet Major Nathan Towson, brevet lieutenant colonel. July 5, 1814. Gallant conduct in the Battle of Chippawa.

2nd Lieutenant H. M. Campbell, brevet 1st lieutenant. July 5, 1814. Gallant conduct — Battle of Chippawa.

2nd Lieutenant Jacob Schmuck, brevet 1st lieutenant. July 25, 1814. Gallant conduct — Battle of Niagara.

Major Jacob Hindman, brevet lieutenant colonel. July 15, 1814. Gallant conduct in the defense of Fort Erie.

Captain Alexander C. W. Fanning, brevet major. August 15, 1814. Gallant conduct in the defense of Fort Erie.

Captain Thomas Biddle, brevet major. August 15, 1814. Gallant conduct in the defense of Fort Erie.

1st Lieutenant R. A. Zantzinger, brevet captain. August 15, 1814. Gallant conduct in the defense of Fort Erie.

2nd Lieutenant Reynold M. Kirby, brevet 1st lieutenant. August 15, 1814. Gallant conduct in defense of Fort Erie.

2nd Lieutenant John G. Watmough, brevet 1st lieutenant. August 15, 1814. Gallant conduct defending Fort Erie.

Captain Alexander S. Brooks, brevet major. September 11, 1814. Gallant conduct — Battle of Plattsburgh.

1st Lieutenant John Mountfort, brevet captain. September 11, 1814. Gallant conduct — Battle of Plattsburgh.

1st Lieutenant Harold Smith, brevet captain. September 11, 1814. Gallant conduct — Battle of Plattsburgh.

1st Lieutenant Chester Root, brevet captain. September 11, 1814. Gallant Conduct — Battle of Plattsburgh.

2nd Lieutenant J. G. Cromwell, brevet 1st lieutenant. September 11, 1814. Gallant conduct — Battle of Plattsburgh.

Major George Armistead, brevet lieutenant colonel. September 12, 1814. Gallant conduct defending Fort McHenry.

Major Roger Jones, brevet lieutenant colonel. September 17, 1814. Gallant conduct — Sortie from Fort Erie.

Brevet 1st Lieutenant Reynold M. Kirby, brevet captain. September 17, 1814. Gallant conduct, Fort Erie sortie.

1st Lieutenant David B. Douglass, brevet captain. September 17, 1814. Gallant conduct, sortie from Fort Erie.

2nd Lieutenant Horace C. Story, brevet 1st lieutenant. September 17, 1814. Gallant conduct, sortie from Fort Erie.

Captain Enoch Humphreys, brevet major. December 23, 1814. Gallant conduct during the siege of New Orleans.

1st Lieutenant Samuel Spotts, brevet captain. January 15, 1815, Gallant conduct during the siege of New Orleans.

1st Lieutenant Luther Scott, brevet captain. February 20, 1815. Distinguished and meritorious services.

2nd Lieutenant Francis O. Byrd, brevet 1st lieutenant. February 20, 1815. Distinguished and meritorious services.

Brevet Major John B. Walbach, brevet lieutenant colonel. May 1, 1815. Meritorious services.

Brevet Lieutenant Colonel Jacob Hindman, brevet colonel. May 17, 1815. Meritorious services.

Archival

RG94, Roll 6. Letters. National Archives. Samuel B. Archer, 1814–1815.
RG94, Roll 94. Letters. National Archives. George Armistead, 1814–1815.
RG94, Roll 20. Letters. National Archives. Samuel Champlain, 1813–1815.
RG94, Roll 32. Letters. National Archives. James S. Swearingen, 1814–1815.
RG98, No. 195/27. Company book. National Archives. Capt. James H. Boyles, 1814–1815.
RG98, No. 180/14. Company book. National Archives. Capt. James R. Hanham, 1814–1815.
RG98, No. 196/28. Company book. National Archives. Capt. Richard A. Zantzinger, 1814–1815.

Manuscript

Armistead, George. Papers. Fort McHenry. Special Collection No. 35; 1812–1815.
Byrd, Francis O. Letters. Virginia Historical. Mss1 B9963 b; 1839–1848, past service.
Hindman, Jacob. Letters. Lilly Library. War of 1812 Collection; 1814–1815.
Mitchell, George E. Letter, 1814. Clements Library. War of 1812 Collection, Niagara.
Sands, Abraham L. Letter book. Nassau County Historical. Mobile, Fort Bowyer; 1813–1815.
Towson, Nathan. Letters. Lilly Library. War of 1812 Collection; 1814.
Towson, Nathan. Letter, 1815. Massachusetts Historical. Jacob Brown Papers; Niagara.
Williams, Alexander J. Letters. Lilly Library. Jonathan Williams Papers; 1814.

Printed Primary

Anonymous. "The Siege of Fort Erie." *United States Military Magazine* 2 (March 1840): 65–73.

Armistead, George. "Official Report of the Bombardment of Fort McHenry." *Patriotic Marylander* 1 (September 1914): 20–23.

Churchill, Frank H. *Sketch of the Life of Bvt. Brig. General Sylvester Churchill, Inspector General, United States Army.* New York: Willis McDonald, 1888.

Hall, James. "A Reminiscence." *Knickerbocker Magazine* 6 (July 1835): 10–19.

Hall, James. "Reminiscences of the Last War." *Illinois Monthly Magazine* 2 (February 1832): 202–207.

Livingston, John. *Portraits of Eminent Americans.* New York: Craighead, 1854, 411–412. [Captain Nathan Towson letter, 1841]

O'Reilly, Isabelle M., ed. "A Hero of Fort Erie: The Correspondence of Lt. Patrick McDonough." *Buffalo Historical Society Publication* 5 (1902): 63–93.

Richards, George H. *A Vindication of His Motives from the Aspersions of His Enemies.* N.p. N.d.

Select Secondary

"Biography of Colonel Jacob Hindman." *Portico* 3 (January 1817): 38–52.

Birkhimer, William E. *Historical Sketch of the Artillery, U. S. Army.* Washington, D.C.: James J. Chapman, 1899.

Fredriksen, John C. "Colonel Childs and His Quadrant: Reflections on the Career of a Distinguished American Soldier." *Military Collector and Historian* 39, no. 3 (Fall 1987): 122–124.

Graves, Donald E. "Field Artillery of the War of 1812: Equipment, Organization, Tactics, and effectiveness." *Arms Collecting* 30, no. 2 (1992): 39–48.

Graves, Donald E. "American Ordnance of the War of 1812: A Preliminary Investigation." *Arms Collecting* 31, no. 4 (1993): 111–120.

Hall, James. "Biographical Sketch of Major Thomas Biddle." *Illinois Monthly Magazine* 1 (September 1831): 549–561.

McKenny, Janice P. *The Organizational History of the Field Artillery.* Washington, D. C.: Center of Military History, United States Army, 2006.

McBarron, H. Charles. "U. S. Corps of Artillery, 1814–1821." *Military Collector and Historian* 2 (1950): 55.

Sheads, Scott. *Guardian of the Star Spangled Banner: Lt. Col. George Armistead and the Fort McHenry Flag.* Baltimore: Toomey Press, 1999.

Taylor, Blaine. "The Rocket's Red Glare." *Military Heritage* 8, no. 2 (2006): 24–31.

Wade, William. "Early Systems of Artillery." *Ordnance Notes* 25 (May 1874): 137–167.

Watmough, John G. *A Brief Sketch of the Services of J. G. Watmough…. When an Officer in the United States Army.* Philadelphia: N.p., 1835.

Regiment of Light Artillery

Raised: April 12, 1808
Recruited: two companies, Massachusetts and New Hampshire; two companies New York and New Jersey; two companies Pennsylvania and Delaware; two companies, Maryland and Virginia; two companies, Kentucky, Ohio Indiana Territory, Michigan Territory; Illinois Territory, Missouri Territory; principal rendezvous, Dedham, Massachusetts.

BATTLE HONORS

1812: Queenston Heights
1813: Fort George, Sacketts Harbor (det.), Beaver Dams (det.), French Creek, Crysler's Farm
1814: La Colle Mill, Oswego, Plattsburgh

The Regiment of Light Artillery was a pre-war formation authorized at ten companies. It was also designated an elite unit with blue jackets trimmed by the requisite black collars and cuffs. The regiment was initially led by Colonel Moses Porter, a colorful Revolutionary War veteran whose propensity for swearing led to the moniker "Old Blowhard." By the fall of 1812 the companies of Captain Gibson and McIntosh were present at the Niagara frontier under Lieutenant Colonel John R. Fenwick (a Marine Corps veteran), and they lost heavily at the Battle of Queenston Heights on October 13, 1812. Fenwick himself was severely wounded, losing an eye and an arm, and captured in a boat, along with 40 of his men. The survivors were soon after reinforced by an additional company commanded by Captain Luther Leonard, which wintered at Fort Niagara. Several other detachments remained at Greenbush Cantonment outside of Albany, New York, under the command of Major Abraham Eustis. Previously, Luther's command was active in the November 22, 1812 bombardment of Fort George and, on November 28, a detachment ferried over to Squaw Island in mid-stream to assisted the failed crossing of General Alexander Smyth's force.

The following spring witnessed a detachment fighting at York, April 27, 1813, under Major Eustis, while the company of Captain McDowell fought at the capture of Fort George, Upper Canada, on May 27, 1813, losing one dead and one injured. McDowell's command subsequently accompanied the 2nd Artillery Regiment to Stoney Creek where, on June 6, 1813, it lost an additional three killed and seven wounded. This detachment passed into captivity at Beaver Dams on June 24, 1813, losing two officers and 33 men as prisoners, along with one 12-pounder and one six-pounder cannon. Several elements were also present at Sackets Harbor on May 29, 1813, and helped repel a determined British attack. By September additional companies were deployed there under Colonel Porter and they accompanied General James Wilkinson's main force down the St. Lawrence River during his Montreal offensive. Here they formed part of General Jacob J. Brown's advanced brigade. Due to the shortage of horses and cannon, the Regiment of Light Artillery frequently fought as light infantry, although they manned several pieces at French Creek on November 2, 1813, driving off two brigs, two schooners, and eight gunboats loaded with infantry. Moreover, the companies of Captains Leonard and McPherson actively fought at Crysler's Farm on November 13, 1813, where a 6-pounder under Lieutenant W. W. Smith was captured. The youthful Smith, a West Point graduate, was fatally wounded. The regiment next wintered at French Mills, New York, with the bulk of the northern army before continuing to Plattsburgh.

That Spring several companies marched to Sacketts Harbor while a detachment was present during the attack upon La Colle Mill, Lower Canada, on March 30, 1814, sustaining five wounded. The gunners had pushed forward one 12-pounder and a 5½ inch howitzer to within 200 yards of the stone mill, only to watch their fire harmlessly glance off. Captain George W. Melvin's company also accompanied four companies of the 3rd Artillery Regiment to Oswego, New York, May 5–6, 1814, distinguishing itself in combat. On May 13, 1814, the company of Lieutenant Arthur W. Thornton, manning seven 12-pounders on naval carriages, repelled Captain Pring's squadron at Otter Creek, Vermont. Captain Luther's company also fought at the battle of Plattsburgh, September 11, 1814, losing three dead and one wounded. However, the bulk of the regiment, organized as infantry, accompanied General George Izard's Right division on its march to the Niagara frontier, and saw no further combat. By war's end the unit relocated back to Greenbush Cantonment, where it was consolidated with the 15th, 26th, 30th, 31st, 34th, and 45th Infantries under the same name. The regiment was finally abolished in 1821 as a cost-cutting measure.

Promotions

Lieutenant colonel John R. Fenwick, brevet colonel. March 18, 1813. Gallant conduct — Niagara frontier.

Colonel Moses Porter, brevet brigadier general. September 10, 1812. Distinguished services in the Campaign of 1813

Major Abraham Eustis, brevet lieutenant colonel. September 10, 1813. Meritorious services.

Captain Robert H. McPherson, brevet major. November 11, 1813. Services in the St. Lawrence Campaign in 1813.

Brevet Major Robert H. McPherson, brevet lieutenant colonel. March 30, 1814. Gallant conduct, La Colle Mill.

Archival

RG94, Roll 9. Letters. National Archives. John R. Fenwick, 1812–1815.
RG94, Roll 33. Letters. National Archives. Samuel Washburn, 1813, 1815.
RG98, Item 79. Orderly book. National Archives. March–June, 1814.
RG98, No. 169/3. Company book. National Archives. Capt. Luther Leonard, 1812–1815.
RG98, No. 170/4. Company book. National Archives. George N. Morris/John R. Bell, 1814–1815.
RG98, No. 363/205A. Morning reports. National Archives. October, 1814–February, 1815.
RG98, No. 41/206. Misc reports. National Archives. Returns, registers, 1811–1821.

Manuscript

Eustis, Abraham. Letter, 1811. Boston Public. *Ms.Am.158, Fort Adams, Boston.
Fenwick, John R. Letter, 1813. Alderman Library. 9667, Ebenezer Stevens Papers; New York.
Fenwick, John R. Diary, 1814. Library of Congress. Toner Collection.
McPherson, Robert H. Letter, 1815. Oberlin College. No. 74, Orrin June Coll., anger at Congress.
Porter, Moses. Letter, 1813. Boston Public. Ms.Am. 1094 (3); Boston defenses.
Porter, Moses. Papers. Danvers Archival. PR/PO/C; Moses Porter Papers, 1812–1814.
Porter, Moses. Letters. Massachusetts Historical. 1815–1817.

Printed Primary

Eustis, Abraham. "The Capture of York." *Massachusetts Historical Society Proceedings* 11 (December 1876): 492–495.
"Reminiscences of the Late War." *The Casket* 10 (June 1835): 353.

Select Secondary

"Biographical Notice of Lieut. W. W. Smith." *Analectic Magazine* 8 (July 1816): 52–54.
Campbell, J. Duncan. "Second Pattern Cap Plate, U. S. Light Artillery, 1814." *Military Collector and Historian* 26 (Spring 1974): 6–9.
Chartrand, Rene, and Eric I. Marsden. "U.S. Light Artillery, 1814–1821." *Military Collector and Historian* 48 (Summer 1996): 86–87.
Larter, Harry C. "Material of the First American Light Artillery." *Military Collector and Historian* 4 (1952): 53–63.
Porter, Moses. *Mess Regulations Adopted by the First Regt. Of United States Light Artillery.* Boston: Thomas F. Bangs, 1817.
Putnam, Alfred A. "General Moses Porter, 1756–1822." *Danvers Historical Society Collection* 15 (1927): 1–25.
Todd, Frederick P. "Notes on the Dress of the Regiment of Light Artillery, U. S. A., 1808–1811." *Military Historian and Collector* 2 (1950): 10–11.

CAVALRY

1st Regiment of Light Dragoons

Raised: April 12, 1808
Recruited: one troop, Maryland and Pennsylvania; two troops, North Carolina, South Carolina, Georgia; two troops Kentucky, Ohio, Michigan Territory, Missouri Territory, Indiana Territory, Illinois Territory

BATTLE HONORS

1813: Fort Meigs, Sacketts Harbor

The 1st Regiment of Light Dragoon was the army's principal mounted arm up through 1812. It had an authorized strength of eight troops, with several being deployed at Pittsfield, Massachusetts, over the winter. Throughout this period many troopers were detached to serve as dispatch riders in the St. Lawrence and Niagara regions. The unit seems to have suffered from a chronic shortage of mounts and was frequently trained and equipped to fight as infantry. Colonel Leonard Covington commanded several detachments in Louisiana before being promoted to brigadier general in August 1813 and venturing north to fight. A detachment of cavalry was apparently present throughout the April–May siege of Fort Meigs, Ohio, where it lost three killed and 17 wounded in the fighting. Meanwhile, Lieutenant Colonel Electus Backus led a detachment of around six troops — over 300 men — at Greenbush, when they were finally ordered to Sacketts Harbor, New York, in May 1813. The dragoons were present at that post when British forces attacked on May 29, 1813. Backus fell mortally wounded from grapeshot during initial phases of the battle, but his troopers were capably led by Captain Arthur P. Hayne and, fighting on foot, stubbornly defended several blockhouses. Along with recruits of the 9th Infantry under Major Thomas Aspinwall, they were a major contributor to the American victory there. Several troops were next brigaded with men from the 2nd Regiment of Light Dragoons during General James Wilkinson's

Arthur P. Hayne, 1st Light Dragoons. Courtesy Arthur H. Mitchell.

offensive down the St. Lawrence River. However, the bulk of American cavalry rode apace with the flotilla by riding down along the New York shore and the 1st Regiment saw no combat. After wintering in Brownsville, New York, the unit was consolidated into the new Regiment of Light Dragoons as of May 1, 1814.

Promotions

Captain Arthur P. Hayne, brevet major. August 1, 1813.

1st Lieutenant Charles J. Nourse, brevet captain. August 15, 1813. Meritorious services.

1st Lieutenant Henry Whiting, brevet captain. March 17, 1814. Meritorious services.

Archival

RG94, Roll 12. Letters. National Archives. Capt. Jacint Laval, 1812–1814.
RG98, No. 166/1. Company book. National Archives. Capt. William Littlejohn, 1813.

Manuscript

Austin, Loring. Diary. Lilly Library. War of 1812 Papers; St. Lawrence, 1813.
Birch, George. Journal. Historical Society (Pa). Birch Family Papers; Sacketts Harbor, 1813.
Covington, Leonard. Papers. Mississippi Department. Covington-Wailes Papers; 1812–1813.
Hayne, Arthur P. Biography. Georgia Historical. Ms 1213, McIntosh Family Papers, fld. 1.

Printed Primary

Brandon, Nellie W., and W. W. Drake. *Memoir of Leonard Covington, edited by L. C. Wailes; Also Some of General Covington's Letters.* Natchez, Miss.: Natchez Printing, 1928.

Select Secondary

A Brief Sketch of the Life and Services of Arthur P. Hayne of Charleston, South Carolina. New York: J. F. Trow, 1852.
McBarron, H. Charles, and Detmar Finke. "United States Light Dragoons, 1808–1810." *Military Collector and Historian* 32 (Fall 1980): 124–125.
Thatcher, Joseph M. "U. S. Light Dragoon Belts, Plates, and Helmets, 1808–1812." *Military Collector and Historian* 27 (Spring 1975): 16–19.
Wilder, Patrick A. *The Battle of Sacketts Harbor.* Baltimore: Nautical and Aviation Press, 1994.

2nd Regiment of Light Dragoons

Raised: January 11, 1812
Recruited: three troops, Massachusetts and New Hampshire; two troops, Rhode Island and Connecticut; two troops Pennsylvania and Delaware; two troops, New York and Vermont.

Battle Honors

1812: Mississinewa (det.)
1813: Fort Meigs, Fort George, Stoney Creek, Crysler's Farm

This unit was authorized six months before the outbreak of hostilities, but recruiting went slowly and it deployed along the northern front in driblets. The first combat-ready element was Captain Samuel G. Hopkins's troop, raised in Kentucky as part of a mixed regular/volunteer squadron under Major James V. Ball. The whole accompanied Lieutenant Colonel John B. Campbell's winter expedition against the Miami Indians of Indiana where, on December 17, 1812, it fought conspicuously at the battle of Mississinewa, losing one dead and six injured. Hopkins subsequently joined the garrison at Fort Meigs, Ohio, under General William H. Harrison, losing an additional three killed and 12 wounded during the siege, April–May 1813. Major Ball was also detached as an escort for messengers going between Fort Meigs and Fort Stephenson, Ohio, when, on July 31, 1813, he was ambushed by a large party of Indians. Ball sounded the charge and completely dispersed his adversaries, killing 11 for a loss of two wounded. Meanwhile, four newly-raised troops appeared along the Niagara frontier under Colonel James Burn, and these participated in the attack upon Fort George, Upper Canada, on May 27, 1813, fighting as infantry. Captain Joseph Seldon's troop then spearheaded the pursuit of British forces inland, losing one killed and two wounded in heavy skirmishing. The troopers were posted well to the rear of the American line during the nighttime attack on their camp at Stoney Creek, June 6, 1813, and not seriously engaged. However, Colonel James Burn became the de facto senior American officer following the capture of Generals John Chandler and William H. Winder, and he ordered an ignominious withdrawal back to Fort George. A detachment of light dragoons next accompanied the advance of Lieutenant Colonel Charles G. Boerstler to Beaver Dams on June 23, 1813, where one cornet and 20 troopers were taken prisoner. The remainder were united with several other troops under Major John T. Woodford, and members of the 1st Regiment of Light Dragoons, where they formed the cavalry reserve of General James Wilkinson's army. After moving down the St. Lawrence River on the New York side, the 2nd Regiment swam across and made a desperate charge at Crysler's Farm, November 11, 1813, saving the American artillery from capture. This was one of only two conventional cavalry charges of the war and the squadron lost 18 killed and wounded out of 130 troopers present. The survivors subsequently wintered at Sacketts Harbor and Watertown, New York. Meanwhile, a detachment of two troops under Captain Hall accompanied the division of General Wade Hampton on his

James Burn, 2nd Light Dragoons. Courtesy Skinner, Inc.

march to Lower Canada, and was present at the October 26, 1813, Battle of Chateauguay. These fell back with the main army and spent the winter at Plattsburgh, New York. On March 30, 1814, the 1st and 2nd Regiments of Light Dragoons were consolidated into the new Regiment of Light Dragoons.

Promotions

Major James V. Ball, brevet lieutenant colonel. December 18, 1812. Gallant conduct — battle of Mississinewa.

Captain Joseph Selden, brevet major. February 21, 1814. Meritorious services.

Archival

RG94, Roll 38. Letters. National Archives. Captain John Butler, 1812–1814.

RG98, No. 167/2A. Company book. National Archives. Captain John A. Burd, 1812–1813. 2nd Light Dragoons. Issue Book. New England Historic. Safe Loc. Hist. UNI 16; 1812–1814.

Manuscript

Ball, James V. Letter, 1813. Library of Congress. William H. Harrison Papers.
Burn, James. Letter, 1814. New York State. Charles K. Gardner Papers, Box 2.
Coles, Walter. Letters. Huntington Library. Gerry and Coles Families; 1813.
Harris, Samuel D. Letters. Buffalo and Erie. A00-201; 1812–1814.
Harris, Samuel D. Letters. Massachusetts Historical. Charlestown Papers, II; 1812–1814.
Nourse, Charles J. Letters. Alderman Library. 3490-a, Nourse Family Papers; 1812–1814.

Printed Primary

Fredriksen, John C., ed. "Colonel James Burn and the War of 1812: The Letters of a South Carolinian Officer." *South Carolina Historical Magazine* 90 (October 1989): 299–312.
Harris, Samuel D. "Service of Capt. Samuel D. Harris: A Sketch of His Military Career as Captain in the Second Regiment of Light Dragoons during the War of 1812." *Buffalo Historical Society Publications* 24 (1921): 327–342.

Select Secondary

Graves, Donald E. "The Second Regiment of U. S. Light Dragoons, 1812–1814." *Military Collector and Historian* 34 (1982): 101–108.
Lake, Martin. *The Mississinewa Expedition, December 17–18, 1812.* Marion, Ind.: Grant County Historical Society, 1997.
Lang, William. *History of Seneca County from the Close of the Revolutionary War to July 1880.* Springfield, Oh.: Transcript Printing Co., 1880, 144–145, 523. [description of James V. Ball and his skirmish, 1813]
Todd, F. P. "2d U. S. Light Dragoons," *Military Collector and Historian* 2 (June 1953): 45.

Regiment of Light Dragoons

Raised: May 12, 1814
Recruited: as previously

Battle Honors

1814: Chippawa, Lundy's Lane, Fort Erie, Cook's Mills

The Regiment of Light Dragoons arose on May 12, 1814, when the two existing regiments were consolidated into a new formation under Colonel James Burn, previously colonel of the 2nd Regiment. The first troop to achieve distinction belonged to Captain Samuel D. Harris, which accompanied the Left Division of General Jacob J. Brown in the famous Niagara campaign. His troopers performed useful service as couriers at Chippawa on July 5, 1814, then were directly engaged in combat at Lundy's Lane on July 25, 1814, losing one killed and two wounded. Previously, Harris had participated in several hot skirmishes against Canadian partisans hovering on the flanks of the American army. His men subsequently fought in the defense of Fort Erie, August–September 1814, where another trooper fell wounded on the September 17 sortie. Later that year several troops under Captain Hall marched from Plattsburgh to Niagara with the Right Division of General George Izard. Simultaneously, a "battalion" of dismounted troopers under Major Thomas Helms marched overland from Sacketts Harbor, New York, to the same destination. During the battle of Cook's Mills, October 19, 1814, several troopers under Lieutenant Anspaugh served as couriers. Further south, a squadron of 130 newly-recruited troopers under Lieutenant Colonel Jacint Laval deployed at the Battle of Bladensburg, August 24, 1814, but saw no combat and restricted their activities to scouting. Things changed on October 31, 1814, when the troop of Captain John A. Burd espied a British landing party at Deep Creek, Maryland, scattered them, and took five prisoners at a cost of three wounded and nine horses dead. In May 1815, Congress disbanded the Regiment of Light Dragoons and the army would not possess another regular cavalry unit until the 1st U.S. Dragoons were reconstituted in 1833.

Promotions

Captain Samuel D. Harris, brevet major. July 5, 1814. Gallant conduct — Battle of Chippawa.

2nd Lieutenant George Watts, brevet 1st lieutenant. Gallant conduct — Battle of Chippawa.

Brevet Major Samuel D. Harris, brevet lieutenant colonel. July 25, 1814. Gallant conduct — Battle of Niagara.

Captain John A. Burd, brevet major. October 31, 1814. Gallant conduct.

Major Arthur P. Hayne, brevet lieutenant colonel, December 23, 1814. Gallant conduct during New Orleans.

Archival

RG94, Roll 12. Letters. National Archives. Jacint Laval, 1814–1815.
RG94, Roll 49. Letters. National Archives. Louis Laval, 1814–1815.

RG94, Roll 144. Letters. National Archives. Henry Whiting, 1812, 1814–1815.
RG98, No. 168/2B. Company book. National Archives. Capt. John A. Burd, 1814–1815.
RG98, No. 166/1. Company book. National Archives. Capt. William Littlejohn, 1814–1815.

Manuscript

Harris, Samuel D. Papers. Buffalo and Erie. A00-201; 1812–1814.
Harris, Samuel D. Letter, 1814. Lilly Library. War of 1812 Papers; Lundy's Lane.
Harris, Samuel D. Letters. Massachusetts Historical. Charleston Papers, II; 1812–1814.
Watts, George. Letter, 1814. Buffalo and Erie. A00-201; Winfield Scott's wounds.

Printed Primary

Ball, James V. *A Refutation of the Charges by Sundry Charges of the Late Regiment of Light Dragoons Against Brevet Colonel James V. Ball.* Winchester, Va.: J. Heiskell, 1815.
Hall, Henry, Captain. *A Brief Reply to the False and Slanderous Charges made by Brevet. Lieut. Col. Ball of the U. S. Army, Against Certain Officers of the United States Dragoons, in a Pamphlet Ascribed to Him, and Circulated in a Clandestine Manner.* Philadelphia, N.p., 1816.
Harris, Samuel D. "Service of Capt. Samuel D. Harris; A Sketch of His Military Career as Captain in the Second Regiment of Light Dragoons During the War of 1812." *Buffalo Historical Society Publications* 24 (1921): 327–342.

Select Secondary

Chartrand, Rene. "U. S. Light Dragoons." *Military Collector and Historian* 42 (Summer 1990): 64–65.
Steffen, Randy. *The Horse Soldier, 1776–1943.* 3 vols. Norman: University of Oklahoma Press, 1977. Vol. 1.

ENGINEERS

U.S. Corps of Engineers

Raised: March 16, 1802
Recruited: all states, graduates of the U. S. Military Academy, West Point, New York.

BATTLE HONORS

1813: Fort Meigs
1814: Fort Erie, Plattsburgh

In 1802 President Thomas Jefferson founded the U. S. Military Academy, West Point, New York, for two specific reasons. The first was to establish a military school for imbuing the prospective officers corps with proper republican precepts, thereby insuring that the army would comfortably coexist within the framework of political democracy. Second, and equally important, was Jefferson's desire for a cadre of trained military engineers that would construct roads, forts, and bridges for the nation, especially in distant reaches of the western frontier. In said fashion, engineers could help shape and sustain what Jefferson felt would ultimately be an "Empire of Liberty" out west. Professional military instruction continued at West Point for a decade and, by the time hostilities with Great Britain commenced in June 1812, the army possessed only seventeen engineering graduates. These were dispersed at various points around the country, primarily along the coast, and were engaged in building fortifications. However, their impact on ensuing military events belies their actual numbers.

Colonel Jonathan Williams, a nephew of Benjamin Franklin, served as the first Chief Engineer of the Army and he oversaw the strengthening of harbor defenses in New York City, particularly Castle Williams on Governors Island. A contempt erupted, unfortunately, after Williams insisted on asserting his rank by assuming control of that post. The War Department, subscribed

Joseph G. Swift, Corps of Engineers. West Point Museum Art Collection, United States Military Academy.

to the notion that engineers, as military technicians, more or less approximated staff officers and could not assert command prerogatives at the expense of line officers, even while outranking them. Williams bitterly resigned his commission in consequence but, as the war ground on, the regulations were gradually relaxed.

Williams's successor was Colonel Joseph G. Swift, who had been actively involved in the Southern Department before transferring north to work in the New York City area. He thus became Chief Engineer of the Army in July, 1812, aged 29 years. Swift labored effectively to enhance defenses of the nation's largest city, and in 1813 he was appointed commander of line units on Staten Island, a sign that the status of engineering officers was improving. He subsequently served as commandant of Fort Richmond and the Hudson Battery before venturing north in the fall of 1813 to participate in General James Wilkinson's St. Lawrence campaign. On November 11, 1813, Swift fought at Crysler's Farm and directed several artillery pieces. The following spring he advanced to brevet brigadier general, becoming the first U.S. Military Academy graduate to reach that grade, then assumed control of all defenses in New York City. City fathers were so pleased by his efforts that they commissioned a full length portrait of Swift, which continues hanging in City Hall.

Army engineers rendered particularly active service in campaigns throughout the Northwest. Captain William Partridge assisted the army of General William Hull by constructing a road from Dayton, Ohio, to Detroit, Michigan. However, he was taken prisoner in August 1812 when Hull surrendered and died in captivity. Meanwhile, Captain Eleazar D. Wood performed yeoman work as part of General William Henry Harrison's staff. He actively led a company of spies in the Lake Erie area during the fall of 1812, and the following spring he designed and constructed Fort Meigs on the Maumee River, Ohio. This spacious bastion successfully defied two British sieges during the spring and summer of 1813. After the crushing American victory at the Thames in October 1813, Captain Charles Gratiot sporadically assumed command of all forces in the Michigan Territory in tandem with General Lewis Cass, while also serving as civil and military administrator of westernmost Upper Canada. Further south, Lieutenant Colonel Walter K. Armistead directed batteries at Craney Island, Virginia, which helped repulse a large British raid conducted by Admiral John Warren in June 1813. His brother, Lieutenant Colonel George Armistead, commanded the artillery detachments deployed there.

Military affairs further east were assisted by a handful of notable officers, particular Captain Joseph G. Totten, who mapped the St. Lawrence region during the American offensive there. After it failed, Totten, assisted by Lieutenants James Gadsden (of Gadsden's Purchase fame) and Rene E. De Russy, constructed badly-needed housing at French Mills, New York, over the winter of 1813–1814. Similar efforts at Sacketts Harbor were abetted by Captains William McRee and Wood, who had also transferred east. These two officers particularly distinguished themselves throughout the 1814 Niagara Campaign under General Jacob J. Brown. They were particularly successful in converting tottering Fort Erie into an impregnable position that repelled the August

15, 1814, attack by Lieutenant General Gordon Drummond with almost 1,000 casualties. Wood, positioned at the left flank of the American camp, directed the 21st Infantry into combat at Snake Hill, inflicting heavy losses on five determined charges by the DeWatteville Regiment. On September 17, 1814, Wood died while participating in General Brown's successful sortie into the British trenches and, after the war, Brown arranged for a memorial to be constructed at West Point in his honor. That September, another chain of fortifications constructed at Plattsburgh, New York, stymied a major attack by British forces under Governor General Sir George Prevost. Previously, Totten had accompanied the Right Division of General George Izard to Niagara, where he arranged for the demolition of Fort Erie in October 1814. To the south, Fort McHenry, Baltimore, which was another product of West Point engineering, defied a severe British bombardment and contributed signally to the American victory there. The Corps of Engineers compiled a splendid wartime record and its cadre continued dominating military and civilian engineering efforts over the next half-century. As Jefferson anticipated, they proved instrumental in facilitating western expansion throughout the age of "Manifest Destiny."

An interesting subdivision of the Corps of Engineers was the Company of Bombardiers, Sapper, and Miners, which were enlisted men led by academy graduates. This force, which only numbered 62 men, remained at West Point for the first two years of the war before transferring to the Left Division at Niagara in July 1814. They were commanded by Lieutenant David B. Douglass, a West Point graduate, and fought at Lundy's Lane and the siege of Fort Erie. On August 15, 1814, they occupied the "Douglass Battery" on the far right of the American camp and bloodily repulsed several British charges under Colonel Hercules Scott. This small but useful force was finally disbanded for reason of economy in 1821.

Another unusual unit attached to the engineers was the Corps of Artificers, a collection of masons, carpenters, blacksmiths, boat-builders, ship carpenters, armories and laborers under Alexander Paris. Paris never received a regular commission, but he led this little band throughout the war and even designed a distinct, green uniform for its members. The Corps of Artificers was disbanded by Congress on March 3, 1815.

Promotions

Captain Joseph G. Totten, brevet major. June 6, 1813. Meritorious services.
Captain Eleazar D. Wood, brevet major. May 6, 1813. Gallant conduct—distinguished services, defense of Fort Meigs.
Colonel Joseph G. Swift, brevet brigadier general. February 19, 1812. Meritorious services.

Major William McRee, brevet lieutenant colonel. July 25, 1814. Gallant conduct — Battle of Niagara.
Brevet Major Eleazar D. Wood, brevet lieutenant colonel. July 25, 1814. Gallant conduct — Battle of Niagara.
Brevet lieutenant colonel William McRee, brevet colonel. August 15, 1814. Distinguished service at Fort Erie.
Brevet Major Joseph G. Totten, brevet lieutenant colonel. September 11, 1814. Gallant conduct at Plattsburgh.
1st Lieutenant Edward De Russy, brevet captain. September 11, 1814. Gallant conduct — Battle of Plattsburgh.
2nd Lieutenant George Trescott, brevet 1st lieutenant. September 11, 1814. Gallant conduct — Plattsburgh.
Major George Bomford, brevet lieutenant colonel. December 22, 1814 Distinguished service, Ordnance Department.
Captain Sylvanus Thayer, brevet major. February 20, 1815. Distinguished and meritorious services at Norfolk.

Archival

RG77, M-417. Letters. National Archives. Buell Collection, 1812–1815.
RG94, Roll 29. Letters. National Archives. Alden Partridge, 1813–1815.
RG94, Roll 5. Letters. National Archives. Joseph G. Swift, 1812–1815.

Manuscript

Douglass, David B. Papers. Clements Library. Niagara, 1814.
Douglass, David B. Papers. U.S. Military Academy. No. 114; some Niagara, 1814.
Drew, Seth. Papers. Clements Library. Superintendent, Plymouth, Mass.
Dumas, Hipolite. Papers. Beinecke Library. Ms. 1422; 1813–1815; Fort Bowyer.
Gratiot, Charles. Letters. Burton Historical.
Gratiot, Charles. Letters. Manuscripts and Archives. Mss. 631, Joseph Wheaton Papers; 1813.
Gratiot, Charles. Letter, 1812. Ohio Historical. VFM92; convoy orders, Mansfield, Ohio.
Parris, Alexander. Letters. New England Historical. Corps of Artificers; 1812–1814.
Partridge, Alden. Papers. Library of Congress. 1812–1815.
Partridge, Alden. Papers. U.S. Military Academy. 1812–1815.
Story, Horace C. Letter, 1814. E. C. Barker History. Joseph Story Papers; Fort Erie.
Swift, Joseph G. Papers. U.S. Military Academy. No. 313; 1812–1815; maps.
Thayer, Sylvanus. Papers. U.S. Military Academy. No. 318; 1812–1815.
Wendell, Abraham. Papers. U.S. Military Academy. No. 392; 1813–1815.
Williams, Jonathan. Papers. Lilly Library. 1812–1815.
Williams, Jonathan. Papers. U.S. Military Academy. No. 398; 1812–1814.
Wood, Eleazar D. Papers. Wisconsin Historical. 1813–1814; Ohio, Fort Erie.
Wood, Eleazar D. Letters. Gilder Lehrman. 1813–1814; Ohio, Fort Erie.

Printed Primary

Cullum, George W. *Campaigns of the War of 1812–1815 Against Great Britain, Selected and Criticized.* New York: J. Miller, 1879, 362–417. [Lieutenant Colonel Eleazar D. Wood narrative, 1813]

Douglass, David B. "Reminiscences of the Campaign of 1814 on the Niagara Frontier." *Historical Magazine* 2 (July 1873); 1–12; 2 (August 1873): 65–76; 2 (September 1873): 127–142; 2 (October 1873): 216–224.

Ellery, Harrison, ed. *The Memoirs of General Joseph Gardner Swift, LL. D., U. S. A.* Worcester, Mass.: Privately printed, 1890.

Horton, John F., ed. "An Original Narrative of the Niagara Campaign of 1814." *Niagara Frontier* 11, no. 1 (1964): 1–36. [David B. Douglass]

Select Secondary

Buzzard, Raleigh B. "Insignia of the Corps of Engineers." *Military Engineer* 42 (1950): 101–103.

Cullum, George W. *Biographical Sketch of Brigadier General Joseph G. Swift, Chief Engineer of the United States Army, July 31, 1812 to Nov. 12, 1818.* New York: C. A. Coffin, 1877.

Gaines, William C. "Second System Fortification Construction at Savannah, Georgia, 1807–1815." *Journal of America's Military Past* 27, no. 2 (2000): 19–39.

Griswold, William A. "A Reasoned Approach to the Defense of New York Harbor in the War of 1812." *Journal of America's Military Past* 30, no. 1 (2004): 26–42.

McBarron, H. Charles, and Detmar Finke. "Corps of Engineers, Enlisted Men, 1803–1811." *Military Collector and Historian* 3 (1951): 81–83.

McBarron, H. Charles, and Detmar Finke. "U. S. Corps of Artificers, 1812–1815." *Military Collector and Historians* 9 (1957): 104–105.

McCarthy, S. M. "The Insignia of the Corps of Engineers." *Military Engineer* 36 (1942): 343–344.

Memoir of Colonel William McRee, United States Engineers. Wilmington, N. C., N.p., 1854.

Smith, Mark A. "The Corps of Engineers and National Defense in Antebellum America, 1815–1860." Unpublished Ph.D. dissertation, University of Alabama, 2004.

Smith, Mildred L. *General Charles Gratiot: Acres and Avenues Bear His Name.* Ithaca, Mi.: Gratiot County Historical Society, 1987.

Thomas, Mary M. "'Science, Military Style': Fortifications, Science, and the Corps of Engineers, 1802–1861." Unpublished Ph.D. dissertation, University of Minnesota, 2002.

Wade, Arthur P. "Artillerists and Engineers: The Beginnings of the American Seacoast Fortifications, 1744–1815." Unpublished Ph.D. dissertation, Kansas State University, 1977.

Walker, Charles. "The Other Good Guys: Army Engineers in the War of 1812." *Military Engineer* 70, no. 455 (May–June 1978): 178–183.

United States Army. Corps of Engineers. Office of History. *The U. S. Army Corps of Engineers: A History.* Alexandria, Va.: U. S. Army Corps of Engineers, 2007.

INFANTRY

1st Regiment of Infantry

Raised: September 29, 1789
Recruited: New Brunswick, New Jersey

BATTLE HONORS

1812: Maguaga (det.), Detroit (det.), Fort Dearborn (det.), Detroit (det.), Fort Wayne (det.), Fort Madison (det.)
1813: Fort Madison (det.)
1814: Campbell's Island (det.), Lundy's Lane, Fort Erie

The War of 1812 found the 1st Regiment of Infantry, the army's senior formation, parceled out in penny-packets at various forts dotting the western frontier. It waged its first battle at Maguaga on August 9, 1812, when two small detachments fought alongside the 4th Regiment in repelling a major body of British and Indians, and Captain Daniel Baker was wounded. On August 15, 1812, Captain Nathan Heald, ordered to abandon Fort Dearborn (Chicago) in the Illinois Territory, marched his 54-man company out accordingly and was annihilated by hostile Indians, losing 26 dead and one wounded. Among the slain was Ensign George Ronan, the first West Point graduate killed in combat. The following day General William Hull surrendered Detroit, placing two detachments of the 1st Regiment into captivity. Thereafter the Indians began a systematic strategy of attacking and besieging American forts along the frontier. On September 4, 1812, a company of the 1st Regiment successfully defended Fort Wayne, Indiana Territory, while on September 5–8, another company clung to Fort Madison in present-day Iowa after losing one man killed. Fort Madison was again attacked on July 5–9, 1813, yet, despite the obvious dangers it posed to the garrison, that lonely outpost was not abandoned until the fall of 1814. Elsewhere, on September 13, 1814, Lieutenant Colonel Robert C. Nicholas gathered several companies

Jacob Kingsbury, 1st Infantry. The Society of the Cincinnati, Washington, D.C.

together for an offensive up the Illinois River; they briefly tangled with Indians on September 28th, but without loss. The regiment then fulfilled a long period of garrison duty, principally in the Missouri Territory. On July 21, 1814, a party of 42 men accompanied Major John Campbell up the Mississippi River in boats until they were ambushed on Campbell's Island and retreated with a loss of eight killed and 16 wounded. Soon after, Lieutenant Colonel Nicholas was ordered to gather three companies and march to the Niagara Frontier as part of General Jacob J. Brown's Left Division. They arrived there on July 25, 1814, just as the battle of Lundy's Lane raged, losing 11 killed, 20 wounded, and two missing in a very confused affair. The 1st Regiment continued on as part of the Fort Erie garrison, and fought well in the sortie of September 17, 1814, losing five killed and 10 wounded. Previously, a further three wounded had been sustained through the British bombardment. The unit returned to Sacketts Harbor, New York, in mid-winter, and in May 1815, it was consolidated with the 17th, 19th, 24th, 28th and 39th Regiments to form the new 3rd U.S. Infantry.

Promotions

Captain Daniel Baker, brevet major. August 9, 1812. Gallant conduct — Battle of Brownstown.
Captain Charles Larrabee, brevet major. August 9, 1812. Gallant conduct — Battle of Brownstown.

Archival

RG94, Roll 46. Letters. National Archives. Capt. Nathan Heald, 1813.
RG94, Roll 5. Letters. National Archives. Capt. Horatio Stark, 1812–1813.
RG94, Roll 34. Letters. National Archives. Capt. John Whistler, 1813–1815.
RG98, No. 53/41. Company Book. National Archives. John Symmes/Eli B. Clemson, 1812–1815.
RG98, No. 52/40. Company Book. National Archives. Capt. Simon Owens, 1812–1814.
RG98, No. 223/83A. Company Book. National Archives. Capt. Horatio Stark, 1812–1815.
RG98, No. 54/42. Company book. National Archives. L. Taliaferro/Linai T. Helm, 1813–1814.
RG98, No. 54/43. Company book. National Archives. John Whistler/James Rhea, 1812–1815.
RG98, No. 226/85. Company book. National Archives. Capt. John Whistler, 1812; Detroit.
RG153, K-1. Court martial. National Archives. Lt. Col. Robert C. Nicholas.
1st U.S. Infantry. Orderly Book. U.S. Military Academy. Fort Madison, 1812–1813.

Manuscript

Baker, Daniel. Papers. Burton Historical. Detroit, 1812.
Bissell, Daniel. Letter book. Missouri Historical. A0127, Daniel Bissell Papers; 1812–1814.
Bissell, Lewis. Papers. Missouri Historical. A0818, Kingsbury Collection.
Bissell, Lewis. Memoir, 1866. Missouri Historical. A2057; Lewis Bissell Papers.
Curtis, Daniel. Letter, 1812. Indiana Historical. M298; Fort Dearborn.
Clemson, E. B. Letters. Wisconsin Historical. John Cleves Symmes Papers, 1 WW.
Curtis, Daniel. Papers. Wisconsin Historical. Tecumseh Papers, 5 YY.
Heald, Nathan. Letters. Burton Historical.
Heald, Nathan. Letters. Chicago Historical. Fort Dearborn Collection; 1812.
Heald, Nathan. Letters. Wisconsin Historical. Frontier Wars Papers, 8 U, 17 U, 24U.

Heald, Nathan. Deposition. Wisconsin Historical. Thomas Forsyth Papers, 1 T; Fort Dearborn.
Helm, Linai. Letter. Wisconsin Historical. Thomas Forsyth Papers, 1 T; Fort Dearborn.
Jordan, Walter K. Letter, 1812. Indiana State. S746; Fort Dearborn.
Kingsbury, Jacob. Papers. Library of Congress. 1812–1814.
Kingsbury, Jacob. Papers. New York Historical. 1812–1814.
Kingsbury, Jacob. Papers. Burton Historical.
Kingsbury, Jacob. Papers. Chicago Historical.
Kingsbury, Jacob. Papers. Lilly Library. Kingsbury Mss; Rhode Island, 1811–1815.
Kingsbury, Jacob. Papers. Missouri Historical. James W. Kingsbury Collection; 1812–1814.
Kingsbury, Jacob. Letter, 1812. New York Historical. Misc Mss K, Fort Adams, RI.
Kingsbury, Jacob. Letters. Wisconsin Historical. John Cleves Symmes Papers, 1 WW.
Nicholas, Robert C. Letter, 1814. New York State. Charles K. Gardner Papers; Fort Erie.
Nicholas, Robert C. Letters. Wisconsin Historical. John Cleves Symmes Papers, 1 WW.
Stark, Horatio. Letters. Wisconsin Historical. John Cleves Symmes Papers, 1 WW.
Symmes, John C. Letters. Library of Congress. John C. Symmes Papers; 1807–1812.
Symmes, John C. Letters. Wisconsin Historical. John Cleves Symmes Papers,1 WW, 2 WW.
Symmes, John C. Journal. Wisconsin Historical. Frontier War Papers, 9U.
Vasquez, Baronet. Papers. Missouri Historical. A1683, Vasquez Family Papers, 1812–1814.
Whistler, James. Letters. Chicago Historical. James Whistler Papers; 1812–1815.
Whistler, James. Letters. Chicago Historical. Fort Dearborn Collection; 1812.

Printed Primary

Barnhart, John D., ed. "A New Letter About the Massacre at Fort Dearborn." *Indiana Magazine of History* 41 (June 1945): 187–199.
Dearborn, Friend. *Early Days in Detroit.* Detroit: Hunt, June, 1906, 880–885. [Ensign Daniel Curtis letter, August 1812]
Gordon, Nellie K. *The Fort Dearborn Massacre, Written in 1814 by Lieut. Linai T. Helm, One of the Survivors.* Chicago: Rand McNally, 1912.
Jacobs, John G. *The Life and Times of Patrick Gass.* Wellsburg, Va.: Jacobs, Smith, 1859, 175–178.
Peckham, Howard, ed. "An Eyewitness Account of the Siege of Fort Wayne." *Indiana Magazine of History* 44 (December 1948): 409–419. [Ensign Daniel Curtis letter, September 21, 1812]
Pen in Hand, Letters from Old Fort Madison and Others Regarding the Fort, 1808–1813. Fort Madison, Ia.: Northlee County Historical Society, 1974.
Quaife, Milo M., ed. "The Story of James Corbin, A Soldier at Fort Dearborn." *Mississippi Valley Historical Review* 3 (September 1916): 219–226.
Quaife, Milo M. *Chicago and the Old Northwest, 1673–1835.* Chicago: University of Chicago Press, 1913. [Lieutenant Linai T. Helm letter, 416–419]

Van Horne, James. *Narrative of the Captivity and Sufferings of James Van Horne, Who Was Nine Months A Prisoner by the Indians on the Plains of Michigan.* Middlebury, Vt.: N.p., 1817.

SELECT SECONDARY

Jackson, Donald. "Old Fort Madison, 1808–1813." *Palimpsest* 47, no. 3 (1966): 1–64.
Livingston, John. *Portraits of Eminent Americans.* New York: Craighead, 1854, 375–405 [William Christy]
Meese, William A. *The Battle of Campbell's Island.* Moline, Ill.: Desaulniers, printers, 1904.

2nd Regiment of Infantry

Raised: March 3, 1791
Recruited: Natchez, Louisiana

BATTLE HONORS

1814: Fort Bowyer
1815: Fort Bowyer

The 2nd Regiment of Infantry consisted of seven companies when war commenced in June 1812, and the bulk of these were located around Fort Stoddert, Alabama Territory. They performed garrison duty until April 1813, when General James Wilkinson ordered them to besiege Spanish forces at Fort Charlotte, Mobile. After this post secured, a new fortification called Fort Bowyer was erected on Mobile Point, overlooking the harbor and garrisoned by 158 men of the 2nd Regiment under Major William Lawrence. On September 12–15, 1814, a large British fleet under Captain William H. Percy bombarded Fort Bowyer and landed a 60-man detachment of Royal Marines who attacked the fort. Lawrence's garrison, manning cannons, easily repulsed the Marines and sank the 22-gun sloop HMS *Hermes.* Percy drew off with a loss of 24 dead and 44 wounded to an American tally of four killed and five wounded. The British army returned in overwhelming strength on February 8, 1815, however, and worked their guns to within 100 yards of the fort. Lawrence, judging his position hopeless, surrendered on February 12, 1815, after inflicting a further 13 killed and 18 wounded on the enemy. The American lost 320 men as captives, along with their regimental colors. This act concluded the 2nd Regiment's wartime activities and in May 1815, it was amalgamated with the 3rd, 7th, and 44th Regiments to form the new 1st U.S. Infantry.

William Lawrence, 2nd Infantry. Frick Art Reference Library.

Promotions

Major William Lawrence, brevet lieutenant colonel. September 15, 1814. Gallant conduct defending Fort Bowyer.

Archival

Fort Bowyer. Correspondence. Alabama Department. SGO13377, Folders 11–12. RG94, Roll 8. Letters. National Archives. Henry Conway, 1812, 1815.

RG98, No. 130/374. Orderly book. National Archives. Capt. William Lawrence, 1812–1813.
RG98, No. 475/376. Orderly book. National Archives. Capt. William Lawrence, 1812–1815.
RG98, No. 485/386. Orderly book. National Archives. Capt. William Lawrence, 1812–1815.
RG98, No. 123/247. Orderly book. National Archives. Capt. William Lawrence, 1812–1815.
RG98, No. 471/370. Orderly book. National Archives. Capt. William Lawrence, 1812–1815.
RG98, No. 122/248. Orderly book. National Archives. Capt. William Lawrence, 1812–1815.
RG98, No. 490/391. Orderly book. National Archives. Unidentified company, 1813–1814.
RG98, No. 111/59B. Company book. National Archives. Capt. William R. Boote, 1812–1814.
RG98, No. 42/244. Company book. National Archives. William R. Boote/W. Lawrence, 1812–1814.
RG98, No. 108/57. Company book. National Archives. John Brahan/William Lawrence, 1812–1813.
RG98, No. 104/54. Company book. National Archives. John Campbell/John R. Luckett, 1812–1813.
RG98, No. 107/56. Company book. National Archives. Capt. Reuben Chamberlain, 1813–1815.
RG98, No. 109/58. Company book. National Archives. Hezekiah Bradley/Alex. Gray, 1812–1815.
RG98, No. 121/246. Morning reports. National Archives. Capt. William Lawrence, 1812.

Manuscript

Baker, Isaac L. Letter, 1812. Filson Historical. A G994/1; Camp Miami, Ohio, scouting.
Brevoort, Henry B. Papers. Burton Historical.
Lawrence, William. Letters. Library of Congress. Andrew Jackson Papers; 1814–1815.
Sparks, Richard. Letters. Library of Congress. Andrew Jackson Papers; Jan.–Nov., 1814.

Printed Primary

Lee, W. *Trial of Col. Thomas H. Cushing Before a General Court Martial Which Sat at Baton Rouge on the Charges Preferred Against Him by Brig. Gen. Wade Hampton.* Philadelphia: Moses, Thomas, 1812.

Select Secondary

Buchwald, Donald M. "History of the First United States Infantry Regiment, 1791–1860." Unpublished master's thesis, Farleigh Dickinson University, 1966.

Coker, William F. "The Last Battle of the War of 1812: New Orleans? No, Fort Bowyer!" *Alabama Historical Quarterly* 43 (1981): 42–63.
Ricketts, Robert. "The Men and Ships of the British Attack on Fort Bowyer — February, 1815." *Gulf Coast Historical Review* 5, no. 2 (1990): 7–17.
Roberts, Gerald F. "William O. Butler, Kentucky Cavalier." Unpublished master's thesis, University of Kentucky, 1971.
Savell, John P. "Protecting the Gateways: The Biography of Fort Morgan." Unpublished master's thesis, University of South Alabama, 2002.
Shaw, Frederick B. *One Hundred Years of Service in Peace and War: History of the Second Infantry, U. S. Army*. Detroit: Strathmore Press, 1940.

3rd Regiment of Infantry

Raised: April 12, 1808
Recruited: Natchez, Mississippi Territory, Louisville, Georgia

BATTLE HONORS

1813: Eccanachaca (Holy Ground)
1814: Pensacola

The 3rd Regiment of Infantry was stationed at Baton Rouge, Louisiana, when the War of 1812 commenced, and only mustered four companies until parts of the 5th Regiment were transferred to it. The men spent several months in garrison at New Orleans, and in April 1813 the unit accompanied General James Wilkinson in his brief campaign against Spanish-held Mobile, Alabama Territory. The onset of the Creek War in August 1813 left the Americans scrambling to assemble troops for an offensive into Indian territory and that November the 3rd Regiment was ordered to join General Ferdinand Leigh Claiborne's militia forces at Fort Claiborne. Striking inland, the regiment fought at Eccanachaca (Holy Ground) on December 23, 1814, against Creeks and escaped slaves under Chief Red Eagle (William Weatherford). Both were dispersed by a bayonet charge; casualties were light, only one dead and six wounded, while Indian losses were computed at 30. The 3rd Regiment continued performing garrison duty at various points throughout the South until the fall of 1814, when General Andrew Jackson deployed them during his capture of Pensacola Florida, on November 7, 1814. Captain William Laval's company distinguished themselves as the forlorn hope, capturing a two-gun battery, while Lieutenant Robinson hauled down the Spanish colors. This act concluded the unit's wartime activities and in May, 1815, it was consolidated with the 2nd, 7th, and 44th Regiments to form the new 1st U.S. Infantry.

Promotions

Captain William Laval, brevet major. November 7, 1814. Gallant conduct at Pensacola.

Captain Henry Chotard, brevet major. December 23, 1814. Gallant conduct during the siege of New Orleans.

Archival

RG98, No. 360/420. Provisions. National Archives. 1812–1815; New Orleans.

RG98, No. 120/245. Orderly book. National Archives. Capt. Matthew Arbuckle, 1812–1813.

RG98, No. 165/252. Orderly book. National Archives. Capt. Samuel W. Butler, 1815.

RG98, No. 498/400. Orderly book. National Archives. Capt. James Dinkins, 1812–1814.

RG98, No. 474/375. Orderly book. National Archives. Capt. James Dinkins, 1812–1814.

RG98, No. 163/250. Orderly book. National Archives. Capt. Joseph Woodruff, 1813–1814.

RG98, No. 164/251. Orderly book. National Archives. Capt. Joseph Woodruff, 1813–1814.

RG98, No. 438/335. Orderly book. National Archives. Unidentified company, 1814–1815.

RG98, No. 496/398. Orderly book. National Archives. Unidentified company, 1814–1815.

RG98, No. 155/63. Company book. National Archives. Capt. William Butler, 1812–1814.

RG98, No. 156/64. Company book. National Archives. Capt. William Butler, 1812–1814.

RG98, No. 157/65. Company book. National Archives. Sam. Butler/Wm. Laval, 1812–1815.

RG98, No. 160/68. Company book. National Archives. Capt. James E. Dinkins, 1812–1815.

RG98, No. 159/67. Company book. National Archives. Capt. Joseph Woodruff, 1812–1815.

RG98, No. 158/66. Company book. National Archives. Robert B. Moore/H. Chotard, 1812–1815.

RG98, No. 154/62. Company book. National Archives. Capt. Joseph Woodruff, 1812–1815.

RG98, Item 171. Muster rolls. National Archives. Various companies, 1812–1813.

Woodruff, Joseph. Morning reports. Historic New Orleans. William C. Cook Collection; 1814–1815.

Manuscript

3rd U. S. Infantry. Correspondence. Alabama Department. SG013378, Folder 10.
Anonymous. Journal. Huntington Library. BR17, surgeon, Pass Christian; 1812.

Arbuckle, Matthew. Letters. Library of Congress. Andrew Jackson Papers, July–Dec., 1814.
Arbuckle, Matthew. Letter, 1813. Perkins Library. U. S. Army Papers, Creek War.
Milton, Homer V. Letters. Library of Congress. Andrew Jackson Papers; April–Oct., 1814.
Milton, Homer V. Letters. Tennessee State. War of 1812 Collection.
Russell, Gilbert C. Letters. Library of Congress. Andrew Jackson Papers; March–July, 1814.
Russell, Gilbert C. Letter, 1815. Lilly Library. Choctaw allies in Creek War.
Russell, Gilbert C. Letters. Mississippi Department. Papers of Governors; Series A, 1813–1814.
Russell, Gilbert C. Letters. Tennessee State. War of 1812 Collection.

Printed Primary

A Narrative of the Life and Death of Lieutenant Joseph Morgan Wilcox, Who Was Massacred by the Creek Indians on the Alabama River on the 15th of January, 1814. Marietta, Oh.: R. Prentiss, 1816.

4th Regiment of Infantry

Raised: April 12, 1808
Recruited: Concord, New Hampshire

Battle Honors

1812: Brownstown, Detroit
1813: Chateauguay, French Creek, Champlain Village
1814: La Colle Mill

The 4th Regiment of Infantry formed the nucleus of General William Hull's western army at the commencement of hostilities. It had been recruited largely in New England from unemployed sailors and quickly acquired the reputation of a well-disciplined outfit. This was partly the result of Colonel John Parker Boyd's insistence on outfitting his men with the latest shakos and belly-style cartridge boxes to distinguish them from other units. It experienced its baptism under fire at Tippecanoe in 1811 under then Governor William Henry Harrison, acquitting itself well in combat. Of roughly 300 men present, the regiment sustained 77 dead and wounded. A long march to Ohio ensued until the 4th Regiment united with Hull's largely militia force in July 1812. It then accompanied the American invasion of Canada and, on August 9, 1812, the unit was dispatched to clear American lines of communications south of the River Raisin. Acting under Lieutenant Colonel James Miller, 6th regiment, it dislodged a strong British and Indian force at Maguaga and suffered 10 killed and 48 wounded. On August 16, 1812, it enjoyed the melancholy distinction of becoming the first U.S. Army unit to surrender its colors to the enemy after Hull timorously capitulated to General Isaac Brock. Efforts were undertaken to recruit a new regiment, which materialized at Burlington, Vermont in the summer of 1813 and accompanied General Wade Hampton's invasion of Lower Canada. On October 26, 1813, the new 4th Regiment was lightly engaged at Chateauguay before wintering at Plattsburgh, New York. On March 30, 1814, the regiment again fought at La Colle Mill, losing one man wounded. Afterwards it was assigned to the Light Division of General Thomas Adams Smith at Chazy, New York, and on July 18–19, 1814, a 20-man detachment under 3rd Lieutenant Charles F. Shelburne beat back an attack by superior enemy forces, losing three dead and four wounded. In the late summer, the 4th Regiment accompanied General George Izard on his march to the Niagara Frontier, seeing no additional fighting. However, a detachment had remained behind and fought in the battle of Plattsburgh on September 11, 1814, losing one killed and one wounded. In May, 1815, the 4th Regiment was consolidated with the 9th, 13th, 21st, 40th, and 46th Regiments to form the new 5th U.S. Infantry.

Promotions

Captain Josiah Snelling, brevet major. August 9, 1812. Gallant conduct — Battle of Brownstown.

Archival

Boyd, John P. Record book. Indiana Historical. BV95; 1808–1812.
RG94, Roll 41. Letters. National Archives. John Darrington, 1813–1814.
RG94, Roll 5. Letters. National Archives. Robert Purdy, 1811–1815.
RG98, No. 685. Letters sent. National Archives. April, 1811–May, 1812.
4th U. S. Infantry. Paymaster. Portsmouth Athenaeum. S0694; subsistence, forage, clothing.

Manuscript

Larabee, Charles. Letters. Wisconsin Historical. Frontier Wars Papers, 5 U, 9 U, 1811–1812.
Miller, James. Letters. Lilly Library. 1811–1815.
Miller, James. Letters. U. S. Military Academy. No. 235; 1811–1812.
Neef, Alexander. Letters. Clements Library. Good on Chateauguay, 1813, La Colle, 1814.
Norton, Jacob P. Papers/Journal. Wisconsin Historical. Plattsburgh-Niagara; 1814.

Peckham, Lewis. Letter, 1814. Indiana Historical. SC1192; Chippawa Creek, Fort Erie.
Renney, Stephen. Letters. Philips Library. Mss 11, Box 15, Folder 12; Plattsburgh.

Printed Primary

Biel, John G., ed. "The Savage Preface to 1812." *Society of Indiana Pioneers Yearbook* (91956): 5–11. [Lieutenant Colonel James Miller letters]
Boyd, John P. "Orderly Book of Colonel John P. Boyd and Extracts, 1811–1812, Fort Independence and Wabash." *Burton Historical Collection Bulletin* 1 (1917): 147–187.
Carlson, Richard G., ed. "George P. Peter's Version of the Battle of Tippecanoe." *Vermont History* 45 (Winter 1977): 38–43.
Gero, Anthony F., and Philip G. Maples. "Notes on the Dress of the 4th Regiment, United States Infantry, 1809–1813." *Military Collector and Historian* 41 (Summer 1989): 80–81.
"History of the Old Fourth Regiment." *House Reports, 322. 27th Congress (1841–1843).* 2nd Session, I: 1–7. [Private Marshal S. Durkee]
Lambert, Robert S., ed. "The Conduct of the Militia at Tippecanoe: Elihu Stout's Controversy with Colonel John P. Boyd." *Indiana Magazine of History* 51 (September 1955): 237–250.
Porter, Daniel R., ed. "Jacob Porter Norton: A Yankee on the Niagara Frontier." *Niagara Frontier* 12 (Summer 1965): 51–57.
Snelling, Josiah. *Remarks on General Hull's Memoir of the Northwestern Army.* Detroit: Sheldon, Wells, 1825.
Walker, Adam. A *Journal of Two Campaigns of the Fourth Regiment of U. S. Infantry in the Michigan and Indiana Territories under the Command of Colonel John Boyd and Lt. Col. James Miller During the Years 1811 & 1812.* Keene, N. H.: Sentinel Press, 1816.
Watts, Florence G., ed. "Lieutenant Charles Larabee's Account of the Battle of Tippecanoe." *Indiana Magazine of History* 57 (September 1961): 225–247.

Select Secondary

Barry, F. W. "Captured Flags in the Royal Hospital, Chelsea." *Journal of the Society of Army Historical Research* 7 (1929): 110–117.
Powell, William H. *A History of the Organization and Movements of the Fourth Regiment Infantry, United States Army, from May 30, 1796 to December 31, 1870.* Washington, D. C.: M'Gill & Witherow, 1871.
Powell, William H. "The Story of A Flag." *United Service* 1 (1899): 229–252.

5th Regiment of Infantry

Raised: April 12, 1808
Recruited: Harrisburg, Pennsylvania

Battle Honors

1813: Stoney Creek, French Creek, Chateauguay
1814: La Colle Mill, Chippawa River, Cook's Mills

The onset of hostilities found the 5th Regiment of Infantry scattered in various detachments throughout the South, including Baltimore, Norfolk, and Baton Rouge. Several companies were transferred to the 3rd Infantry Regiment while new companies were ordered recruited in Pennsylvania to replace them. These arrived along the Niagara Frontier in October 1812 and were temporarily consolidated with the 13th Regiment. After wintering at Buffalo, New York, the 5th Regiment was assigned to General John P. Boyd's 1st Brigade in time to fight at Fort George on May 27, 1813; no casualties are recorded. The unit was next closely engaged at Stoney Creek on June 6, 1813, as part of General William H. Winder's brigade, losing two killed and nine wounded. Here it formed in reserve under Colonel Homer V. Milton and, despite some close action, did not have a man captured. The regiment remained with Boyd's brigade that fall and on November 1–2, 1813, fought at French Creek against marauding British gunboats. The 5th Regiment subsequently wintered at French Mills, New York. Meanwhile, a detachment also accompanied General Wade Hampton's division during his ill-fated offensive into Lower Canada, and was present at Chateauguay on October 26, 1813. Both sections of the regiment united in time for the Battle of La Colle Mill, March 30, 1814, where they were heavily engaged and lost four dead and 32 injured. The 5th infantry next repaired back to Plattsburgh as part of General Daniel Bissell's brigade, and accompanied him to the Niagara Frontier that fall. The regiment lost one man killed during the bombardment of Chippawa River on October 15, 1814, and was also closely engaged at Cook's Mills on October 19, 1814, sustaining an additional five dead and 14 wounded. The regiment spent its final winter at Buffalo, New York, and in May 1815, it was amalgamated with the 18th and 35th Regiments to form the new 3rd U.S. Infantry.

Archival

Bissell, Daniel. Letter book. Missouri Historical
RG94, Roll 31. Letters. National Archives. James Sauders, 1813–1815.
RG94, Roll 22. Letters. National Archives. James Dorman, 1813–1815.
RG98, No. 209/71. Company book. National Archives. Capt. Richard H. Bell, 1812–1814.
RG98, No. 208/70. Company book. National Archives. James Dorman/John Jamison, 1814–1815.
RG98, Item 175. Monthly returns. National Archives. Capt. Benjamin Rope, 1814–1815.

Manuscript

Bissell, Daniel. Papers. Missouri Historical. 1812–1814.
Bissell, Daniel. Papers. Mercantile Library.
Blair, Alexander. Letters. Heinz History Center. MFF0082; Surgeon.
Johnson, John. Letter, 1813. Massachusetts Historical. Charles E. French Collection; Stoney Creek.

Select Secondary

Zell, Carl J. "Daniel Bissell." Unpublished Ph.D. dissertation, St. Louis University, 1971.

6th Regiment of Infantry

Raised: April 12, 1808
Recruited: New York and Reading, Pennsylvania

Battle Honors

1812: Queenston Heights
1813: York, Fort George, Beaver Dams, French Creek
1814: La Colle Mill, Plattsburgh

In the opening months of the war, the 6th Regiment of Infantry was concentrated at Greenbush Cantonment (Albany), New York, prior to marching on to Plattsburgh that fall. However, two companies commanded by Captains John Machesney and George Nelson were present along the Niagara frontier and fought at Queenston Heights on October 13, 1812. Casualties are not recorded, but Nelson died in combat. The remaining companies at Plattsburgh subsequently served as part of General Joseph Bloomfield's brigade. The following spring, the 6th Regiment marched to Sacketts Harbor and partook of General Zebulon M. Pike's amphibious expedition against York, Upper Canada. It fought conspicuously in combat, losing 13 dead and 103 wounded, principally to the infamous magazine explosion. The 6th Regiment next served under Lieutenant Colonel James Miller during the capture of Fort George on May 27, 1813, losing an additional six killed and 16 wounded. It remained a part of General John P. Boyd's 1st Brigade at Fort George over the summer, although on June 23, 1813, Captain Machesney and 58 soldiers were captured at Beaver Dams. By fall the unit had transferred back to Sacketts Harbor in time to participate in General James Wilkinson's St. Lawrence expedition. It was known to have been present at French Creek, November 1–2, 1813, as part of General Jacob J. Brown's 2nd Brigade, and subsequently wintered at French Mills, New York. The 6th Regiment next fought at La Colle Mill, Lower Canada, on March 30, 1814, as part of a consolidated battalion, suffering six wounded. It then returned to Plattsburgh as part of General Alexander Macomb's brigade. During the battle there on September 11, 1814, four companies garrisoned Fort Moreau and suffered four killed and 18 wounded. In May 1815, the 6th Regiment was consolidated with the 16th, 22nd, 23rd, and 32nd Regiments to form the new 2nd U.S. Infantry.

Promotions

Lieut. Col. James Miller, brevet colonel, August 9, 1812. Gallant conduct — Battle of Brownstown.

Captain Gerard D. Smith, brevet major. July 25, 1814. Gallant Conduct — Battle of Niagara.

Archival

RG94, Roll 9. Letters. National Archives. Isaac L. Dubois, 1812, 1814.
RG94, Roll 26. Letters. National Archives. Thomas Lawson, 1813–1815.
RG94, Roll 5. Letters. National Archives. Horatio Stark, 1813–1814.
RG98, Item 176. Letters sent. National Archives. June, 1811–October, 1813.
RG98, No. 211/73. Company book National Archives. Capt. John Chapman, 1814–1815.
RG98, No. 212/74. Company book. National Archives. Gad Humphreys/James Bailey, 1813–1815.
RG98, No. 210/72. Company book. National Archives. Capt. James Masters, 1811–1815.
6th U. S. Infantry. Muster rolls. New York State. CQ161-222; 1812–1815.
Wendell, Henry R. Orderly book. New York State. 11319 & 12350; 1812–1813.
Wendell, Henry R. Orderly book. New York State. 14775, March 1814–July 1815; Plattsburgh.
6th U. S. Infantry. Orderly book. Owen D. Young. Mss. Coll. 132, Box 2.1; March–July, 1814.
Wendell, Henry R. Orderly book. Ticonderoga Historical.
6th U. S. Infantry. Orderly book. U.S. Army Military. 1810–1811.

Manuscript

Beaumont, William. Letters. U.S. Army Military. Arch Coll 101, Plattsburgh; 1813–1814.
Beaumont, William. Letters. Cushing/Whitney. BMC Ms Coll 2, Plattsburgh; 1813–1815.
Coburn, Nathan. Memoir. Rensselaer County. B2-Box 3 #53.19; 1812.

Lawson, Thomas. Letter, 1813. Huntington Library. HN29689, surgeon, to Jonas Simonds.
Miller, James. Letter, 1813. Library of Congress. Benham-McNeil Papers; Fort George.
Miller, James. Letters. Lilly Library. 1811–1815.
Miller, James. Letter, 1813. New York Historical. Misc Mss M, to Jonas Simonds.
Miller, James. Letters. U.S. Military Academy. No. 235; 1813–1814.
Walworth, John. Letters. Library and Archives. MG24, F16; 1812–1813.
Wendell, Henry R. Papers. New York State. 10398; recruiting, 1812–1813, Schenectady.
Wendell, Henry R. Papers. New York State. (N) SC9831, 1812–1814.

Printed Primary

"Extracts from Court Martial Records: Trouble in the Sixth Infantry, 1811." *Army and Navy Life* 9 (1906): 513–528.
Miller, Genevieve, ed. *William Beaumont's Formative Years: Two Early Notebooks, 1811–1824*. New York: Henry Schulman, 1946, 1–51.
Myer, Jesse S. *Life and Letters of Dr. William Beaumont*. St. Louis: V. V. Mosby Company, 1912.
Voorkers, James. *Address of James J. Voorkers, a First Lieutenant, Sixth Regiment Infantry of the United States: To a Court of Inquiry Instituted for the Purpose of Inquiring into the Specifications herein Contained*. New York: Printed at the Apollo Office, 1812.

Select Secondary

Babcock, Elkanah. *A War History of the Sixth U. S. Infantry from 1798 to 1903*. Kansas City, Mo.: Hudson-Kimberly Pub. Co., 1903.
Holden, Robert J. "James Miller, Collector of the Port of Salem." *Essex Institute Collections* 104 (1968): 253–302.
Horsman, Reginald. *Frontier Doctor: William Beaumont, America's First Great Medical Scientist*. Columbia: University of Missouri Press, 1996.
Kenney, Alice P. "The Bathtub Courtmartial." *New York Historical Quarterly* 50, no. 3 (1966): 281–297.

7th Regiment of Infantry

Raised: April 12, 1808
Recruited: Eddyville and Hopkinsville, Kentucky

Battle Honors

1812: Fort Harrison, Lake Peoria Expedition
1814: Prairie du Chien, Rock River, Villere's Plantation
1815: New Orleans, Fort St. Philip

As a part of the pre-war military establishment, the 7th Regiment of Infantry was recruited, trained and deployed in Louisiana and was occupying numerous western posts when hostilities commenced. On September 4–5, 1812, Captain Zachary Taylor, a future president, skillfully defended Fort Harrison, Indiana Territory, from a large Indian attack. His small detachment lost two dead and two injured. Colonel William Russell subsequently rounded up several companies of rangers, mounted riflemen, and his own soldiers to launch a large raid against Pimartam's Town on the shores of Lake Peoria. They attacked on November 11, 1812. Little resistance was encountered, the village was burned, and the expedition returned safely. In June 1814, General Benjamin Howard led 60 soldiers of the 7th Regiment up the Mississippi River and established Fort Shelby in the Wisconsin Territory. This post was rapidly surrounded by British and Indian forces, so Major Taylor was ordered to relieve the garrison if possible. He assembled 350 soldiers and rangers in eight boats and rowed up as far as Rock River where, on September 4, 1814, they were attacked by large numbers of Indians and three British cannon. Taylor, whose boat was holed, retreated back downstream with 11 wounded; Fort Shelby surrendered to the British.

The bulk of the 7th Regiment's manpower remained in Louisiana throughout the war, and for many months it garrisoned such diverse locations such as New Orleans, Baton Rouge, Mobile, and Pass Christian. In the fall of 1814, it joined General Andrew Jackson's main force and on December 23, 1814, fought conspicuously at the night battle of Villere's Plantation, losing seven dead and 28 wounded. The company of Lieutenant McClelland initiated the conflict by charging through the De la Ronde Gate and driving British pickets back. The Americans then withdrew to a defensive line along the Rodriguez Canal and on January 1, 1815, the 7th Regiment helped repel a British reconnaissance in force, losing one wounded. Throughout the memorable battle on January 8, 1815, the 7th regiment occupied a line between batteries No. 1 and 2 on the right flank, repelled a determined attack by Colonel Rennie, and suffered two killed and one wounded. Immediately afterwards, the companies of Captains Narcissus Broutin and William Wade, then garrisoning Fort St. Phillip below the city, were bombarded by the British sloops HMS *Herald*, *Sophia*, and two bomb vessels from January 9–18, suffering two wounded. In May 1815, the 7th Regiment was combined with the 2nd, 3rd, and 44th Regiments to form the new 1st U.S. Infantry.

Promotions

Captain Zachary Taylor, brevet major. September 5, 1812. Gallant Conduct in the defense of Fort Stephenson.

3rd Lieutenant Joseph Leach, brevet 2nd lieutenant. December 23, 1814. Gallant conduct during New Orleans.

Captain George C. Allen, brevet major. January 8, 1815. Gallant conduct during the siege of New Orleans.

Captain Elijah Montgomery, brevet major. January 8, 1815. Gallant conduct during the siege of New Orleans.

Captain Samuel Vail, brevet major. January 8, 1815. Gallant conduct during the siege of New Orleans.

Archival

RG98, No. 428/325. Orderly book. National Archives. Unidentified, 1813–1815.
RG98, No. 95. Orderly book. National Archives. Unidentified, 1813–1815.
RG98, No. 378/262. Orderly book. National Archives. Unidentified, 1813–1815.
RG98, No. 372/256. Orderly book. National Archives. Capt. Richard Oldham, 1812, 1814.
RG98, No. 100. Orderly book. National Archives. Capt. Richard Oldham, 1812, 1814.
RG98, No. 486/387. Orderly book. National Archives. Capt. Samuel Vail, 1814–1815.
RG98, No. 96. Orderly book. National Archives. Capt. Samuel Vail, 1814–1815.
RG98, No. 375/259. Orderly book. National Archives. Capt. Wm McClellan, 1813–1814.
RG98, No. 370/253. Orderly book. National Archives. Unidentified company, 1812–1814.
RG98, No. 374/258. Orderly book. National Archives. Unidentified company, 1812–1814.
RG98, No. 97. Orderly book. National Archives. Unidentified company, 1812–1814.
RG98, No. 371/255. Orderly book. National Archives. Unidentified company, 1812–1814.
RG98, No. 373/257. Orderly book. National Archives. Unidentified company, 1812–1814.
RG98, No. 376/260. Orderly book. National Archives. Unidentified company, 1812–1814.
RG98, No. 214/76. Company book. National Archives. Capt. James Doherty, 1813–1815.
RG98, No. 213/75. Company book. National Archives. Capt. Walter H. Overton, 1811–1815.
RG98, No. 425/312. Morning reports. National Archives. Various.
RG98, No. 355/254. Morning reports. National Archives. Various.
RG98, No. 377/261. Morning reports. National Archives. Various.
RG98, No. 379/263. Morning reports. National Archives. Various.

Manuscript

Baughman, John. Diary. U.S. Army Military. War of 1812 Misc, 1812–1814.
Jesup, Thomas S. Papers. Library of Congress. 0318C, Detroit memoranda; 1812–1813.
Kercheval, Samuel. Muster roll. Ohio Historical. March, 1813.

Russell, William. Letters. Alabama Department. SGO13378, Folder 17.
Russell, William. Letters. Indiana Historical. M98; William H. English Coll.
Russell, William. Letters. Indiana State. L127, V91, Box4–5; Lasselle Family Papers.
Russell, William. Letters. Library of Congress. Andrew Jackson Papers; 1813–1815.
Russell, William. Letter, 1814. Library of Congress. William Henry Harrison papers.
Taylor, Zachary. Letters. Kentucky Historical. 1812–1815.
Taylor, Zachary. Letter, 1813. Gilder Lehrman. GLC00040; mentions Fort Meigs, York.
Taylor, Zachary. Letter, 1812. Indiana Historical. SC2161; Fort Harrison.
Taylor, Zachary. Letters. Library of Congress. 0506E Zachary Taylor Papers; 1814.
Taylor, Zachary. Letters. Missouri Historical. A1250 President's Collection; 1814–1815.
Taylor, Zachary. Letters. William T. Young. 1VF87M17; 1812–1814.

Printed Primary

Taylor, Zachary. "Letter of General Zachary Taylor, November 9, 1812." *Collector* 22 (April 1909): 62.

Select Secondary

Bauer, K. Jack. *Zachary Taylor: Soldier, Planter, and Statesman of the Old Southwest.* Baton Rouge: Louisiana State University Press, 1985.
Bennett, David C. "Fort Harrison under Siege—1812." *Journal of America's Military Past* 25, no. 2 (Fall 1998) 19–28.
Kieffer, Chester L. *Maligned General: The Biography of Thomas Sidney Jesup.* San Rafael, Calif.: Presidio Press, 1979.
Meese, William A. "Credit Island, 1814–1914." *Illinois State Historical Society Journal* 7 (January 1915): 348–373.

8th Regiment of Infantry

Raised: January 11, 1812
Recruited: Fort Hawkins, Georgia, North Carolina, South Carolina; Georgia

Battle Honors

Not engaged

The 8th Regiment of Infantry was raised in the South and spent its entire service life garrisoning strategic points along the coast, including Beaufort, South Carolina, and Savannah, Georgia. Its mettle was never tested in combat and in May, 1815, it was consolidated with the 10th, 36th, and 38th Regiments to form the new 7th U.S. Infantry. Ironically, its most noted alumnus, Captain David Emanuel Twiggs, remained a career army officer and rose to brigadier general by 1861, and gained notoriety by tamely surrendering all U.S. Installations in Texas to Confederate authorities.

Archival

RG94, Roll 21. Letters. National Archives. William C. Cumming, 1813–1814.
RG94, Roll 28. Letters. National Archives. Lawrence Manning, 1812–1813.
Jones, William. Orderly Book. Georgia Department. 1812–1815.

Manuscript

Anderson, William P. Records. Alabama Department. Weekly report, 1812.
Jones, William. Letters. Georgia Historical. Ms 448, William Jones Papers; recruiting.
Pinder, Joseph W. Papers. Georgia Historical. Ms 620; military supplies.

Printed Primary

Fredriksen, John C., ed. "A Georgian Officer in the War of 1812: The Letters of William Clay Cumming." *Georgia Historical Quarterly* 71 (Winter 1987): 668–692.

Select Secondary

Heidler, Jeanne T. "The Military Career of David Emanuel Twiggs." Unpublished Ph.D. dissertation, Auburn University, 1988.

9th Regiment of Infantry

Raised: June 26, 1812
Recruited: Boston and Pittsfield, Massachusetts, and New Hampshire

Battle Honors

1813: Sacketts Harbor, Crysler's Farm
1814: Chippewa, Lundy's Lane, Fort Erie

After recruiting, the 9th Regiment of Infantry marched to Plattsburgh, New York, as part of General John Chandler's brigade, and wintered there. The following spring it marched to Sacketts Harbor and was in the act of arriving when British forces attacked on May 29, 1813. Several canoe-loads of men were captured on Lake Ontario, but Major Thomas Aspinwall escaped with several companies and occupied a line of block houses in the enemy's path. His recruits then defied all British attempts to evict them and, in con-

Henry Leavenworth, 9th Infantry. Frontier Army Museum, Fort Leavenworth, Kansas.

cert with the 1st Light Dragoons under Captain Arthur P. Hayne, were largely responsible for saving Sacketts Harbor from capture. Its casualties here are not recorded. The unit remained at Sacketts Harbor until the fall, when it joined General Leonard Covington's 3rd Brigade and participated in the St. Lawrence Campaign of General James Wilkinson. The 9th was heavily engaged at Crysler's Farm on November 11, 1813 and, while its losses are not known, paymaster Captain David S. Townsend was wounded and captured. After wintering at French Mills, New York, the regiment slogged overland to

Buffalo New York, under Major Henry Leavenworth. There it became part of General Winfield Scott's 1st Brigade and underwent intense training. Leavenworth, bolstered by several companies of the 22nd Regiment of Infantry, then fought at the Battle of Chippawa, July 5, 1814, contributing to the victory and losing 13 killed and 45 wounded. Three weeks later the regiment was in the thick of fighting at Lundy's Lane, July 25, 1814, where it lost an additional 16 killed, 90 wounded, and 13 missing. Among the slain was Captain Abraham Fuller Hull, son of the disgraced General William Hull. The 9th Regiment was present throughout the siege of Fort Erie, losing one wounded during the nighttime attack of August 15, 1814, and eight dead and 24 wounded during the sortie of September 17, 1814. British bombardments accounted for another eight killed and 17 wounded. The unit subsequently marched back to Sacketts Harbor in the middle of winter and, in May, 1815, it was amalgamated with the 4th, 13th, 21st, 40th, and 46th Regiments to form the new 5th U.S. Infantry.

Promotions

Captain Turner Crooker, brevet major. July 4, 1814. Gallant conduct in repelling a charge of British dragoons.

Major Henry Leavenworth, brevet lieutenant colonel. July 5, 1814. Distinguished services at the Battle of Chippawa.

Captain Thomas J. Harrison, brevet major. July 5, 1814. Gallant conduct — Battle of Chippawa.

Brevet Lieutenant Colonel Henry Leavenworth, brevet colonel. July 25, 1814. Gallant conduct — Battle of Niagara.

1st Lieutenant Joseph Gleason, brevet captain. August 15, 1814. Gallant conduct in the defense of Fort Erie.

Lieutenant Colonel Thomas Aspinwall, brevet colonel. September 17, 1814. Gallant conduct, Fort Erie sortie.

Ensign Patrick O'Flyng, brevet 2nd Lieutenant. August 15, 1814. Distinguished conduct in defense of Fort Erie.

Brevet 2nd Lieutenant Patrick O'Flyng, brevet 1st lieutenant. September 17, 1814. Gallant conduct, Fort Erie sortie.

Archival

RG94, Roll 12. Letters. National Archives. Henry Leavenworth, 1814–1815.

RG98, No. 219/80B. Company book. National Archives. George Bender/Samuel Allen, 1813–1815.

RG98, No. 224/83B. Company book. National Archives. Lieut. David Chandler, 1814–1815.

RG98, No. 222/82. Company Book. National Archives. Capt. William L. Foster, 1814.

RG98, No. 221/81B. Company book. National Archives. Capt. Abraham F. Hull, 1814.
RG98, No. 220/81A. Company book. National Archives. Abraham F. Hull/Moses Hoit, 1812–1815.
RG98, 218/80A. Enlistments. National Archives. Capt. Chester Lyman, 1812–1813.
9th U. S. Infantry. Paymaster. Portsmouth Athenaeum. S0694; subsistence, forage, clothing.

Manuscript

Aspinwall, Thomas. Letter, 1813. New York Public. Townsend-Gerry Papers; Crysler's Field.
Carr, Robert. Letter, 1813. Boston Public. *Ch.C.11.3; Fort Ontario.
Carr, Robert. Diary. Historical Society (Pa.). 1812–1813.
Leavenworth, Henry. Letter, 1815. Library of Congress. Thomas S. Jesup Papers; Lundy's Lane.
Leavenworth, Henry. Letter, 1814. New York State. Charles K. Gardner Papers; Lundy's Lane.
Townsend, David S. Papers. New York Public. Townsend-Gerry Papers; St. Lawrence.

Printed Primary

Bates, George C. "Reminiscences of the Brady Guards." *Michigan Pioneer* 13 (1888): 530–546.
Cruikshank, Ernest A., ed. *Documentary History of the Campaigns Upon the Niagara Frontier*. 9 vols. Welland, Ont.: Tribune Press, 1896–1908. Vol. 9, 335–343. [Lieutenant Colonel Henry Leavenworth's letter]
Hurd, D. Hamilton. *History of Norfolk County, Massachusetts*. Philadelphia: J. W. Lewis, 1884, 864–865. [Lieutenant Colonel Thomas Aspinwall letter, 1814]

Select Secondary

Brown, Fred R. *History of the Ninth U. S. Infantry, 1789–1909*. Chicago: R. R. Donnelley, 1909.
Parker, Henry S. "Henry Leavenworth, Pioneer General." *Military Review* 50 (December 1970): 56–68.
Smith, C. Charles. "Memoir of Colonel Thomas Aspinwall." *Massachusetts Historical Society Proceedings* 3 (November 1891): 30–38.
Wilder, Patrick A. *The Battle of Sacketts Harbor, 1813*. Baltimore: Nautical and Aviation Publishing, 1994.

10th Regiment of Infantry

Raised: January 11, 1812
Recruited: Wilkesboro, North Carolina

Battle Honors

1813: Chateauguay
1814: La Colle Mill

The 10th Regiment of Infantry was authorized to raise two battalions, although both remained consistently under-strength during the war years. Several elements performed garrison duty along the Virginia, Georgia, and Carolina coasts for a year before a battalion-sized unit mustered at Norfolk under Lieutenant Colonel Duncan L. Clinch and hiked northwards. The unit reached Burlington, Vermont, as part of General Wade Hampton's division and took post with General George Izard's brigade. Thus situated, it fought at Chateauguay on October 26, 1813, before wintering at Plattsburgh, New York. The extreme northern clime played havoc on the Southerners and the 10th proved to be an extremely sickly formation. The following spring only a detachment was present at La Colle Mill on March 30, 1814, before the unit proceeded back to Plattsburgh for reassignment as part of General Thomas Adams Smith's Light Brigade. In the late summer of 1814, the 10th Regiment accompanied General Izard's march from Plattsburgh to the Niagara Frontier, and while it was present during the bombardment of British positions at Chippawa Creek, the unit saw no further combat. After wintering at Black Rock, New York, the 10th Regiment was consolidated with the 8th, 36th and 38th Regiments to form the new 7th U.S. Infantry. Little is known of the activities of the 2nd battalion, save for periodic appearances at Richmond and Baltimore throughout 1813.

Archival

RG94, Roll 24. Letters. National Archives. William S. Hamilton, 1813–1814.
RG98, No. 225/84. Company book. National Archives. Capt. George Vashon, 1813–1815.

Manuscript

Atkinson, Henry. Letter, 1813. Historical Society (PA). Dreer Collection; to Wade Hampton.
Atkinson, Henry. Letter, 1814. Southern Historical. No. 805, Bartlett Yancey Papers.
Hamilton, William S. Papers. Hill Library. Mss 1029.3167; 1812–1813.
Hamilton, William S. Papers. Southern Historical. 1471; 1812–1813.
McKinzie, A. R. Letter, 1814. Southern Historical. 578, Jones-Patterson Papers; Chippawa.
Pickens, Andrew. Letter, 1813. South Carolina Historical. 43/465; conditions in East Florida.

Printed Primary

Keith, Alice B., and William H. Masterson, eds. *The Papers of John Gray Blount.* 4 vols. Raleigh: North Carolina Department of History and Archives, 1952–1984. Vol. 4, 219. [Lieutenant John G. Blount letter, 1813]

Select Secondary

Lemmon, Sarah M. *Frustrated Patriots: North Carolina and the War of 1812.* Chapel Hill: University of North Carolina Press, 1973.

Patrick, Rembert W. *Aristocrat in Uniform: General Duncan L. Clinch.* Gainesville: University of Florida, 1963.

11th Regiment of Infantry

Raised: January 11, 1812
Recruited: Bennington, Vermont

Battle Honors

1813: Crysler's Farm
1814: La Colle Mill, Chippewa, Lundy's Lane, Fort Erie

The 11th Infantry Regiment was authorized to recruit two battalions which were initially stationed at Burlington in their native state. There they functioned as part of General John Chandler's brigade until the spring of 1813, when the 1st Battalion proceeded to Sacketts Harbor, New York, as part of General Robert Swartwout's 4th Brigade. Meanwhile, the 2nd Battalion, which remained at Burlington, was understrength and temporarily merged with the 29th Regiment of Colonel Melancton Smith. This composite unit accompanied General Wade Hampton's ill-fated foray into Lower Canada and was present at Chateauguay on October 26, 1813. The unit subsequently wintered at Plattsburgh, New York, before fighting at La Colle Mill on March 30, 1814, with Colonel Isaac Clark's consolidated formation. In April 1814, the remainder of both battalions finally united at Buffalo, New York, as part of General Winfield Scott's 1st Brigade. On July 5, 1814, they advanced into combat on the plains of Chippawa under Colonel John B. Campbell until he fell severely wounded, then Major John McNeil took over. They fought fiercely in close combat, losing 15 dead and 65 wounded. Three weeks later at Lundy's Lane, July 25, 1814, McNeil had his kneecap shot out by canister while the 11th Regiment temporarily broke under intense artillery fire, then rallied. They suffered an additional 28 killed, 103 wounded, and 12 missing in the biggest stand up engagement of the war. The

John McNeil, 11th Infantry. Collections of the State of New Hampshire, Division of Historical Resources.

survivors next served in the defense of Fort Erie under Lieutenant Colonel Moody Bedel, sustaining three dead and 10 wounded in the night attack of August 15, 1814, and four dead and 25 wounded during the sortie of September 17, 1814. The British bombardment also inflicted an additional nine killed and 39 wounded. In the winter of 1814, the 11th Regiment made an overland march back to Sacketts Harbor and, in May, 1815, it was consolidated with the 25th, 27th, 29th, and 37th Regiments to form the new 6th U.S. Infantry.

Promotions

Major John McNeil, brevet lieutenant colonel. July 5, 1814. Distinguished services at the Battle of Chippawa.

Brevet Lieutenant Colonel John McNeil, brevet colonel. July 25, 1814. Gallant conduct — Battle of Niagara.

1st Lieutenant Newman S. Clarke, brevet captain. July 25, 1814. Gallant conduct — Battle of Niagara.

Captain William S. Foster, brevet major. August 15, 1814. Gallant conduct in the defense of Fort Erie.

Archival

RG94, Roll 39. Letters. National Archives. Col. John B. Campbell, 1814.
RG98, No. 234/91. Company book. National Archives. Richard Bean/Malachi Corning, 1813–1814.
RG98, No. 231/90A. Company book. National Archives. Capt. John Bliss, 1813–1814.
RG98, No. 233/90C. Company book. National Archives. Capt. John Bliss, 1813–1814.
RG98, No. 235/92. Company book. National Archives. Capt. William Foster, 1814–1815.
RG98, No. 232/90B. Company book. National Archives. V. R. Goodrich/John Bliss, 1812–1814.
RG98, No. 161. Company book. National Archives. Capt. Samuel Gordon, 1812–1813.
RG98, No. 229/87. Company book. National Archives. Joseph Griswold/Wm. S. Foster, 1812–1815.
RG98, No. 230/88. Company book. National Archives. Capt. Benjamin Snead, 1812–1815.
RG98, No. 227/86. Company book. National Archives. Capt. John W. Weeks, 1812–1814.
RG98, No. 228/86. Company book. National Archives. John W. Weeks/Malachi Corning, 1814.
RG153, K-4. Court martial. National Archives. Blake, Henry J.
McNeil, John. Orderly book. New Hampshire. French Mills; 1813–1814.

Manuscript

Bedell, Moody. Letters. Lilly Library. 1814.
Bedell, Moody. Orders. Maine Historical. Coll. 1555, John M. Fogg Papers; 1812.
Bedell, Moody. Letters. New Hampshire. Bedell Family Papers.
Bliss, John. Letter, 1813. U.S. Military Academy. David Crawford Papers; Sacketts Harbor.
Clark, Isaac. Papers. Bailey/Howe Library. Wilbur Collection; 1812–1815, Champlain.
Clark, Isaac. Letter, 1813. Massachusetts Historical. C.E. French, Folder 6; Burlington, Vt.
Clark, Isaac. Letters. New York Historical. Henry Dearborn letter books; 1812–1813.
Crawford, David. Letter, 1843. Vermont Historical. Battle of Chippewa to John McNeil; 1843.

McNeil, John. Letters. Library of Congress. Benham-McNeil Papers.
McNeil, John. Letters. New York Historical.
McNeil, John. Letters. New Hampshire. 1814.
Sawyer, James S. Letters. Library of Congress. Horace B. Sawyer Papers; 1812–1814.
Sheldon, Walter. Papers. Vermont State Archives. Henry Stevens, Sr., Collection; 1812–1815.
Sheldon, Walter. Papers. Sheldon Museum. Walter Sheldon Papers, paymaster.
Staniford, Thomas. Letters. New York Historical. Misc Mss Staniford, Burlington; 1812–1813.
Weeks, John W. Letters. Rauner Library. ML-1, Weeks Family Papers; 1812–1814.
Weeks, John W. Letters. New Hampshire. Hibbard Collection; 1812–1814.
Weeks, John W. Letters. U.S. Army Military. E361.W44 1937, transcripts; 1814.

Printed Primary

Ellis, Arthur B., ed. "Letter of John W. Blake Describing the Battle of Lundy's Lane." *Massachusetts Historical Society Proceedings* 26 (January 1891): 257–259.
"Garrison Orders; Burlington, Vermont, July 13–August 4, 1813." *Moorsfield Antiquarian* 1 (August 1937): 79–103.
Hemenway, Abby B. *Vermont Historical Gazette*. 5 vols. Burlington: A. M. Hemenway, 1887. Vol. 1, 574–581. [Private John Price]
Parker, Wilmond W., ed. "Letters of the War of 1812 in the Champlain Valley." *Vermont Quarterly* 12 (April 1944): 104–124. [Private A. G. Cogswell]
Peach, Arthur W., ed. "War of 1812." *Vermont Quarterly* 21 (January 1953): 48–51. [Sergeant Jesse P. Harmon letters]
Smith, Lester W., ed. "A Drummer Boy in the War of 1812: The Memoirs of Jarvis Frary Hanks." *Niagara Frontier* 7 (Summer 1960): 53–62.

Select Secondary

Biography of General John McNeil. N.p., N.d.
Doan, Daniel. "The Enigmatic Moody Bedell." *Historical New Hampshire* 25 (Fall 1970): 27–36.
Sites, Karen A. "Isaac Clark of Castleton: A Controversial Figure in Early Vermont History." Undergraduate thesis, University of Vermont, 1987. Typescript at Vermont Historical Society Archives.

12th Regiment of Infantry

Raised: January 29, 1812
Recruited: Staunton, Virginia, and Maryland

Battle Honors

1813: French Creek, Crysler's Farm
1814: La Colle Mill, Odletown, Bladensburg

The 12th Regiment of Infantry completed its recruitment and arrived along the Niagara Frontier in late fall of 1812. Colonel Thomas Parker then directed its operations during General Alexander Smyth's botched Niagara River crossing to Frenchman's Creek on November 28, 1812, although losses are not recorded. It was subsequently brigaded with the 20th Regiment of Infantry over the winter, which they passed at Williamsville. The 12th remained inactive at Niagara until May 27, 1813, when Lieutenant Colonel James P. Preston led it across back the Niagara River and captured recently evacuated Fort Erie without a shot. That fall the 12th Regiment transferred to Sacketts Harbor to join General John P. Boyd's 1st Brigade in anticipation of joining General James Wilkinson's St. Lawrence Campaign. The unit fought at Crysler's Farm on November 11, 1813, although losses are not recorded, and it wintered again at French Mills, New York. A small detachment of the regiment was also present at La Colle Mill, Lower Canada, on March 30, 1814, then the entire regiment marched to Plattsburgh to serve in General Thomas Adams Smith's Light Brigade at Chazy. On June 28, 1814, a detachment, fighting as light infantry, participated in a heavy skirmish at Odletown, Lower Canada, where celebrated raider Lieutenant Colonel Benjamin Forsyth was killed. The 12th Regiment next accompanied General George Izard's march from Plattsburgh to the Niagara Frontier in August 1814, although it saw no additional combat. However, a company of 80 men under Captain Morgan was present at Bladensburg, Maryland, on August 24, 1814, and a detachment also endured the bombardment of Fort McHenry on September 13, 1814. In May, 1815, the 12th Regiment was consolidated with the 5th, 18th, and 35th Regiments to form the new 8th U.S. Infantry.

Promotions

Major Alexander A. White, brevet lieutenant colonel. December 23, 1814. Gallant conduct during New Orleans.

Archival

Paxton, James. Orderly Book. Library of Congress. 0314, Peter Force Papers; 1813–1815.
RG94, Roll 13. Letters. National Archives. Thomas P. Moore, 1812–1814.
RG94, Roll 15. Letters. National Archives. Joseph Shommo, 1812, 1815.
RG98, No. 243/98B. Orderly book. National Archives. Capt. A. L. Madison, 1813–1814.

RG98, No. 240/96. Company book. National Archives. James Charlton/Thom. Sangster, 1813–1815.
RG98, No. 242/98A. Company book. National Archives. Capt. Andrew Madison, 1812–1815.
RG98, No. 244/99A. Company book. National Archives. Capt. Thomas Moore, 1813–1814.
RG98, No. 239/95. Company book. National Archives. Capt. James Paxton, 1812–1815.
RG98, No. 236/93A. Company book. National Archives. Capt. Thomas Post, 1813–1815.
RG98, No. 237/93B. Company book. National Archives. Capt. Thomas Post, 1814–1815.
RG98, No.241/97. Company Book. National Archives. Capt. Thomas Sangster, 1815.
RG98, No. 245/99B. Company book. National Archives. Capt. Lewis B. Willis, 1814–1815.
12th U. S. Infantry. Orderly book. Owen D. Young. Mss. Coll. 132, Box 2.1; March–July, 1814.

Manuscript

Campbell, David. Papers. Perkins Library. Niagara and St. Lawrence; 1812–1814.
Campbell, David. Letters. Wisconsin Historical. Draper 10DD.
Campbell, David. Letters. Massachusetts Historical. Thomas Jefferson Papers; 1812–1813.
Coles, Isaac A. Letters. Chicago Historical. Edward Coles Papers; 1812–1814.
Coles, Isaac A. Letters. Tennessee State. War of 1812 Collection.
Coles, Isaac A. Papers. Virginia Historical.
Preston, James P. Letters. Virginia Historical. Mss1 P9267 d 7-255 (A-L); 1812–1813.
Preston, James P. Letters. Virginia Historical. Mss1 P9267 d 7-255 (M-W); 1812–1813.
Preston, James P. Letter, 1813. Virginia Historical. Mss1 P9267 D 271-274; protests Coles.
Strother, John. Minutes. Library of Congress. U. S. Army Coll., court martial, 1815.
Wager, Philip. Diary. Library of Congress. Misc. Mss., St. Lawrence; 1812–1814.

Printed Primary

Coles, Isaac A. *Letters &c. Published by Isaac A. Coles, Colonel of the 12th Regiment, Concerning His Arrangement for Trial Before a Military Court in September, 1814.* Washington, D. C., N. p., 1814.
Coles, Isaac A. *Mr. President and Gentlemen of the Court: I stand Before you Charged with Crimes....* N.p., 1813.
A Sketch of the Life of Lieut. Mathew Hughes, Late of the United States Army, Serving on the Niagara Frontier During the Late War Between This Country and Great Britain. Alexandria, Va.: J. Course, N. Rounsavell, 1815.

Select Secondary

Runge, William H. "Isaac A. Coles." *Albemarle County Historical Society Papers* 14 (1954–1955): 49–60.

13th Regiment of Infantry

Raised: January 11, 1812
Recruited: Albany, New York

Battle Honors

1812: Queenston Heights, French Creek
1813: Fort George, Crysler's Farm
1814: La Colle Mill, Plattsburgh

The first combat elements of the 13th Regiment of Infantry were conducted to the Niagara Frontier in the early fall of 1812 by Colonel Philip P. Schuyler. Several companies under Lieutenant Colonel John Chrystie next participated in the disastrous Battle of Queenston Heights on October 13, 1812. Chrystie managed to ferry over nearly 300 men in 11 boats and most of these were captured, although Captain John E. Wool's company successfully stormed a British battery. Additional losses were incurred during General Alexander Smyth's abortive Niagara River crossing to Frenchman's Creek on November 28, 1812. The survivors were subsequently attached to the 5th Regiment of Infantry over the winter, which was spent at Williamsville, New York. The following spring several detachments fought at the storming of Fort George, May 27, 1813, at which post it also served as a garrison unit. It was then reassigned as part of General William H. Winder's brigade during the advance to Stoney Creek, but missed that battle on June 6, 1813, by being detached to the lake shore, three miles distant, to guard boats and stores. Chrystie next sortied from Fort George in an attempt to save American forces trapped at Beaver Dams on June 24, 1813, but withdrew after perceiving their surrender. On July 8, 1813, disaster struck again when a picket under Lieutenant Joseph C. Elbridge was cut off and massacred by Indians with a loss of 12 dead and three wounded. That fall, the 13th Regiment ventured to Sacketts Harbor where it became part of General John P. Boyd's 1st Brigade. It then sailed down the St. Lawrence River as part of General James Wilkinson's Montreal expedition and fought at Crysler's Farm on November 11, 1813. Its losses have not been recorded but it is known that the company of Cap-

John Chrystie, 13th Infantry. Frick Art Reference Library.

tain Mordecai Myers lost 23 men out of 89 present. After wintering at French Mills, New York, the unit proceeded to Plattsburgh and, on March 30, 1814, it fought again at La Colle Mill on March 30, 1814, losing six men wounded. Afterwards it formed part of General Alexander Macomb's brigade at Plattsburgh, until it was reassigned to General Thomas Adam Smith's brigade and accompanied his march to Niagara in late summer. The 13th Regiment ended the war posted at Sacketts Harbor to bolster the garrison and saw no further combat. However, a company under Captain John Sproull remained behind at Plattsburgh and fought capably at Beekmantown Road on September 6, 1814, suffering, three dead and six wounded. In May 1815, it was amalgamated with the 25th, 27th, 29th, and 37th Regiment to form the new 6th U.S. Infantry.

Archival

RG98, No. 247/101. Company book. National Archives. Capt. William Adams, 1814–1815.
RG98, 246/100. Company Book. National Archives. Capt. Myndert M. Dox, 1813–1815.
RG98, No. 251/105A. Company book. National Archives. Capt. Stephen Kearny, 1814–1815.
RG98, No. 252/105B. Company book. National Archives. Capt. Stephen Kearny, 1814–1815.
RG98, No. 248/102. Company book. National Archives. Capt. John K. Paige, 1814–1815.
Dox, Myndert M. Muster roll. New York Historical. BV War of 1812; 1812–1813.
13th U. S. Infantry. Orderly book. Owen D. Young. Mss. Coll. 132; Box. 2.1; March–July, 1814.
Martin, Hugh K. Muster rolls. U.S. Military Academy. 1812–1813.

Manuscript

Chrystie, John. Vouchers. Georgia Department. AC55-101M, Few Collection; 1812–1813.
Chrystie, John. Letters. Mudd Library. Microfilm 10821.254; 1812–1813.
Chrystie, John. Letters. New York Historical. Albert Gallatin Papers, Queenston, 1812.
Chrystie, John. Letters. Oberlin College. Nos. 11, 21, Orrin June Coll.; 1812–1813.
Claude, John. Letter, 1815. Clements Library. War of 1812 Collection.
Dox, Mynery M. Issuances. Feinberg Library. Records books; 1813–1815.
Myers, Mordecai. Letters. Clements Library. Myers–Mason–Baily Papers.
Myers, Mordecai. Papers. Clements Library. 1812–1814.
Reab, John. Letters. Perkins Library. Walter L. Sutton Papers; parole matters.
Schuyler, Peter P. Letters. Maine Historical. No. 33, Henry Dearborn Papers; 1812–1813.
Wool, John E. Letter, 1812. Buffalo and Erie. A64-286, Queenston Heights.
Wool, John E. Papers. New York State. 15361, John E. Wool Papers, 1812–1814.
Wool, John E. Letters. Feinberg Library. 1814.

Printed Primary

Armstrong, John. *Notices of the War of 1812*. 2 vols. New York: G. Dearborn, 1836–1840. Vol. 2, 207–219. [Lieutenant Colonel John Christie letter, October 13, 1812]

"The Battle of Queenston Heights, By An Officer in the Army." *United Service Journal* 2 (May 1851): 161–164.

Fredriksen, John C., ed. "'Plough-joggers for Generals': The Experiences of a New York Ensign in the War of 1812." *Indiana Magazine of History* 11 (October 1986): 16–27. [Ensign Joseph Hawley Dwight]

Myers, Mordecai. *Reminiscences, 1780–1814, Including Incidents in the War of 1812–14.* Washington, D. C.: Crane Press, 1900.

St. Denis, Guy. "Robert Walcot: The Man Who Could Not Possibly Have Shot General Brock." *Journal of the Society for Army Historical Research* 83, no. 336 (2005): 280–290.

Wool, John E. "The Battle of Queenston." *Historical Magazine* 2 (November 1867): 283–285.

Wool, John E. "Major General John Ellis Wool to W. L. Stone on the Battle of Queenston Heights, October, 1812." *New York Public Library Bulletin* 9 (April 1905): 120–122.

Select Secondary

Clarke, Dwight L. *Stephen Watts Kearny: Soldier of the West.* Norman: University of Oklahoma Press, 1961.

Hinton, Harwood P. "The Military Career of John Ellis Wool." Unpublished Ph.D. dissertation, University of Wisconsin, 1960.

McAlexander, Ulysses G. *History of the Thirteenth Regiment, United States Infantry.* N.p., 1905.

14th Regiment of Infantry

Raised: January 11, 1812
Recruited: Baltimore, Maryland, Virginia

Battle Honors

1812: Fort Niagara, French Creek
1813: Fort George, Beaver Dams, Crysler's Farm
1814: La Colle Mills, Cooks Mills

The 14th Regiment of infantry spent nearly nine months recruiting and training before it arrived on the Niagara Frontier under Colonel William H. Winder. On November 21, a small detachment was present during the British bombardment of Fort Niagara, and seven days later Colonel Winder participated in the aborted Niagara River crossing of General Alexander Smyth. In confused fighting along Frenchman's Creek, the regiment lost six killed and 22 wounded. After wintering at Black Rock, New York, the 14th Regiment was brigaded with the 12th and 20th Regiments, and subsequently fought at

Isaac D. Barnard, 14th Infantry. Chester County Historical Society.

the capture of Fort George on May 27, 1813. The following month it joined newly-promoted General William H. Winder's brigade and advanced to Stoney Creek. However, it was detached from the main force lake to guard boats and stores along the lakefront, so missed the heavy fighting there. However, the unit suffered a major disaster when Lieutenant Colonel Charles G. Boerstler led nearly a force of 460 men out from Fort George (including 332 from the 14th) and directly into a snare set for them at Beaver Dams. Apparently, American plans had been overheard by Canadian heroine Laura Secord, who walked several miles through the wilderness to alert British authorities.

On June 24, 1813, Boerstler was obliged to surrender his men and regimental flag to inferior numbers of British troops and Indian allies. Other detachments remained at Sacketts Harbor where, in the fall, they formed part of General Robert Swartwout's 4th Brigade. These fought at Crysler's Farm on November 11, 1813 (casualties are not recorded) then spent an arduous winter at French Mills, New York. The 14th Regiment subsequently fought again at La Colle Mill on March 30, 1814, before marching on to Plattsburgh as part of General Daniel Bissell's brigade. In late summer the regiment accompanied General George Izard's march to the Niagara Frontier, and on October 15, 1814, it lost one man wounded during the bombardment of the Chippawa River. Four days later Bissell was directed to outflank British positions along the river, which culminated in a small but intense clash at Cook's Mills on October 19, 1814. Here Major Isaac D. Barnard led his men on a spectacular frontal charge, suffering seven dead and 19 wounded, which partially induced the British to withdraw. The unit next wintered at Niagara and in May 1815, was consolidated with the 12th and 20th Regiments to form the new 4th U.S. Infantry.

Archival

RG98, No. 253/106. Company book. National Archives. Capt. Samuel Lanes, 1812–1815.
RG153, G-9. Court martial. National Archives. Colonel Charles G. Boerstler.

Manuscript

Carr, Robert. Diary. Historical Society (Pa). Oswego, St. Lawrence; 1812–1813.
Barnard, Isaac D. Letters. Burton Historical. Letter fragments, 1812–1814; Plattsburgh.
Barnard, Isaac D. Letter, 1814. Oberlin College. No. 63, Orrin June Collection; Cook's Mills.
Gilder, Reuben. Papers. McKeldin Library. Postwar complaints; 1815.
Gilder, Reuben,. Letter, 1815. New York State. 160; prisoners of war.
Grindage, Henry. Letters. Minnesota Historical. A H396, Box 1, Hawley Family; 1812–1814.
Randall, Thomas. Letters. Maryland Historical. Ms. 1912; 1813–1814.
Winder, William H. Letter, 1813. Historical Society (Pa). Townsend-LeMaistre Coll., officer duties.
Winder, William H. Regt. Orders. Maryland Historical. 1813.

Printed Primary

Barry, F. W. "Captured Flags in the Royal Hospital, Chelsea." *Journal of the Society of Army Historical Research* 7 (1929): 110–117.
Chapin, Cyrenius. *Chapin's Review of Armstrong's Notices of the War of 1812*. Black Rock, N.Y.: D. P. Adams, 1836.

Dix, Morgan, ed. *The Memoirs of John Adams Dix.* 2 vols. New York: Harper and Bros., 1853. Vol. 1, 38–56.

Winder, William H. *Statement of Occurrences on the Niagara Frontier in 1812.* Washington, D. C., Duff Green, 1829.

15th Regiment of Infantry

Raised: January 11, 1812
Recruited: Trenton, New Jersey

Battle Honors

1813: York, Fort George, Frenchman's Creek, Crysler's Farm
1814: La Colle Mill, Cook's Mills

The 15th Regiment of Infantry reported for duty at Plattsburgh, New York, in the early fall of 1812, where it was initially assigned to the brigade of General Joseph Bloomfield. Colonel Zebulon M. Pike then led it north during General Henry Dearborn's aborted offensive into Lower Canada where, on the evening of November 19, 1812, it mistook other American units for the enemy and fired into them. The following spring the 15th Regiment rode sleds to Sacketts Harbor to serve in newly promoted Brigadier General Pike's amphibious descent upon York, Upper Canada, on April 27, 1813. The unit was closely engaged, losing 12 dead and 28 injured, many of them to a magazine explosion. Shortly afterwards, the 15th Regiment unit was assigned to General John Chandler's brigade, where it fought at the capture of Fort George on May 27, 1813, losing one killed and seven wounded. After transferring back to Sacketts Harbor that fall, the 15th Regiment formed part of General Jacob J. Brown's 2nd Brigade. It accompanied General James Wilkinson's main force down the St. Lawrence River towards Montreal, saw no additional fighting, then wintered at French Mills, New York. In the spring of 1814, the regiment marched to Plattsburgh, where it was initially posted as part of General Alexander Macomb's brigade. That August, when General George Izard marched the Right Division to Niagara, the 15th Regiment was reassigned to General Daniel Bissell's brigade. There, on October 19, 1814, it fought well at Lyon's Creek, losing one wounded. Previously, a single company of 50 men had been left behind at Plattsburgh under Captain George McGlassin. On the evening of September 9, McGlassin, though bed-ridden, volunteered to lead a sortie against a nearby British rocket battery being erected only 500 yards from Fort Brown. This little action proved entirely successful, and the battery was stormed without the loss of a man. This action concluded the 15th Regiment's combat career and in May 1815, it was consolidated into the Regiment of Light Artillery.

Promotions

1st Lieutenant David Riddle, brevet captain. July 25, 1814. Gallant conduct — Battle of Niagara.
1st Lieutenant Donald Frazer, brevet captain. July 25, 1814. Gallant conduct — Battle of Niagara.
Captain George McGlassin, brevet major. September 11, 1814. Gallant conduct — Battle of Plattsburgh.
Captain White Youngs, brevet major. September 11, 1814. Gallant conduct — Battle of Plattsburgh.
Brevet Captain David Riddle, brevet major. September 17, 1814. Gallant conduct — Sortie from Fort Erie.
Brevet Captain Donald Frazer, brevet major. September 17, 1814. Gallant conduct — Sortie from Fort Erie.
3rd Lieutenant Samuel Riddle, brevet 2nd lieutenant. September 17, 1814. Gallant conduct, Fort Erie sortie.

Archival

RG94, Roll 1. Letters. National Archives. Zebulon M. Pike, 1812–1813.
Memorandum Book. Muster rolls. New Jersey Historical. MG1; Capt. John M. Scott; 1812–1814.
Vanderhoof, Cornelius. Record Book. New Jersey Historical. MG496; May, 1812.

Manuscript

Bloomfield, Moses O. Journal. Morristown National. Micro Reel 5, 1027–1035; pre-York, 1813.
Carr, Robert. Diary. Historical Society (Pa). Oswego, St. Lawrence; 1812–1813.
Carr, Robert. Letters. Maryland Historical. War of 1812 Collection; recruiting, 1814.
Frazer, Donald. Letter, 1813. Lilly Library. War of 1812 Collection; Stoney Creek.
Pike, Zebulon M. Letters. Boston Public. Ch.A.9.37, to William Eustis, 1812.
Pike, Zebulon M. Letters. Beinecke Library.
Pike, Zebulon M. Letters. Oneida Historical.
Pike, Zebulon M. Letters. Western Reserve.
Scott, John M. Letters. New Jersey Historical. MG 1044, York, Fort George; 1812–1813.

Printed Primary

"A British Deserter." *North Country Notes* (January 1968). [Captain Charles W. Hunter letter]

Fredriksen, John C., ed. "The Letters of Captain John Scott, 15th U. S. Infantry: A New Jersey Officer in the War of 1812." *New Jersey History* 107 (Fall/Winter 1989): 61–82.

Zlatich, Marko. "Uniform of the 15th United States Infantry regiment, 1812." *Military Collector and Historian* 54 (Fall 2002): 130–131.

16th Regiment of Infantry

Raised: January 11, 1812
Recruited: Philadelphia and Easton, Pennsylvania

Battle Honors

1813: York, Fort George, Stoney Creek, Crysler's Farm
1814: Cook's Mills

The 16th Regiment of Infantry originated as a two-battalion organization, with each formation mustering a handful of companies. In the fall of 1812, the 1st Battalion arrived at Plattsburgh, New York, functioning as part of General Joseph Bloomfield's brigade. The unit next participated in General Henry Dearborn's failed offensive that fall, which advanced no further than the Canadian border before turning around. In the spring of 1813, Colonel Cromwell Pearce marched the 1st Battalion to Sacketts Harbor, where it joined General Zebulon M. Pike's amphibious expedition against York, Upper Canada. The regiment fought well at York on April 27, 1813, losing five dead and 36 injured, and Colonel Pearce assumed control of occupation forces following the death of Pike. By May 1813, the 1st Battalion had been reassigned to General John P. Boyd's 1st Brigade, which then fought at Fort George, Upper Canada, on May 27, 1813; losses here were eight killed and 10 wounded. Advancing inland with General William H. Winder's brigade, part of the regiment was present at Stoney Creek on June 6, 1813, where a gallant charge led by Lieutenant McChesney recaptured an American artillery piece. On August 24, 1813, Captain William Davenport's company also had a heavy skirmish with British light troops and Indians outside Fort George, losing two dead. That fall, the 1st and 2nd battalions merged at Sacketts Harbor and were assigned to General Leonard Covington's 3rd Brigade. The new unit fought at Crysler's Farm on November 11, 1813, although casualties are unrecorded. After wintering at French Mills, New York, Pearce marched his men to Plattsburgh, New York, where they were initially posted with General Alexander Macomb's brigade. In August 1814, General George Izard was ordered to the Niagara Frontier with the bulk of his Right Division, and the 16th Regiment transferred again to the brigade of General Daniel Bissell. On October 19, 1814, it performed admirably at Cook's Mills, sustaining nine wounded. The regiment wintered at Black Rock, where Colonel Pearce succeeded General Izard as theater commander, and in May 1815, joined the 22nd, 23rd, and 32nd Regiments to form the new 2nd U.S. Infantry.

Archival

RG98, No. 261/112B. Company book. National Archives. Jon. Aitken/Thomas Horrell, 1814–1815.

RG98, No. 260/112A. Company book. National Archives. John Baldy/Thomas Horrell, 1814–1815.

RG98, No. 256/109A. Company book. National Archives. Capt. Wm Davenport, 1813–1815.

RG98, No. 257/109B. Company book. National Archives. Capt. Wm Davenport, 1813–1815.

RG98, No. 255/108. Company book. National Archives. Capt. James McElroy, 1814–1815.

RG98, No. 259/111. Company book. National Archives. Capt. N. McLaughlin, 1814–1815.

RG98, No. 258/110. Company book. National Archives. Lieut. Thomas Powers, 1813–1815.

Manuscript

Carr, Robert. Letter, 1813. Boston Public. *Ch.C.11.3; Fort Ontario, NY.
Carr, Robert. Diary. Historical Society (Pa). Robert Carr Papers; 1812–1813.
Pearce, Cromwell. Letter, 1815. Historical Society (Pa). Postwar complaints.

Printed Primary

Fredriksen, John C., ed. "'A Poor But Honest Sodger': Colonel Cromwell Pearce, the 16th U. S. Infantry, and the War of 1812." *Pennsylvania History* 52 (July 1985): 131–161.

17th Regiment of Infantry

Raised: January 11, 1812
Recruited: Lexington, Kentucky, Chillicothe, Ohio

Battle Honors

1813: Frenchtown, Fort Meigs, Fort Stephenson
1814: Mackinac

George Croghan, 17th Infantry. Frick Art Reference Library.

For a western army unit, the 17th Regiment of Infantry was relatively strong and mustered 400 men by the time it marched to the relief of Fort Wayne, Indiana, in September 1812. On September 14, Colonel Samuel Wells led the his men on a retaliatory expedition against the village of Chief Elkhorn, which he found abandoned, and completed his 60-mile round trip march in only four and a half days. That fall a detachment comprising of Captains Hightower, Collier, and Sebree, the whole commanded by Colonel Wells, accompanied General James Winchester on his ill-fated offensive to recapture Detroit. This endeavor came to grief at the Battle of Frenchtown (River Raisin), on January 18–22, 1813, which cost the 17th Regiment 119 killed and wounded with an additional 60 captured. The surviving companies next fought at the siege of Fort Meigs, April–May 1813, being brigaded with the 19th Regiment of Infantry for administrative/tactical purposes. On May 5, 1813, the 17th/19th battalion successfully sortied and stormed a British battery, along with 41 prisoners, although at a cost of 39 dead and 90 wounded. It was subsequently broken up into various detachments across Ohio, the largest being Captain James Hunter's company at Fort Stephenson. On August 2, 1813, Major George Croghan bloodily repulsed an attack there by the British 41st Regiment, inflicting over 100 casualties while losing one killed and seven wounded. The unit continued holding various strong points over the winter and, becoming seriously undermanned, it was combined with the 19th, 26th, and 28th Regiment to form a new 17th and 19th Regiment. The new unit remained deployed in small detachments throughout Ohio, Michigan, and Upper Canada, although several companies fought at the failed attack on Michilimackinac on August 4, 1814, losing five dead and 19 injured. By fall several more companies were brought together under Colonel John Miller and sailed from Detroit to Fort Erie to bolster Captain John T. Chunn's Company, already there. The battalion was assigned to General Thomas Adams Smith's brigade, saw no further fighting, and in May 1815, it was consolidated with the 1st, 13th, 24th, 28th, and 33rd Infantries to form the new 3rd U.S. Infantry.

Promotions

Major George Croghan, brevet lieutenant colonel. August 2, 1813. Gallant conduct in the defense of Fort Stephenson.
Captain John T. Chunn, brevet major, August 15, 1814. Gallant conduct in the defense of Fort Erie.

Archival

17th U.S. Infantry. Records. Center for Archival. MMS 610; July–August 1814.
RG94, Roll 28. Letters. National Archives. John Miller, 1813–1814.
RG94, Roll 15. Letters. National Archives. Edmund Shipp, 1812.
17th U.S. Infantry. Monthly return. Ohio Historical. OVS7268-9, Captain David Holt; 1814.
17th U.S. Infantry. Prisoner lists. Wisconsin Historical. Frontier Wars Papers, 9 U.

Manuscript

Butler, William O. Letters. Kentucky Historical. Poem about River Raisin Massacre.
Croghan, George. Letters. Clements Library. Croghan Family Papers.
Croghan, George. Letters. Filson Historical. A C941; 1813, Lake Erie events, Canada.

Croghan, George. Papers. Library of Congress. Misc Mss. 3005.
Croghan, George. Papers. New York Public. 1812–1814.
Croghan, George. Letter, 1813. New York State. War of 1812 Coll.; to William H. Harrison.
Croghan, George. Letters. Rutherford B. Hayes. Fort Stephenson.
Croghan, George. Papers. Wisconsin Historical. William Croghan Papers, 1 N; 1811–1815.
Graham, Richard. Papers. Missouri Historical. A0601; 1813–1815.
Miller, John. Letters. Burton Historical.
Miller, John. Letters. Library of Congress. William H. Harrison Papers; Oct.–Nov. 1813.
Scott, Chasteen. Letter, 1814. Indiana Historical. Arthur G. Mitten Coll.; whips a Yankee!
Tod, George. Papers. Ohio State Library.
Tod, George. Papers. Library of Congress. Duncan McArthur Papers; enlistments.
Tod, George. Papers. Western Reserve. MS. 3203.
Todd, Charles S. Papers. Filson Historical. A T633; 1813, Thames map.
Todd, Charles S. Papers. Wisconsin Historical. Frontier Wars Papers, 7 U.
Trimble, David. Papers. Ross County Historical. 1990.08; aide to William Henry Harrison.

Printed Primary

Putnam, Elizabeth D., ed. "The Life and Service of Joseph Duncan, Governor of Illinois, 1834–1838." *Illinois State Historical Society Transactions* No. 26 (1919): 107–187. [110–111]
Quaife, Milo M., ed. "A Diary of the War of 1812." *Mississippi Valley Historical Review* 1 (September 1914): 272–278.

Select Secondary

Bowlus, Bruce A. "A Signal Victory Gained: The Battle of Fort Stephenson, August 1 & 2, 1813." *Northwest Ohio Quarterly* 63 (1991): 43–47.
Clift, Garret G. *Remember the Raisin!* Frankfort: Kentucky Historical Society, 1961.
Griffin, G. W. *Memoir of Col. Charles S. Todd.* Philadelphia: Claxton, Remsen, 1874.
Jelsma, Sherry K. "The Making of Imperishable Honor: Charles S. Todd in the War of 1812." *Register of the Kentucky Historical Society* 105, no. 2 (Spring 2007): 195–228.
Johnson, Eric. "The Twin Regiments: A Short History of the 17th and 19th Regiments of Infantry." *Journal of the War of 1812* 8, no. 2 (Spring/Summer 2004):5–11.
Parson, Thomas W. "George Croghan in the War of 1812." *Northwest Ohio Quarterly* 22 (1948): 192–202.

18th Regiment of Infantry

Raised: June 26, 1812
Recruited: Columbia, South Carolina

Battle Honors

Not engaged

This unit was recruited and deployed at Charleston, South Carolina, throughout the war. It saw no combat and after May 1815, was amalgamated with the 5th and 35th Regiments to form the new 8th U.S. Infantry. However, Colonel William Drayton became a noted political figure afterwards and an opponent to President Andrew Jackson during the so-called "Bank Wars" of the 1830s.

Archival

RG94, Roll 13. Letter. National Archives. Thomas P. Moore, 1813–1815.
RG98, No. 684. Company book. National Archives. Capt. Robert Fenner, 1814–1815.
Brown, Hamilton. Records. Southern Historical. 1090 2.1; 1814–1815.

Select Secondary

Chastaine, Ben H. *History of the 18th United States Infantry, First Division, 1812–1919*. New York: The Hymans Pub. Co., 1919.

19th Regiment of Infantry

Raised: January 11, 1812
Recruited: Zanesville, Ohio, Kentucky

Battle Honors

1812: Detroit (det.); Mississinewa (det.)
1813: Frenchtown (det.), Fort Meigs, Fort Niagara (det.)
1814: Chippawa (det.), Lundy's Lane (det.), Fort Erie, Mackinac (det.)

Following an initial spate of recruitment, the 19th Regiment spent the bulk of its service life in various detachments. Several soldiers were attached to the army of General William Hull when it surrendered Detroit on August 15, 1812, while Captain Elliot's company marched with Lieutenant Colonel John B. Campbell against the Miami Indians along the Mississinewa River. On December 18, 1812, the unit helped repulse an Indian attack on the American encampment, losing three wounded. On January 22, 1813, a further three companies fought at the Battle of Frenchtown, Michigan Territory, where they were destroyed. The surviving companies under Colonel John Miller

William Allen Trimbell, 19th Infantry. Courtesy Ohio Historical Society.

were then brigaded with the 17th Regiment of Infantry in time for the siege of Fort Meigs, Ohio. On May 5, 1813, Miller's force sortied and captured a siege battery and 41 British soldiers while suffering a combined loss of 39 dead and 90 wounded. A part from the regiment apparently accompanied General William Henry Harrison's invasion of Upper Canada in the fall of 1813 and spent the winter at Sacketts Harbor, New York. A small detachment under Lieutenant Fredericks was also captured at Fort Niagara during the surprise assault by British forces on December 19, 1813. The following May the 17th, 19th, 26th and 27th Regiments were consolidated to form new 17th and 19th Regiments, although both continued serving in scattered detachments. One company accompanied the ill-fated expedition of Lieutenant Colonel George Croghan against Michilimackinac, losing one killed and 19 wounded there on August 4, 1814. Another company was attached to the 21st Regiment during the 1814 Niagara Campaign, losing three killed and two wounded at Chippawa, July 5, 1814. This force was subsequently augmented by several companies under by Major William A. Trimble, and were posted within Fort Erie proper. Through newly-recruited, they fought bravely during the August 15, 1814, night attack upon the American camp, repulsing several determined attempts by the 103rd Regiment, and killed Colonel William Drummond in the process. Total losses for the siege and sortie amounted to 11 dead and 22 wounded, after which the unit relocated to Detroit and Malden, Upper Canada, for the winter. In May 1815, the 19th Regiment joined the 1st, 17th, 24th, 28th, and 33rd Regiments to form the new 3rd U.S. Infantry.

Promotions

Lieutenant Colonel John B. Campbell, brevet colonel. December 18, 1812. Gallant conduct — Battle of Mississinewa.

Captain William McDonald, brevet major. July 25, 1814. Gallant conduct — Battle of Niagara.

3rd Lieutenant Charles Cissna, brevet 2nd lieutenant. August 15, 1814. Gallant conduct defending Fort Erie.

Major William A. Trimble, brevet lieutenant colonel. September 19, 1814. Gallant conduct, sortie from Fort Erie.

Archival

McArthur, Duncan. Orderly Book. Library of Congress. Duncan McArthur Papers; 1813–1814.

RG94, Roll 39. Letters. National Archives. John B. Campbell, 1812–1814.

RG94, Roll 46. Letters. National Archives. Nathan Heald, 1813–1814.

RG94, Roll 28. Letters. National Archives. John Miller, 1813–1815.

Manuscript

Campbell, John B. Letter, 1813. Library of Congress. William H. Harrison Papers; Ohio.
Jesup, Thomas S. Letters. U.S. Army Military. Arch Coll 101; 1813–1814.
McDonald, William. Letter, 1814. Ross County Historical. Fort Erie.
Shannon, James. Papers. William T. Young. 55W22.
Trimble, William A. Letters. Ohio Historical. MSS267, William A. Trimble Papers.
Trimble, William A. Letters. Western Reserve. Ms. 3205, Allen Trimble Papers.
Will, George. Roster. Filson Historical. Special Collections, CW; January, 1815.

Printed Primary

Brown, Ashley, ed. "The Expedition of Colonel John B. Campbell of the 19th U. S. Infantry in November 1812, from Franklintown to the Mississinewa Villages." *Northwest Ohio Historical Quarterly* 8 (January 1936): 1–6.

Davis, Johnda T., ed. "Memoirs of Col. John Cochran." *Pickaway Quarterly* 7 (Fall 1967): 7–20.

"Papers Relating to the War of 1812: Major George Tod." *Western Reserve Historical Society Tracts* No. 15 (April 1873): 1–3; No. 17 (November 1873): 1–5; No. 19 (November 1873): 1–4; No. 28 (October 1875): 1–4; No. 51 (December 1879): 115–123.

Tuttle, Mary M. "William Allen Trimble." *Ohio Archaeological and Historical Society Publications* 14 (July 1905): 225–246. [letter, 1814, 234–235]

Select Secondary

Graves, Donald E. "William Drummond and the Battle of Fort Erie." *Canadian Military History* 1, nos. 1–2 (1992): 25–43.

Griffin, William W. "Destruction of Delaware and Miami Towns in the Aftermath of Tippecanoe: The Impact of Perspective on History." *Papers of the Algonquian Conference* No. 31 (2000): 68–76.

Johnson, Eric. "The Twin Regiments: A Short History of the 17th and 19th Regiments of Infantry." *War of 1812 Journal* 8, no. 2 (Spring/Summer 2004): 5–11.

20th Regiment of Infantry

Raised: June 26, 1812
Recruited: Fredericksburg, Virginia

Battle Honors

1812: French Creek
1813: Fort Erie
1814: La Colle Mill

The first detachment of the newly-recruited 20th Regiment of Infantry arrived along the Niagara frontier in the fall of 1812, and several detachments participated in General Alexander Smyth's abortive crossing of the Niagara River on November 28, 1812. Over the winter the unit was brigaded with the 12th Regiment of infantry at Williamsville, New York, and the following spring it was joined by the 14th Regiment. In May, 1813, this force crossed the Niagara River and bloodless occupied the recently-evacuated Fort Erie. It remained at Niagara until September, 1813, when it joined the St. Lawrence expedition of General James Wilkinson; any combat or casualties are not recorded. Following a difficult winter at French Mills, New York, the 20th Regiment participated in the Battle of La Colle Mill on March 30, 1814, emerging unscathed. The bulk of men then transferred over to the 12th Regiment at Plattsburgh, while its officers returned to Virginia on recruiting service for the rest of the war. In May 1815, it was consolidated with the 12th and 14th Regiments to form the new 4th U.S. Infantry.

Promotions

2nd Lieutenant Edward B. Randolph, brevet 1st lieutenant. July 25, 1814. Gallant conduct — Battle of Niagara.

Archival

Peyton, Bernard. Orderly Book. Library of Virginia. 1812–1814.
RG98, No. 264/115. Company book. National Archives. Captain William S. Jett, 1812–1814.
RG98, No. 262/113. Company book. National Archives. John Stanard/John Macrae, 1812–1814.
RG98, No. 263/114. Company book. National Archives. Capt. Byrd C. Willis, 1813–1814.

Manuscript

Campbell, David. Papers. Perkins Library. 1812–1813.
Coles, Isaac A. Letters. Tennessee State. War of 1812 Collection.
Coles, Isaac A. Papers. Virginia Historical.
Randolph, Edward B. Memoir. Mitchell Memorial. Randolph-Sherman Papers; Lundy's Lane.
Randolph, Thomas M. Letters. Tennessee State. War of 1812 Collection.

Select Secondary

Gaines, William H. *Thomas Mann Randolph, Jefferson's Son-in-Law*. Baton Rouge: Louisiana State University Press, 1966, 82–100.

21st Regiment of Infantry

Raised: June 26, 1812
Recruited: Massachusetts, Portsmouth, New Hampshire

Nathaniel N. Hall, 21st Infantry. Kent-Delord House Museum.

Battle Honors

1813: York, Fort George, Sacketts Harbor, Crysler's Farm
1814: Chippawa, Lundy's Lane, Fort Erie

In October 1812, Colonel Eleazar W. Ripley led nine companies of the 21st Regiment of Infantry from Massachusetts to Plattsburgh, New York, where they formed part of General John Chandler's brigade. They were then detached to accompany General Zebulon M. Pike's amphibious attack upon York, Upper Canada, on April 27, 1813, and took post in the reserve. Ripley came ashore following Pike's untimely death and so effectively restored order that, afterwards, British authorities subsequently released Lieutenant Peter Pelham, who had been captured at Crysler's Farm. Ripley also remained in reserve at Fort George on May 27, 1813, while another detachment helped defend Sacketts Harbor from a determined British attack two days later. In the fall the 21st Regiment functioned as part of General Robert Swartwout's 4th Brigade, and was conspicuously engaged at Crysler's farm on November 11, 1813, although its losses are unrecorded. At the close of the engagement, General James Wilkinson ordered Lieutenant Colonel Timothy Upham up from the reserve to stabilize the wavering American line. Apparently, the regiment's steady conduct prevented the defeat from turning into a rout. In the spring of 1814 the unit departed French Mills, New York, for Sacketts Harbor, where it was assigned to newly promoted General Ripley's 2nd Brigade under Colonel James Miller, formerly of the 6th Regiment. Miller then accompanied his charge to Buffalo, New York, as part of General Jacob J. Brown's invigorated Left Division. It missed fighting in the battle of Chippawa on July 5, 1814, but bore a central role at Lundy's Lane on July 25th. Miller was called upon by General Brown (and then General Ripley) to storm a British battery crowning the lane, which was performed in dramatic style. The regiment then held its own against several determined British counterattacks until Ripley brought up the 23rd Regiment in support. Losses here totaled 15 dead, 70 wounded, and 19 missing. The 21st Regiment subsequently fought with distinction at the defense of Fort Erie on August 15, 1814, while under the leadership of Brevet Lieutenant Colonel Eleazar D. Wood. This talented engineer officer had been entrusted with the defense of Snake Hill, and the extreme left flank, and he lost two killed and six wounded while inflicting hundreds of casualties on the flintless DeWatteville Regiment. On September 17, 1814, Lieutenant Colonel Upham once again commanded the 21st in reserve and covered the American withdrawal, although its losses are not recorded. A further 21 killed and 32 wounded had been sustained during the British bombardment. The unit wintered at Sacketts Harbor after a difficult winter march from Buffalo, and in May, 1815, it was consolidated with the 4th, 9th, 13th, 40th, and 45th Regiments to form the new 5th U.S. Infantry. Colonel Miller's exclamation "I'll try, Sir," uttered at Lundy's Lane, is enshrined as the regimental motto.

Promotions

Colonel James Miller, brevet brigadier general. July 25, 1814. Distinguished services at the Battle of Niagara.

Captain Sullivan Burbank, brevet major. July 25, 1814. Gallant conduct — Battle of Niagara.

1st Lieutenant John W. Holding, brevet captain. July 25, 1814. Gallant conduct — Battle of Niagara.

1st Lieutenant Nathaniel N. Hall, brevet captain. August 15, 1814. Gallant conduct in the defense of Fort Erie.

Captain Morrill Marston, brevet major. August 15, 1814. Gallant conduct in the defense of Fort Erie.

2nd Lieutenant Benjamin F. Larned, brevet 1st lieutenant. August 15, 1814. Gallant conduct defending Fort Erie.

Archival

RG98, No. 265/46. Company book. National Archives. Capt. Lemuel Bradford, 1812–1815.

RG98, No. 271/123A. Company book. National Archives. Capt. Lemuel Bradford, 1812–1815.

RG98, No. 272/123B. Company book. National Archives. Lemuel Bradford/Ira Drew, 1814–1815.

RG98, No. 268/120. Company book. National Archives. Capt. Sullivan Burbank, 1814.

RG98, No. 266/118. Company book. National Archives. Capt. Morrill Martson, 1813–1814.

RG98, No. 269/121. Company book. National Archives. Capt. Charles Procter, 1813–1815.

RG98, No. 99/122B. Company book. National Archives. Capt. Joseph Treat, 1813–1815.

RG98, No. 270/122A. Company book. National Archives. Capt. Joseph H. Vose, 1813–1814.

RG98, No. 267/119. Letters sent. National Archives. Capt. Jeremiah Chapman, 1812–1813.

Loring, Pere. Muster roll. Portsmouth Athenaeum. S0614; Fort Constitution, N.H., 1814–1815.

21st U.S. Infantry. Paymaster. Portsmouth Athenaeum. S0694; subsistence, forage, clothing.

Manuscript

Bartlett, Josiah, Jr. Letters. New Hampshire. Wingate Family Papers.
Miller, James. Letter, 1814. Clements Library. War of 1812 Collection; Fort Erie.
Miller, James. Letter, 1814. Gilder Lehrman. GLC03370; Fort Erie attack.
Miller, James. Letters. Lilly Library. War of 1812 Collection; 1812–1814.
Miller, James. Letters. Massachusetts Historical. Jacob J. Brown Papers; Niagara affairs.
Miller, James. Letter, 1814. Ohio Historical. William A. Trimble Papers; Niagara affairs.
Miller, James. Papers. U.S. Military Academy. No. 235; 1812–1815.
Pelham, Peter. Letters. Syracuse University. Osborne Family Papers; 1813.
Trowbridge, Amasa. Papers. Library of Congress. Misc. Mss.; surgeon, York, Fort Erie.
Upham, Timothy. Letter, 1815. Library of Congress. James Madison Papers, to Henry Dearborn.
Upham, Timothy. Letters. Lilly Library. War of 1812 Collection; 1814.
Upham, Timothy. Letters. Manuscripts and Archives Ms. 604, Series III, Box 16; 1813–1815.
Upham, Timothy. Letters. New Hampshire. 1814.

Printed Primary

Anonymous. "The Sortie From Fort Erie." *United States Military Magazine* 1 (February 1840): [5–6].
Cate, Mary R., ed. "Benjamin Ropes' Autobiography." *Essex Institute Historical Collections* 91 (April 1955): 105–127.
Hough, Franklin B. *A History of St. Lawrence and Franklin Counties, New York, from the Earliest period to the Present Time.* Albany: J. Munsell, 1860, 639–649. [Dr. Amasa Trowbridge narrative, St. Lawrence, 1813]
Treat, Joseph. *The Vindication of Captain Joseph Treat, Late of the Twenty-First Regiment, U. S. Infantry, Against the Atrocious Calumny Comprehended in Major General Brown's Official Report of the Battle of Chippewa.* Philadelphia: N.p., 1815.
Trowbridge, Francis B. *The Trowbridge Genealogy.* New Haven: Tuttle, More, Taylor, 1908, 537–538. [Dr. Amasa Trowbridge letters, 1813–1814]

Select Secondary

Hampton, Celwyn E. *The Twenty-first's Trophy of Niagara.* Fort Logan, Colo.: N.p., 1909.
Hampton, Celwyn E. *History of the Twenty-First Infantry.* Columbus: Miller, 1911.
Holden, Robert J. "James Miller, Collector of the Port of Salem." *Essex Institute Collections* 104 (1968): 253–302.
Thayer, Virginia. *War of 1812 Soldiers Index: 21st Regiment.* Concord, N.H.: New Hampshire Division of Records Management & Archives, 1994.
"Timothy Upham." *New England Genealogical and Historical Register* 10 (January 1856): 101–102.

22nd Regiment of Infantry

Raised: June 26, 1812
Recruited: Pittsburgh, Pennsylvania, Delaware

BATTLE HONORS

1812: Fort Niagara
1813: Fort George, French Creek, Crysler's Farm
1814: Chippewa, Lundy's Lane, Fort Erie

Hugh Brady, 22nd Infantry. Burton Historical Collection, Detroit Public Library.

The 22nd Regiment of Infantry first deployed at the Niagara frontier in November 1812, when Lieutenant Colonel George McFeely took 180 men into garrison at Fort Niagara, New York. On November 21, 1812, this detachment performed actively during the bombardment of that post, losing one dead and one injured. The following spring, McFeely's men were assigned to General John P. Boyd's brigade and fought at the May 27, 1813, Battle of Fort George, losing 10 wounded. By fall the unit had been reassigned to the 2nd Brigade of General Jacob J. Brown, and spearheaded the American drive down the St. Lawrence River. A detachment was present at a skirmish along French Creek on November 1–2, 1813, against British gunboats. After wintering in French Mills, New York, 1813–1814, the 22nd Regiment marched overland to Buffalo to become part of General Winfield Scott's 1st Brigade, although the four companies present remained attached to Major Henry Leavenworth's 9th U. S Infantry for tactical purposes. These soldiers participated in the Battle of Chippawa on July 5, 1814, losing eight dead and 44 wounded. Shortly afterwards, Colonel Hugh Brady brought up several more companies in time to fight as a battalion at Lundy's Lane, July 25, 1814, where Brady was severely wounded and his small command lost a staggering 39 dead, 90 wounded, and 22 missing. The 22nd Regiment remained active in the defense of Fort Erie, August–September, 1814, losing an additional 10 killed and 42 wounded to various causes. It finally marched back to Sacketts Harbor in dead winter, and in May, 1815, the 22nd Regiment joined the 6th, 16th, 23rd, and 32nd Regiments in forming the new 2nd U.S. Infantry.

Promotions

Captain John Pentland, brevet major. July 25, 1814. Gallant conduct — Battle of Niagara.

2nd Lieutenant John Brady, brevet 1st lieutenant. February 5, 1815. Gallant conduct.

Archival

Army Collection. Order book. Missouri Historical. A0050; Sacketts Harbor, 1813–1815.

RG98, No. 275/125. Company book. National Archives. George W. Barker/Thomas Sprogell, 1813.

RG98, No. 281/130. Company book. National Archives. Capt. Jacob Carmack, 1814–1815.

RG98, No. 277/127. Company book. National Archives. Capt. Willis Foulk, 1813–1815.

RG98, No. 280/129. Company book. National Archives. Capt. Joseph Henderson, 1813–1815.

RG98, No. 278/128A. Company book. National Archives. Capt. Thomas Lawrence, 1814–1815.

RG98, No. 279/128B. Company book. National Archives. Capt. Thomas Lawrence, 1814–1815.
RG98, No. 276/126. Company book. National Archives. D. McFarland/ David Milliken, 1812–1813.
RG98, No. 273/124A. Company book. National Archives. Capt. John Pentland, 1812–1814.
RG98, No. 274/124B. Company book. National Archives. Capt. John Pentland, 1812–1814.

Manuscript

Henderson, Joseph. Memoir. Lilly Library. War of 1812 Collection; Niagara, 1814.
Pentland, John. Letter, 1816. Historical Society (Pa). Miscellaneous Collection; Lundy's Lane.

Printed Primary

Brady, Hugh. "The Battle of Lundy's Lane." *Historical Magazine* 10 (September 1866): 272.
Crombie, John N., ed. "The Papers of Major Daniel McFarland: A Hawk of 1812." *Western Pennsylvania Historical Society Magazine* 51 (April 1968): 101–125.
Fredriksen, John C., ed. "Chronicle of Valor: The Journal of a Pennsylvania Officer in the War of 1812." *Western Pennsylvania Historical Magazine* 67 (July 1984): 243–284. [Lieutenant Colonel George McFeely]
Howard, Florence, and Mary Howard, eds. "The Letters of John Patterson, 1812–1813." *Western Pennsylvania Historical Magazine* 23 (July 1940): 99–109. [Private John Patterson]
Kyte, E. C. "Fort Niagara in the War of 1812; Sidelights from an Unpublished Order Book." *Canadian Historical Review* 17 (1936): 373–384.
Linn, John B. *Annals of Buffalo Valley, Pennsylvania, 1755–1855*. Harrisburg, Pa.: Lane S. Hart, 1877, 419–420. [Lieutenant Samuel Brady letter, 1814]
Taylor, R. Bruce, ed. "Garrison Orders and Proceedings of Fort Niagara, etc." *Quarterly Journal of the New York State Historical Association* 8 (January–April 1927): 62–80, 152–178. [Lieutenant Colonel George McFeely]

Select Secondary

Bates, George C. "General Hugh Brady." *Michigan Pioneer* 2 (1877–1878): 573–579.
Brady, Hugh. "General Hugh Brady: A Biographical Sketch." *Michigan Pioneer* 3 (1881): 84–87.
Brady, William T. "The 22nd Regiment in the War of 1812." *Western Pennsylvania Historical Magazine* 32 (March–June 1949): 56–60.
Crombie, John N. "The 22nd U. S. Infantry: A Forgotten Regiment in a Forgotten War." *Western Pennsylvania Historical Magazine* 50 nos. 2–3 (April–July 1967): 133–147, 221–231.
McBarron, H. Charles, and James Kochan. "The 22nd U. S. Infantry Regiment, 1812–1813." *Military Collector and Historian* 33 (Winter 1981): 164–165.

23rd Regiment of Infantry

Raised: June 26, 1812
Recruited: Utica, New York, and Vermont

BATTLE HONORS

1812: Queenston Heights, French Creek
1813: Fort George, Sacketts Harbor, Stoney Creek, Beaver Dams
1814: La Colle Mills, Chippewa, Lundy's Lane, Fort Erie

The 23rd Regiment first deployed along the Niagara frontier under Major James R. Mullany in the fall of 1812, where at least 65 soldiers fought at Queenston Heights on October 13, 1812. Casualties are not reported but are assumed to be considerable. The following month elements of the regiment were present during General Alexander Smyth's abortive crossing of the Niagara River to Frenchman's Creek on November 28, 1812, which cost them a further six dead and 22 wounded. A small detachment also fought at Sacketts Harbor, New York, when that post was attacked on May 29, 1813. The unit wintered along the frontier and on May 27, 1813, participated in the capture of Fort George, Upper Canada, as part of General John Chandler's brigade, sustaining a further three killed and six wounded. The 23rd apparently also had a company present under Major Armstrong at Stoney Creek on June 6, 1813, which fought on the left flank and lost one killed and two wounded. Worse, an entire company of 63 men under Captain Isaac Roach was captured at Beaver Dams on June 23, 1813. The remaining soldiers were sent to Sacketts Harbor where they joined the 15th and 22nd Regiments as part of General Jacob J. Brown's 2nd Brigade. After wintering at French Mills, New York, and fighting at La Colle Mill on March 30, 1814, part of the 23rd Regiment returned to Buffalo, New York, as part of General Eleazar W. Ripley's 2nd Brigade, and was lightly engaged at the Battle of Chippawa, July 5, 1814, losing one man wounded. Several days later Major George M. Brooke arrived from Sacketts Harbor with the balance of the regiment, which fought closely at Lundy's Lane, July 25, 1814, losing 10 dead and 52 injured. The regiment was also active during the defense of Fort Erie, losing six wounded on the night attack of August 15, 1814, and 19 dead and 26 wounded during the sortie of September 17, 1814. The month-long British bombardment also inflicted an additional 12 dead and 24 wounded. A small detachment was apparently present at Plattsburgh on September 11, 1814, although details of its service are unknown. The 23rd Regiment endured a harrowing march from Niagara back to Sacketts Harbor in the winter of 1814,

George Mercer Brooke, 23rd Infantry. Tampa Historical Society, Inc.

and in May 1815, it was amalgamated with the 6th, 16th, 22nd, and 32nd Regiments to form the new 2nd U.S. Infantry.

PROMOTIONS

1st Lieutenant William J. Worth, brevet captain. July 5, 1814. Gallant and meritorious conduct, Battle of Chippawa.

Captain Azariah W. Odell, brevet major. July 25, 1814. Gallant conduct — Battle of Niagara.

Brevet Captain William J. Worth, brevet major. July 25, 1814. Distinguished conduct, Battle of Niagara.

1st Lieutenant John P. Livingston, brevet captain. July 25, 1814. Gallant conduct — Battle of Niagara.

Major George M. Brooke, brevet lieutenant colonel. August 15, 1814. Gallant conduct in the defense of Fort Erie.

Brevet lieutenant colonel George M. Brooke, brevet colonel September 17, 1814. Gallant conduct, Fort Erie sortie.

2nd Lieutenant Joshua B. Brant, brevet 1st lieutenant. September 17, 1814. Gallant conduct, sortie from Fort Erie.

2nd Lieutenant John P. Dieterich, February 5, 1815. Gallant conduct.

Archival

Paxton, James. Orderly Book. Library of Congress. 0314, Peter Force Papers; 1813–1815.

RG98, No. 284/133. Company book. National Archives. Capt. Frederick Brow, 1814–1815.

RG98, No. 283/132. Company Book. National Archives. Capt. Richard Goodell, 1814.

RG98, No. 282/131. Company book. National Archives. Lieut. Justus Ingersoll, 1814–1815.

RG98, No. 285/134. Company book. National Archives. Azariah Odell/William Belknap, 1814–1815.

Manuscript

Belknap, William G. Papers. Mudd Library. WC062, Box 1; Fort Erie.
Goodell, Richard. Letters. New York Historical. Misc Mss G, Niagara; 1813–1814.
Hovey, Nathaniel. Letter, 1814. Buffalo and Erie. Niagara matters.
Preston, James P. Letters. Virginia Historical. Mss1 pg267 d 7-255 (A-L); 1812–1813.
Preston, James P. Letters. Virginia Historical. Mss1 pg267 d 7-255 (M-W); 1812–1813.
Tappan, Samuel. Memoir. U.S. Army Military. War of 1812 Misc.; Lundy's Lane, Fort Erie.
Worth, William J. Letter, 1815. Massachusetts Historical. Jacob Brown Papers; Lundy's Lane ending.

Printed Primary

Archer, Mary R., ed. "Military Journal of the War of 1812." *Pennsylvania Magazine of History and Biography* 17, nos. 2–3 (1893): 129–158, 281–315. [Captain Isaac Roach]

Crombie, John N., ed. "The Papers of Major Daniel McFarland: A Hawk of 1812." *Western Pennsylvania Historical Magazine* 51 (April 1968): 101–125.

Foreman, Carolyn T. "General William Goldsmith Belknap." *Chronicles of Oklahoma* 20 (June 1942): 124–142.

Graves, Donald E. *Soldiers of 1814: Enlisted Men's Memoirs of the Niagara Campaign.* Youngstown, N.Y.: Old Fort Niagara Association, 1995. [Private Amasa Ford, 51–58]

Harrington, Isaac R. *To Col. J. R. Mullany, Quarter-master General of the Northern Division of the United States Army.* Burlington, Vt.: I. R. Harrington, 1817.

SELECT SECONDARY

Wallace, Edward S. *William Jenkins Worth, Monterrey's Forgotten Hero.* Dallas: Southern Methodist University Press, 1927.

24th Regiment of Infantry

Raised: June 26, 1812
Recruited: Tennessee, Mississippi Territory, Louisiana Territory, with principal depots at Nashville and Knoxville.

BATTLE HONORS

1813: Fort Stephenson (det.), Fort Niagara (det.)
1814: Longwood (det.), Mackinac, Fort Clark

The 24th Regiment of Infantry spent nearly a year recruiting before it was finally deployed to the field. On June 7, 1813, it arrived at Franklintown, Ohio, with 314 men and a month later it constituted the principal garrison at Fort Meigs when that post was besieged by British and Indians or a second time in July. On August 2, 1813, a detachment was present at the Battle of Fort Stephenson, which was a disastrous repulse for General Henry Procter. Afterwards several companies totaling 280 men arrived to garrison newly-liberated Detroit under Captain Alex Gray, but otherwise the unit remained widely dispersed: two companies under Captains Robert Desha and Allen were present at Belle Fontaine, Missouri, while the companies of Captain Hamilton and Lieutenant Peel garrisoned Fort Niagara, New York. On the evening of December 19, 1813, the latter formations were captured in a surprise British assault by Lieutenant General Gordon Drummond. The 24th Regiment enjoyed better luck under Captain Andrew Hunter Holmes at Longwoods on March 4, 1814, when several companies, partially deployed in square formation, repelled several assaults by British light infantry. For a loss of four killed and three wounded, men of the 24th inflicted 10 dead and 66 wounded on their antagonists. That summer several companies also joined Lieutenant Colonel George Croghan on his amphibious assault against Michilimackinac, losing five dead and 12 wounded to a determined British defense. On August 19, 1814, a company of the 7th Regiment commanded by Lieutenant Joseph

Perkins of the 24th surrendered Fort Clark, Wisconsin Territory, to superior British and Indian forces; they were paroled and sent immediately back to St. Louis under a Canadian escort to prevent the Indians from massacring them. In May 1815, the 24th Regiment joined the 1st, 17th, 19th, 28th, and 39th Regiments to form the new 3rd U.S. Infantry.

Promotions

Captain Andrew H. Holmes, brevet major. March 4, 1814. Gallant conduct.
Captain Robert Desha, brevet major. August 4, 1814. Gallant conduct in the attack upon Fort Michillimackinac.
Major Robert Butler, brevet lieutenant colonel. December 23, 1814. Gallant conduct during New Orleans.

Archival

RG197. Reports. Louisiana State. 10324.1-26; 1814–1815.
RG94, Roll 38. Letters. National Archives. Captain John Butler, 1812–1814.
24th U. S. Infantry. Morning reports. Tennessee Historical. Winchester Papers, Box 6, 1814–1815.

Manuscript

Anderson, William P. Letter, 1813. Chicago Historical. Jackson Papers; complains about militia.
Anderson, William P. Letters. Library of Congress. William Henry Harrison Papers, Ohio; 1813.
Campbell, James H. Letters. Filson Historical. A C187; 1813–1814.
Holmes, Andrew H. Folder. Burton Historical. Details about his death, 1814.
O'Fallon, John. Letters. Burton Historical.
O'Fallon, John. Papers. Filson Historical. A/031; 1812–1815.
O'Fallon, John. Papers. Missouri Historical. A1151; 1812–1814.
O'Fallon, John. General Orders. New York State. N892; Fort Meigs, 1813.
Wilkinson, Walter. Papers. Missouri Historical. A1610, Tesson Collection, recruiting; 1813.

Printed Primary

Keeler, Lucy E. "The Croghan Celebration." *Ohio Archaeological and Historical Society Publications* 16 (January 1907): 1–105. [Private William Gaines, 82–86]

Select Secondary

Dunnigan, Brian L. "The Battle of Mackinac Island." *Michigan History* 59, no. 4 (1979): 239–254.
Jones, F. L. "The Longwoods." *Canadian Army Journal* 12 (1958): 64–76.

Kohler, C. Douglas, and Douglas De Croix. "At the Point of a Bayonet!" The British Capture of Fort Niagara." *Western New York Heritage* 9, no. 4 (2007): 48–56.
Poole, J. I. "The Fight at Battle Hill." *London and Middlesex County Historical Society Transactions* 4 (1913): 7–61.

25th Regiment of Infantry

Raised: June 26, 1812
Recruited: Hartford, Connecticut, Rhode Island

Battle Honors

1813: Stoney Creek, Chateauguay, Crysler's Farm
1814: Chippawa, Lundy's Lane, Fort Erie

The 25th Infantry Regiment was initially deployed to Plattsburgh, New York, and formed part of General John Chandler's brigade. As such they were present at the battle of Fort George on May 27, 1813, but suffered no casualties. Advancing inland, the 25th Regiment was closely employed at Stoney Creek on June 6, 1813, where Major Joseph Lee Smith's prior redeployment to elevated terrain probably saved the army. With campfires back-lighting the oncoming British, they poured a heavy and destructive fire upon them; Smith lost seven dead and 12 wounded. The 25th Regiment marched back to Fort George for service in the ambitious St. Lawrence Campaign of that fall. Here they were led by Colonel Edmund P. Gaines and reassigned to the 3rd brigade of General Leonard Covington. The regiment was present at Crysler's Farm on November 11, 1813, and wintered at French Mills, New York, before marching to Buffalo under the command of Major Thomas S. Jesup. Here they joined the 9th, 11th, and 22nd Regiments as part of General Winfield Scott's brigade and received intense tactical training. On July 3, the 25th was ferried across the Niagara River, where it surrounded Fort Erie and forced its surrender; fire from the garrison inflicted four casualties. Major Jesup next led it at the Battle of Chippawa on July 5, 1814, where he turned the British right, enfiladed them, and contributed to victory at a cost of five dead and 71 wounded. Three weeks later he performed similar work at Lundy's Lane, July 25, 1814, where the light company under Captain Daniel Ketchum captured British general Phineas Riall and his entire suite. The regiment suffered an additional 28 killed and 66 wounded and 22 missing in consequence. The 25th subsequently formed part of the Fort Erie garrison, August–September 1814, losing an additional six dead and 11 wounded, mostly to bombardment.

Thomas S. Jesup, 25th Infantry. Washington National Cathedral, bequest of Mary Jesup Sitgreaves.

In the late fall, Lieutenant Colonel Jesup was ordered to Hartford, Connecticut, by Secretary of War James Monroe. This was ostensibly for recruiting purposes but, in reality, to keep tabs on Federalists during the infamous "Hartford Convention" in that city. Nothing came of this quixotic sojourn, but Jesup was fully prepared to use force and quell any disloyalty from the irascible

New Englanders. In May, 1815, his hard-charging regiment was consolidated with the 11th, 27th, 29th, and 37th Regiments to form the new 6th U.S. Infantry.

Promotions

Major Thomas S. Jesup, brevet lieutenant colonel. July 5, 1814. Distinguished services at the Battle of Chippawa.

Brevet Lieutenant Colonel Thomas S. Jesup, brevet colonel. July 25, 1814. Gallant conduct in the Battle of Niagara.

Captain Daniel Ketchum, brevet major. July 25, 1814. Distinguished services and gallant conduct, Battle of Niagara.

Captain John B. Murdock, brevet major. July 25, 1814. Gallant conduct — Battle of Niagara.

Captain Benjamin Watson, brevet major. July 25, 1814. Gallant conduct — Battle of Niagara.

Major Charles K. Gardner, brevet lieutenant colonel. February 5, 1815. Distinguished and meritorious services.

Archival

RG94, Roll 12. Letters. National Archives. Captain Henry Leavenworth, 1812–1814.

RG98, No.292/141. Company book. National Archives. Captain Jesse Beach, 1814–1815.

RG98, No. 294/143. Company book. National Archives. Captain Daniel Ketchum, 1814–1815.

RG98, No. 291/140. Company book. National Archives. Captain Peter Bradley, 1813–1814.

RG98, No. 288/137. Company book. National Archives. Festus Cone/ Thomas M. Read, 1812–1814.

RG98, No. 293/142. Company book. National Archives. Captain Archibald C. Crary, 1814–1815.

RG98, No. 286/134. Company book. National Archives. Captain George Howard, 1812–1813.

RG98, No. 287/136. Company book. National Archives. Captain Thomas S. Seymour, 1814–1815.

RG98, No. 290/139. Company book. National Archives. Captain Edward White, 1814–1815.

RG98, No. 289/138. Record book. National Archives. Benjamin Watson/J. Burbridge, 1814–1815.

Howard, George. Orderly Book. New York Historical. BV Sec. W; 1813–1814.

Bartlett, David. Reports. Rhode Island. Mss 673, SG 3; Fort Adams, 1812–1813.

Manuscript

Battey, William. Letter, 1812. Rhode Island. Ms 790; describes Cantonment Greenbush.
Gardner, Charles K. Letters. Historical Society (Pa). Daniel Parker Papers.
Gardner, Charles. K. Papers. New York State. KB12914; 1812–1815.
Gifford, John. Letter, 1814. Penfield Library. Gifford Family Papers; Lundy's Lane, 1814.
Howard, George. Journal. Connecticut Historical. Ms 78171, Niagara; 1813–1814.
Jesup, Thomas S. Papers. U.S. Army Military. 1813–1815.
Jesup, Thomas S. Papers. Library of Congress. 0318C; 1812–1815, Niagara memoranda.
Jesup, Thomas S. Letters. New York State. 1814–1815.
Jesup, Thomas S. Papers. Perkins Library. Dalton Coll.
Jesup, Thomas S. Letter, 1825. Virginia Historical. Mss2 J4998 a 1; Lundy's Lane.
Shields, Hector. Letters. American Antiquarian. War of 1812 Collection; Chippawa, 1814.
Sturtevant, Thomas. Letter, 1814. South Carolina Historical. Joshua B. Whitridge Papers; Stoney Creek.
Whitridge, Joshua B. Letters. South Carolina Historical. Joshua B. Whitridge Papers; Niagara, 1813.

Printed Primary

Clarke, Jack A., ed. "Thomas Sidney Jesup: Military Observer at the Hartford Convention." *New England Quarterly* 29 (September 1956): 393–399.
Gardner, Charles K. *Proceedings of a Court Martial Held at Fort Independence, Boston Harbor.* N. P., 1816.
Cruikshank, Ernest A., ed. *Documentary History of the Campaign Upon the Niagara Frontier* 9. Vols. Welland, Ont.: Tribune Press, 1896–1908. Vol. 9, 473–482. [Major Thomas S. Jesup diary]
Fredriksen, John C., ed. "Chronicle of Valor: The Journal of a Pennsylvania Officer in the War of 1812." *Western Pennsylvania Historical Magazine* 67 (July 1984): 243–284. [Colonel George McFeely]
Fredriksen, John C. "Memoirs of Ephraim Shaler: A Connecticut Yankee in the War of 1812." *New England Quarterly* 57 (September 1984): 411–420.
Jesup, Thomas S. "Who Captured General Riall?" *Historical Magazine* 8 (July 1870): 54–55.
Memoir of General Scott, From Records Contemporaneous with Events. Washington, D. C.: C. Alexander, 1852. [Major Thomas S. Jesup letters, 11–22]
Senter, Nathaniel G. M. *A Vindication of the Character of Nathaniel G. M. Senter.* Hallowell, Me.: Ezekiel Gooddale 1815.
United States. Army. Division of the North. *A Pamphlet Being in Circulation, Purporting to Be the Trial of Major Charles K. Gardner, the Following is Intended to be a Supplement to it: Being the Decision of the Court and the Official Approbation of the Same.* New York. N.p., 1816.

Select Secondary

Fredriksen, John C. "Lawyer, Soldier, Judge: Incidents in the Life of Joseph Lee Smith of New Britain, Connecticut." *Connecticut Historical Society Bulletin* 51 (Spring 1986): 103–121.

Kieffer, Chester L. *Maligned General: The Biography of Thomas Sidney Jesup*. San Rafael, Calif.: Presidio Press, 1979.
Kochan, James L., and Don Troiani. "25th United States Infantry Regiment, Spring 1813–Spring 1814." *Military Collector and Historian* 50 (Spring 1998): 42–43.

26th Regiment of Infantry (I)

Raised: January 29, 1813
Recruited: Ohio

Battle Honors

Not engaged

The 26th Regiment of Infantry was beset by a lack of numbers throughout its short service life, despite its status as one of six regular regiments assigned to the army of General William Henry Harrison. Consequently it was restricted to garrison duties, first in Ohio and then Detroit, following the latter's recapture. Its only known encounter proved disastrous: on December 15, 1813, a company under Lieutenant Joseph Larwill was encamped 15 miles from the mouth of the Thames River, when it was surprised by Lieutenant Henry Metcalfe and 33 Norfolk County militiamen. Three officers and 35 soldiers were captured. In May, 1814, the 26th was consolidated with the 17th, 19th, and 27th Regiments to form new 17th and 19th Regiments.

Manuscripts

Baird, William. Memoir. Indiana State. S52; 1812–1813, Detroit.
Brady, Josiah. Letters. Burton Historical. 1813.

26th Regiment of Infantry (II)

Raised: March 30, 1814
Recruited: Burlington, Vermont

Battle Honors

1814: Fort Erie (det.), Plattsburgh (det).

This unit began as the 48th Regiment of Infantry, but was renumbered the 26th in May 1814. After recruiting, it was armed with rifles and deployed in various detachments. Lieutenant Martin Scott, a legendary marksman of the postwar period, was among those serving in the ranks. At least one company of the 26th was active in the defense of Fort Erie, Upper Canada, from August–September 1814, while another detachment of 100 under Captain Grosvener served at Plattsburgh on September 11, 1814. In May 1815, it was consolidated into the Regiment of Light Artillery.

Archival

RG98, No. 295/144. Company book. National Archives. Captain Elijah Boardman, 1814–1815.

RG98, No. 297/146. Company book. National Archives. Captain Ira Williams, 1814–1815.

RG98, No. 296/145. Company book. National Archives. John Levake/Salmon C. Cotton, 1814–1815.

Select Secondary

Sachese, Nancy D. "Frontier Legend: Bennington's Martin Scott." *Vermont History* 34 (1966):157–168.

27th Regiment of Infantry (I)

Raised: January 29, 1813
Recruited: Ohio

Battle Honors

1813: Chatham, Thames
1814: Longwood

After recruiting this unit became one of six regular regiments assigned to General William Henry Harrison's army. In July 1813 it mustered 350 men at Senecatown, on the Lower Sandusky River, Ohio. Lieutenant Colonel George Paull commanded 120 men during the pursuit of fleeing British forces and were present at Chatham, October 4, 1813. During the climactic victory of the Thames on October 5, Paull occupied the extreme right of Harrison's line and was tasked with carrying the enemy artillery, losing two dead and four wounded in the process. The following spring a detachment fought at the Battle of Longwoods on March 4, 1814, although casualties are unknown.

In May 1814, the 27th was consolidated with the 17th, 19th, and 26th Regiments to form new 17th and 19th Regiments.

Manuscript

Atkins, Quintus. Journal. Western Reserve. MS. 2018.
Cass, Lewis. Report. U.S. Army Military. 27th Regiment Papers, 1813.
Shannon, James. Papers. William T. Young. 55W22; 1813–1815.

Printed Primary

Brunson, Alfred. *A Western Pioneer, or, Incidents in the Life and Times of Alfred Brunson.* 2 vols. Cincinnati: Hitchcock, Walden, 1872. Vol.1, 106–148.
Brunson, Alfred. "Death of Tecumseh." *Wisconsin Historical Collections* 4 (1857–1858): 369–374.

27th Regiment of Infantry (II)

Raised: March 30, 1814
Recruited: New York City

Battle Honors

Not engaged

This unit began life as the 47th Regiment of Infantry but was renumbered the 27th as of May 1814. It spent its entire operational life as part of the New York City garrison, with no colonel ever being appointed. In May 1815, the 27th was consolidated with the 11th, 25th, 29th, and 37th Regiments to form the new 6th U.S. Infantry.

Archival

RG98, No. 298/147. Company book. National Archives. Captain Aaron C. Crane, 1814–1815.
RG98, No. 300/149. Company book. National Archives. Captain Thomas Earle, 1814–1815.
RG98, No. 299/148. Company book. National Archives. Captain Christian Hartell, 1814–1815.
RG98, No. 301/150. Company book. National Archives. Captain James Porter, 1814–1815.
RG98, No. 302/151. Company book. National Archives. Captain Allen Reynolds, 1814–1815.

RG98, No. 303/152. Company book. National Archives. Captain Benjamin F. Wood, 1814–1815.

28th Regiment of Infantry

Raised: January 29, 1813
Recruited: Olympian Springs, Kentucky

BATTLE HONORS

1813: Detachment serving as marines on Lake Erie
1814: Longwood, Sturgeon Creek

The 28th Regiment was one of six regular regiments assigned to the army of General William Henry Harrison. In July 1813, it mustered 450 men while posted at Fort Massac under Colonel Thomas D. Owings. On September 5, 1813, Captain George Stockton's company of the 28th accompanied General Harrison during his tour of Commodore Oliver Hazard Perry's fleet at Erie, Pennsylvania, and several soldiers served as marines during the climactic battle of September 10; four were killed and nine wounded. The regiment next saw combat on March 4, 1814, when several detachments under Major Andrew Hunter Holmes fought and won the battle of Longwoods, Upper Canada, against superior numbers of British light troops. On July 12, 1814, another detachment was heavily ambushed by Indians at Sturgeon Creek (Point au Playe) Upper Canada, roughly 40 miles below Malden, suffering nine killed and four wounded. In May 1815, the 28th joined the 1st, 17th, 19th, 24th, and 29th, in forming the new 3rd U.S. Infantry.

PROMOTIONS

Captain Thomas L. Butler, brevet major. January 8, 1815. Gallant conduct during the siege of New Orleans.

ARCHIVAL

RG94. Letters. National Archives. Anthony Butler, 1813–1815.
28th U. S. Infantry. Enlistments. Ross County Historical. N/A103; March–November, 1814.

MANUSCRIPT

Butler, Anthony. Letters. Burton Historical.

Butler, Anthony. Papers. E. C. Barker History. 1813–1814.
O'Fallon, John. Letters. Burton Historical.
O'Fallon, John. Papers. Filson Historical. A/031; 1812–1815.
O'Fallon, John. Papers. Missouri Historical. A1151; 1812–1814.
O'Fallon, John. Letter, 1813. Wisconsin Historical. Tecumseh Papers, 6 YY; Fort Meigs.
Todd, Charles S. Papers. Filson Historical. A T633; 1812–1815.
Todd, Charles S. Letters. Wisconsin Historical. Frontier Wars Papers, 7 U.

Select Secondary

Jelsma, Sherry K. "The Making of Imperishable Honor: Charles S. Todd in the War of 1812." *Register of the Kentucky Historical Society* 105, no. 2 (Spring 2007): 195–228.

29th Regiment of Infantry

Raised: January 29, 1813
Recruited: Albany, New York

Battle Honors

1813: Chateauguay
1814: Plattsburgh

The 29th Regiment of Infantry was formed then marched to Burlington, Vermont, as part of General Wade Hampton's Division. There it was temporarily attached to several companies of the 11th Regiment, and the combined unit was commanded under Colonel Melancton Smith. In this capacity it fought at the Battle of Chateauguay on October 26, 1813, with General George Izard's brigade. After wintering at Plattsburgh, the 29th Regiment was reassigned to the brigade of General Alexander Macomb. On September 6, 1814, a detachment of 250 men under Major John E. Wool engaged a strong British column at Beekmantown Road, New York, supported by a body of riflemen commanded by Lieutenant Colonel Daniel Appling. These troops caused considerable casualties to the British and they made a final stand at Culver Hill, supported by two artillery pieces, before finally retreating. Among the British casualties was Brevet Lieutenant Colonel Willington of the 3rd (Buffs) Regiment, who died bravely at the head of his men. On September 11, 1814, Colonel Smith's men occupied Fort Moreau during the British attack on Plattsburgh. Their determined stand cost the regiment and additional 15 dead and 16 wounded. In May 1815, the 29th was consolidated with the 11th, 25th, 27th, and 37th Regiments to form the new 6th U.S. Infantry.

Promotions

Major John E. Wool, brevet lieutenant colonel. September 11, 1814. Gallant conduct — Battle of Plattsburgh.

Archival

RG98, No. 305/154. Company book. National Archives. Captain John C. Rochester, 1813–1815.
RG98, No. 304/153. Company book. National Archives. Captain James B. Spencer, 1814–1815.
RG98, No. 306/155. Company book. National Archives. Captain Peter B. Van Buren, 1813–1815.

Manuscript

Rochester, John C. Letters. Rush Rhees Library. Plattsburgh; 1813–1814.
Ward, Aaron. Letters. Boston Public. *Ms.Am.141, Chateauguay; 1813–1814.
Wool, John E. Papers. New York State. 15361; 1814.
Wool, John E. Papers. Feinburg Library. 1814.

Printed Primary

"Garrison Orders; Burlington, Vermont, July 13–August 4, 1813." *Moorsfield Antiquarian* 1 (August 1937): 79–103.
Nelson, Gladys G., ed. "The Battle of Plattsburgh." *University of Rochester Library Bulletin* 3 (Winter 1948): 30–34. [Lieutenant Nathaniel Rochester]
Wool, John E. "A Letter from John E. Wool." *Historical Magazine* 2 (October 1873): 243.
Wool, John E. "The Battle of Beekmantown Road in 1814." *North Country Notes* (September 1965).
Wool, John E. "Major Wool's Account of the Battle of Plattsburgh." *North Country Notes* (September 1961).

Select Secondary

Hinton, Harwood P. "The Military Career of John Ellis Wool." Unpublished Ph.D. dissertation, University of Wisconsin, 1960.

30th Regiment of Infantry

Raised: January 29, 1813
Recruited: Burlington, Vermont

Battle Honors

1814: La Colle Mills, Plattsburgh

After recruitment, this formation was brigaded with the 31st Regiment of Infantry as part of General Wade Hampton's division at Burlington, Vermont. It was next posted with General George Izard's brigade and partook of the Battle of Chateauguay on October 26, 1813. The following spring it formed part of a detachment commanded by Colonel Isaac Clark, 11th Regiment, which fought at La Colle Mill on March 30, 1814, losing nine dead and 30 wounded. That summer the regiment constituted part of Daniel Bissell's brigade at Plattsburgh, New York, although it did not accompany him to Niagara. The unit was present during the battle on September 11, 1814, where it garrisoned Redoubt No. 1 and lost one dead and seven injured. In May 1815, the 30th was absorbed into the Regiment of Light Artillery.

Archival

30th U. S. Infantry. Orderly Book. Bailey Howe/Library. Burlington; November 1814–June 1815.

RG98, No. 307/156. Company book. National Archives. Captain William Miller, 1813–1815.

RG98, No. 308/157. Company book. National Archives. Captain David Sanford, 1814–1815.

RG98, No. 309/158. Company book. National Archives. Captain James Taylor, 1815.

Manuscript

Burton, John H. Letters, 1813. Minnesota Historical. P939; 1813 commission.

31st Regiment of Infantry

Raised: January 29,1813
Recruited: Woodstock, Vermont

Battle Honors

1813: Chateauguay
1814: La Colle Mill, Plattsburgh

Shortly after being recruited and deployed at Burlington, Vermont, the 31st Regiment of Infantry was brigaded with the 30th Regiment, and remained so for the rest of the war. In this capacity it formed part of General George Izard's brigade during the Battle of Chateauguay, October 25, 1813, and was also present at La Colle Mill on March 30, 1814. By the summer of 1814 the

31st regiment formed part of General Daniel Bissell's brigade at Plattsburgh, New York, but it remained behind and garrisoned Fort Brown under General Alexander Macomb. It consequently fought in the battle there on September 11, 1814, losing one dead and seven wounded. As of May 1815, the unit was amalgamated into the Light Artillery Regiment.

Archival

31st U. S. Infantry. Muster roll. Cincinnati Historical. Mss VF3129; Plattsburgh, February, 1815.
RG98, No. 312/161. Company book. National Archives. Capt. Andrew Arnold, 1814–1815.
RG98, No. 310/159. Company book. National Archives. Captain Ethan Burnap, 1814–1815.
RG98, No. 311/160. Company Book. National Archives. Captain Rufus Stewart, 1814–1815.
Morrill, Joseph. Record book. Vermont Historical. XMSC 20:3, 1813–1814.

32nd Regiment of Infantry

Raised: January 29,1813
Recruited: Delaware and Pennsylvania

Battle Honors

Not engaged

This regiment appears to spent most of its existence in or near New York City as part of the garrison, although by July 1814 there were 165 soldiers deployed at Plattsburgh. Several ranking officers were detached to other theaters, most notably Lieutenant Colonel Samuel Lane, who served at Fort McHenry, Maryland, and Major Andrew H. Holmes, the victor of Longwoods, who was slain at Mackinac on August 4, 1814. In May 1815, the unit was consolidated with the new 2nd U.S. Infantry.

Archival

32nd U. S. Infantry. Register. Hagley Museum. 1813.
RG98, No. 313/162. Company book. National Archives. Capt. Samuel Borden, 1813–1815.
RG98, No. 314/163. Company book. National Archives. Capt. John Steele, 1814–1815.
RG98, No. 315/164. Orderly book. National Archives. Capt. Charles F. Goodman, 1814–1815.

Manuscript

Holmes, Andrew H. Folder. Burton Historical. Reflections upon his death and burial.

33rd Regiment of Infantry

Raised: January 29, 1813
Recruited: Massachusetts, Saco, Maine Territory

Battle Honors

1813: Chateauguay
1814: La Colle Mill, Plattsburgh

After forming, this regiment marched to the Champlain Valley as part of General Wade Hampton's division. The 33rd Regiment fought off a Canadian attack against the American advanced camp on October 4, 1813, losing Lieutenant Nash and one private killed. It subsequently served in Colonel Purdy's brigade at Chateauguay on October 26, 1813, and sustained no losses, but Lieutenant William Morris was court-martialed and cashiered for poor behavior. The following spring, the 33rd Regiment fought at La Colle Mill on March 30, 1814, and was next assigned as part of General Daniel Bissell's brigade at Plattsburgh, New York. The unit remained behind at Plattsburgh following the departure of General George Izard from that theater and, during the battle of September 11, 1814, it occupied Fort Scott, losing two dead and two injured. After May 1815, it was consolidated into the Light Artillery Regiment.

Archival

Haley, Noah. Record Book. Boston Public. Ms.q.Am.2247; Maine, 1813.
RG94, Roll 5. Letters. National Archives. Captain Horatio Stark, 1813–1815.
RG98, No. 317/166. Company book. National Archives. Captain James Curry, 1814–1815.
RG98, No. 316/165. Company book. National Archives. Captain Benjamin Dunn, 1814–1815.
Goodwin, Jeremiah. Issue book. New England Historical. Safe Loc. Hist YOR 2; 1813–1815.

Manuscript

Goodwin, Jeremiah. Letters. Portsmouth Athenaeum. S0623, Plattsburgh, 1813–1814.

Lane, Isaac. Letters. Maine Historical. Coll. 2244; 1813–1815.
Lane, Isaac. Papers. Maine Historical. Coll. 108; 1813–1815.
Powell, Samuel. Enlistments. New Hampshire. June–December, 1813.
Walworth, John. Letters. Library and Archives. MG24, F16; 1813–1814.

34th Regiment of Infantry

Raised: January 29, 1813
Recruited: Massachusetts, Portland, Maine Territory

BATTLE HONORS

1813: Chateauguay
1814: Plattsburgh

After being raised the regiment reported for duty in the Champlain Valley, where it formed part of General Wade Hampton's Division. As such it was present at Chateauguay on October 26, 1813, but not closely engaged. The following spring a detachment fought at La Colle Mill on March 30, 1814, but sustained no losses. The regiment remained behind at Plattsburgh as part of General Alexander Macomb's brigade and during the battle of September 11, 1814, it occupied Redoubt No. 2, losing two killed and four wounded. In May 1815, the unit was amalgamated with the Light Artillery Regiment.

PROMOTIONS

Major William Piatt, brevet lieutenant colonel. December 23, 1814. Gallant conduct during the siege of New Orleans.

ARCHIVAL

RG98, No. 320/169. Company book. National Archives. Captain Thomas Bailey, 1814–1815.
RG98, No. 321/170. Company book. National Archives. Captain Isaac Carter, 1814–1815.
RG98, No. 319/168. Company book. National Archives. Captain Peter Chadwick, 1814–1815.
RG98, No. 318/167. Company book. National Archives. Captain Robert R. Kendall, 1814–1815.
RG98, No. 322/171. Company book. National Archives. Captain Benjamin Poland, 1814–1815.
34th Regiment. Register. New York Public. U.S. Army Boxes; Capt. Thomas Bailey.

Manuscript

Vinson, Thomas M. Papers. Massachusetts Historical. Vinson, Box 1; 1813.

Printed Primary

Learned, Joseph D. *Report of the Trial of Col. Joseph D. Learned, of the 34th U. S. Regt. Infantry, Convened at Portland, District of Maine, on the 14th Day of November, A. D., 1814.* Portland: A. & J. Shirley, 1815.

35th Regiment of Infantry

Raised: January 29, 1813
Recruited: Petersburg, Virginia

Battle Honors

Not engaged

The 35th Regiment spent the war performing garrison duty at various points along the Virginia coast and saw no action. In May 1815, it was consolidated with the 5th and 18th Regiments to form the new 8th U.S. Infantry.

Archival

Smith, William. Orderly Book. Library of Congress. 0314; Fort Nelson, February–March, 1813.
RG98, No. 323/172. Company book. National Archives. Capt. Walter T. Cocke, 1814–1815.
RG98, No. 324/173. Company book. National Archives. Capt. Francis E. Walker, 1814–1815.

Manuscript

Bolling, Blair. Letters. Virginia Historical. Mss1 B6386 b 8–10; 1813–1814.
Bolling, Blair. Accounts. Virginia Historical. Mss1 B6386 b 11–16; enlistments.
Bolling, Blair. Memoir. Virginia Historical. O.S. Mss5:5 B6383:1, pp. 26–34.

36th Regiment of Infantry

Raised: January 29, 1813
Recruited: Richmond, Virginia, and Georgetown, District of Columbia.

Battle Honors

1814: Bladensburg, Fort McHenry

This unit performed garrison duty throughout the Baltimore-Washington, D. C., area with little interruption until the summer of 1814. That year it mustered only 250 men at St. Mary's, Maryland, and on July 19, 1814, Colonel Henry Carberry marched it to the aid of Commodore Joshua Barney's gunboat flotilla at Leonard's Creek. On August 24, 1814, the regiment deployed under Lieutenant Colonel William Scott as part of General Walter Smith's brigade. At one point, the regiment changed front to face the advancing British and received their fire. Losses have never been ascertained, but Lieutenant Colonel Scott's horse was killed beneath him. His regiment was in the act of returning fire when General William H. Winder hurriedly galloped up and ordered them withdrawn immediately. The 36th Regiment subsequently retired in good order, although a detachment of 80 men posted near the Easton Branch Bridge did not rejoin the main body for some time afterwards. On September 13, 1814, another detachment helped garrison Fort McHenry in Baltimore harbor and withstood the intense British bombardment. In May 1815, the 36th joined the 8th, 18th, and 33rd Regiments to form the new 7th U.S. Infantry.

Archival

Carberry, Henry. Accounts. Ohio Historical. Transportation costs, 1814, 1815.

37th Regiment of Infantry

Raised: January 29, 1813
Recruited: New London and Hartford, Connecticut

Battle Honors

Not engaged

The 37th Regiment served exclusively as a garrison unit in its home state, principally at the port of New London, and saw no action. However, Colonel Henry Atkinson became a leading figure of western military affairs over the next three decades. In May 1815, the 37th was amalgamated with the 11th, 25th, 27th, and 29th Regiments to form the new 6th U.S. Infantry.

Henry Atkinson, 37th Infantry. State Historical Society of Iowa, State Historical Museum.

Archival

37th Infantry. Account book. Connecticut Historical. Acct Books; 1813–1815.
RG98, No. 329/178. Company book. National Archives. Capt. John Brown, 1814–1815.
RG98, No. 330/179. Company book. National Archives. Chauncey Ives/David T. Welch, 1813–1815.

RG98, No. 328/177. Company book. National Archives. Capt. Samuel B. Northrop, 1813–1815.
RG98, No. 325/174. Company book. National Archives. Capt. Christopher Ripley, 1813–1815.
RG98, No. 327/176. Company book. National Archives. Capt. Stephen D. Tilden, 1814–1815.
RG98, No. 326/175. Company book. National Archives. Capt. Elizur Warner, 1813–1815.

MANUSCRIPT

Atkinson, Henry. Letter, 1814. Southern Historical. Yancey Bartlett Papers, 825: promotions.
Ripley, Christopher. Papers. Connecticut Historical. Ms 64088, Fort Griswold, 1813–1815.

SELECT SECONDARY

Nichols, Roger L. *General Henry Atkinson, A Western Military Career*. Norman: University of Oklahoma Press, 1965.

38th Regiment of Infantry

Raised: January 29, 1813
Recruited: Baltimore and Craney Island, Maryland

BATTLE HONORS

1814: Bladensburg, Fort McHenry

This unit spent the bulk of its service life in the Baltimore region as a garrison unit. On July 25, 1814, it marched to the aid of Commodore Joshua Barney's gunboats at Leonard's Creek, Maryland. The 38th saw its only pitched encounter at Bladensburg on August 24, 1814, where it was posted near Barney's naval battery on the left of General William H. Winder's line. The regiment was not closely engaged, suffered no casualties, and withdrew in good order. Several companies next garrisoned Fort McHenry in Baltimore harbor where, on September 13, 1814, they endured a terrific bombardment by the entire British fleet. Once again, no losses were incurred. In May 1815, the unit was consolidated with the 8th, 10th, and 36th Regiments to form the new 7th U.S. Infantry.

ARCHIVAL

RG94, Roll 31. Letters. National Archives. Richard M. Sands, 1813, 1815.
RG98, Item 296. Orders issued. National Archives. Craney Island, Va., 1814–1815.

Manuscript

Watkins, Gassaway. Papers. Maryland Historical. Ms.879; 1814.

Printed Primary

United States. Adjutant-General's Office. *Letter from the Acting Secretary of War Transmitting an Official Report of the Adjutant and Inspector General Relative to the Mutiny Said to Have Taken Place at Norfolk of a Part of the 38th Regiment, United States Infantry.* Washington, D. C.: William A. Davis, 1817.

39th Regiment of Infantry

Raised: January 29, 1813
Recruited: Knoxville, Tennessee

Battle Honors

1814: Horseshoe Bend, Pensacola

The 39th Regiment spent a complete year recruiting before it was committed to combat operations during the Creek War. Its lieutenant colonel, Thomas Hart Benton, was a personal enemy of General Andrew Jackson, who deliberately kept him on recruiting service to deny him any wartime laurels. The unit finally joined Jackson's army at Fort Strother, Alabama Territory, on March 6, 1814, and, on the 27th of that year, several companies fought at the decisive battle of Horseshoe Bend. The soldiers were called upon to storm a fortified Indian position that had been loopholed for musket fire, yet, Colonel John Williams at their head, it was carried at bayonet point. Major Lemuel Montgomery was slain on the parapet while Ensign Sam Houston received an arrow in his thigh; fierce Creek resistance cost the 39th a further 17 dead and 59 wounded. Some time later the regiment formed part of the garrison at Mobile, from which Captains Walker and Long led companies on the attack against Pensacola, West Florida, on November 7, 1814. In May, 1815, the 39th was consolidated with the 1st, 17th, 19th, 24th, and 28th Regiments to form the new 3rd U.S. Infantry.

Archival

RG94, Roll 32. Letters. National Archives. Nathaniel Smith, 1813, 1815.
24th U.S. Infantry. Morning reports. Tennessee Historical. Winchester Papers, Fort Charlotte; 1815.

Manuscript

Benton, Thomas H. Letters. Library of Congress. Andrew Jackson Papers; 1813–1815.
Blue, Uriah. Letters. Library of Congress. Andrew Jackson Papers; 1814–1815.
Houston, Samuel. Letters. E. C. Barker History. Horseshoe Bend; 1815.
Williams, John. Letters. Library of Congress. Andrew Jackson Papers; 1814–1815.

Printed Primary

Day, Donald, and Harry Ullom, eds. *The Autobiography of Sam Houston.* Norman: University of Oklahoma Press, 1947, 9–14.

Select Secondary

Chambers, William N. "Thwarted Warrior: The Last Years of Thomas Hart Benton in Tennessee, 1812–1815." *East Tennessee Historical Society Publications* No. 22 (1950): 22–29.
Kanon, Thomas. "A Slow, Laborious Slaughter: The Battle of Horseshoe Bend." *Tennessee Historical Quarterly* 50, no. 1 (1999): 2–15.
Maiden, Leota D. "Colonel John Williams." *East Tennessee Historical Society Publications* No. 30 (1958): 7–47.
Reid, John A. "The Silk Standards of the 39th U. S. Infantry." *Military Collector and Historian* 50 (Spring 1998): 35–37.
Rucker, Brian R. "In the Shadow of Jackson: Uriah Blue's Expedition into West Florida." *Florida Historical Quarterly* 73, no. 3 (1995): 325–378.

40th Regiment of Infantry

Raised: January 29, 1813
Recruited: Boston, Massachusetts

Battle Honors

1814: Fort Sullivan

This unit performed constant, if quiet, garrison duty in detachments stationed at Boston, Portsmouth, New Hampshire, and Portland and Eastport, Maine Territory. All this changed on July 18, 1814, when a large British expeditionary force under Major General Sir John Coape Sherbrooke and Admiral Edward W. Griffith arrived off Eastport. Fort Sullivan was then garrisoned by Major Perley Putnam's company of 40 men which, after firing several defiant cannon shots, surrendered. On August 20, 1814, the British had moved up in force to Castine where a company under Lieutenant Andrew Lewis occupied a half moon battery. Defying all calls to surrender, Lewis fired several shots at the British, then spiked his cannon, blew up the redoubt, and withdrew in good order to the interior. On September 12, 1814, the company of Captain John Leonard at Machias also retreated without putting up serious resistance. As of May, 1815, the 40th Regiment joined with the 4th, 9th, 13th, 21st, and 46th Regiments to form the new 5th U.S. Infantry.

Archival

40th U. S. Infantry. Roster. American Antiquarian. War of 1812 Papers; Fort MacClary, Maine.
RG98, No. 333/182. Company book. National Archives. Capt. Robert Neale, 1813–1814.
RG98, No. 331/180. Company book. National Archives. Capt. Leonard Ross, 1813–1814.
RG98, No. 332/181B. Company book. National Archives. Mat. N. Sanborn/Wm B. Parker, 1814–1815.
RG98, No. 334/183. Descriptions. National Archives. Capt. Jacob B. Varnum, 1813–1815.
40th U. S. Infantry. Paymaster. Portsmouth Athenaeum. S0694; subsistence, forage, clothing.

Manuscript

George, Charles H. Letter, 1815. Portsmouth Athenaeum. S572; arrest for overstaying leave.
Hodges, Samuel, Jr. Papers. American Antiquarian. Recruiting; Taunton, Boston, 1812–1814.
Mosley, Luke. Letters. Boston Public. Ms.3121 (1); clerk, Fort Independence.
Neal, Robert. Enlistments. New Hampshire. 1813–1814.
Varnum, Jacob B. Memoranda. Chicago Historical. Alphabetical Colls.; Fort Sullivan, 1814.
Varnum, Jacob B. Letters. Buffalo and Erie. A. Conger Goodyear Collection.

41st Regiment of Infantry

Raised: January 29, 1813
Recruited: New York City

Battle Honors

Not engaged

This unit functioned as part of the New York City garrison and saw no combat. In May 1815, it became part of the Corps of Artillery.

ARCHIVAL

RG98, No. 128/349. Orderly book. National Archives. Captain John L. Clark, 1815.
RG98, No. 340/189. Company book. National Archives. Captain Francis Allyn, 1813–1815.
RG98, No. 337/186. Company book. National Archives. Samuel Berrian/John Ingersoll, 1813–1815.
RG98, No. 336/185. Company book. National Archives. Captain Charles Humphrey, 1814–1915.
RG98, No. 341/190. Company book. National Archives. Capt. Mangle M. Quackenbush, 1814–1815.
RG98, No. 338/187. Company book. National Archives. Captain William S. Radcliff, 1814–1815.
RG98, No. 339/188. Company book. National Archives. Captain Gilbert Sherman, 1814–1815.
RG98, No. 335/184. Company book. National Archives. Captain Alpheus Sherman, 1814–1815.

MANUSCRIPT

Allyn, Francis. Papers. New London Historical. Ms K.AL59A; 1813–1815.

42nd Regiment of Infantry

Raised: January 29 1813
Recruited: Sunbury, Pennsylvania, New York City; rendezvous at Newcastle, Delaware.

BATTLE HONORS

Not engaged

This unit formed part of the New York City garrison throughout its service life, and at various times it garrisoned Fort Richmond and Staten Island. In May, 1815, it was amalgamated with the Corps of Artillery.

ARCHIVAL

RG98, No. 344/193. Company book. National Archives. Captain George W. Barker, 1814–1815.
RG98, No. 346/194B. Company book. National Archives. John Biddle/Thomas Hanson, 1813–1815.
RG98, No. 345/194A. Company book. National Archives. Captain Thomas Hanson, 1814–1815.

RG98, No. 342/191. Company book. National Archives. Captain James F. De Peyster, 1814–1815.

RG98, No. 343/192. Company book. National Archives. Captain Edmund B. Duval, 1814–1815.

Manuscript

Irvine, William N. Letters. Historical Society (Pa). Irvine Family Papers; Irvine was colonel.

Stockton, Thomas. Papers. Library of Congress. 1813–1815.

43rd Regiment of Infantry

Raised: January 29, 1813
Recruited: Raleigh, North Carolina

Battle Honors

1815: Point Petre (det.)

This unit performed garrison duty along the coast of North Carolina, South Carolina, and Georgia, for its entire existence. On January 13, 1815, Captain Edward F. Tatnall's company was stationed at Point Petre, Georgia, in concert with a single company of the 1st Rifles under Captain Abram A. Massias. They were attacked by a force of 800 Royal Marines, sailors, and the 2nd West India Regiment, and fell back before being overrun. Captain Tatnall was wounded in the affair, along with two of his soldiers. In May 1815, the 43rd Regiment was consolidated with the Corps of Artillery.

Archival

RG94, Roll 27. Letters. National Archives. William B. Ligon, 1813–1815.
RG94, Roll 29. Letters. National Archives. William G. Oliver, 1813, 1815.
RG98, No. 348/196. Company book. National Archives. Capt. George Dabney, 1814–1815.

Manuscript

Manigault, Gabriel H. Letters. South Carolina Historical. Manigault Family Papers.

44th Regiment of Infantry

Raised: January 29, 1813
Recruited: New Orleans, Louisiana; Nashville, Tennessee

BATTLE HONORS

1814: Pensacola, Villere's Plantation
1815: New Orleans

Nearly eighteen months lapsed between the time that the 44th Regiment of Infantry was authorized and it finally saw action as part of General Andrew Jackson's army. In September, 1814, Colonel George T. Ross led a force of 70 soldiers to Barataria, where they flushed out Jean Lafitte's pirates. At Pensacola, West Florida, on November 7, 1814, Major Henry B. Peire was sent forward with a flag to demand the surrender of the Spanish garrison there. When this demand was refused, the companies of Captains Isaac L. Baker and William O. Butler drew up on the extreme left-hand flank of Jackson's attacking column. 3rd Lieutenant Alfred Flournoy was the only casualty in this brief affair, losing his leg to a cannonball as the battery was stormed. The 44th marched back to Louisiana and next formed part of Jackson's main column during the night action at Villere's Plantation on December 23, 1814. The regiment was in the thick of fighting, losing seven killed and 26 wounded, but performed well. Jackson subsequently fell back and fortified his line along the Rodriguez Canal, where, on January 1, 1815, the British conducted a reconnaissance in force that was brushed back. This affair cost the 44th another one killed and three wounded. Throughout the famous battle of January 8, 1815, the regiment deployed in the middle of the American line, between Batteries No. 4 and No. 5, but its 285 men never fired a shot. A small artillery redoubt near the Mississippi River was also manned by a detachment of the 44th under Lieutenant Marant. In May 1815, the 44th was consolidated with the 2nd, 3rd, and 7th regiments to form the new 1st U.S. Infantry.

PROMOTIONS

1st Lieutenant Richard K. Call, brevet 2nd lieutenant. November 7, 1814. Gallant behavior at Pensacola.
Captain John Reid, brevet major. December 23, 1814. Gallant conduct during the siege of New Orleans.
Captain William O. Butler, brevet major. December 23, 1814. Gallant conduct during the siege of New Orleans.
Captain Isaac L. Baker, brevet major. December 23, 1814. Gallant conduct during the siege of New Orleans.

1st Lieutenant William Gibbs, brevet captain. December 23, 1814. Gallant conduct during the siege of New Orleans.

Manuscript

Baker, Isaac L. Notebook. Library of Congress. Misc. Mss. Coll.; August–September, 1814.
Call, Richard K. Journal. Florida Historical. Pensacola, New Orleans; 1814–1815.
Call, Richard K. Papers. Southern Historical.
Peire, Henry D. Records. Hill Library. Mss. 1097; weekly report, 1815.
Peire, Henry D. Letters. Library of Congress. Andrew Jackson Papers; 1814–1815.
Reid, John. Letters, 1815. Historic New Orleans. William C. Cook Collection.
Reid, John. Papers. Library of Congress. 1814–1815.
Reid, John. Letters. Library of Congress. Andrew Jackson Papers; 1814–1815.
Ross, George T. Letters. Historic New Orleans. William C. Cook Collection; 1815.
Ross, George T. Letters. Library of Congress. Andrew Jackson Papers, 1814–1815.

Printed Primary

Baker, Isaac L. "The Journal of Isaac L. Baker, July–August, 1814." *Southwestern Historical Quarterly* 30 (April 1927): 272–282.
Barker, Eugene C., ed. *The Austin Papers*. 2 vols. Washington, D.C.: Government Printing Office, 1924. Vol. 1, 246 [Capt. Isaac L. Baker letter, 1815]

Select Secondary

Doherty, Herbert J. *Richard Keith Call: Southern Unionist*. Gainesville: University of Florida Press, 1961.
Roberts, Gerald F. "William O. Butler, Kentucky Cavalier." Unpublished master's thesis, University of Kentucky, 1971.
Vogel, Robert C. "The Patterson-Ross Raid on Barataria, September, 1814." *Louisiana History* 33, no. 2 (1992): 157–170.

45th Regiment of Infantry

Raised: March 30, 1814
Recruited: Bath, Maine Territory; Massachusetts

Battle Honors

Not engaged

This unit briefly fell under the purview of Colonel Henry Atkinson, a future frontier officer of note. However, recruitment appears to have been lackluster for the unit only mustered 344 men as of September. The 45th Regiment was initially assigned to General Daniel Bissell's brigade and marched with him to Sacketts Harbor, New York, in August 1814, where it remained behind as part of the garrison. A handful of invalids also served at Plattsburgh and fought there on September 11, 1814. In May 1815, the 45th was amalgamated with the Regiment of Light Artillery.

Archival

RG98, No. 28/199. Company book. National Archives. Capt. Smith Elkins, 1814.
RG98, No. 27/198. Company book. National Archives. Capt. Joseph Flanders, 1814–1815.
RG98, No. 349/197. Company book. National Archives. Capt. Daniel M. Gregg, 1814–1815.
RG98, No. 29/200. Company book. National Archives. Capt. Daniel Holden, 1814–1815.

Manuscript

Bradford, Benjamin. Papers. New Hampshire. Captain, Concord rendezvous; 1814.
Davis, Aquila. Letters. New Hampshire. Lieutenant Colonel; 1814.
Wilson, William H. Letters. Clements Library. Surgeon; 1814.

46th Regiment of Infantry

Raised: March 30, 1814
Recruited: New York City

Battle Honors

Not Engaged

This unit remained in the vicinity of New York City for the duration of its existence as part of the local garrison. In May 1815, it joined the 4th, 9th, 13th, 21st, and 40th regiments as part of the new 5th U.S. Infantry.

Promotions

Captain Loring Austin, brevet major. July 5, 1814. Gallant conduct as aide-de-camp, Battle of Chippawa.

Archival

RG98, No. 31/202. Company book. National Archives. Capt. Moses D. Burnett, 1814–1815.
RG98, No. 32/203. Company book. National Archives. Capt. Peter Miller, 1814–1815.
RG98, No. 30/301. Company book. National Archives. Capt. Job Wright, 1814–1815.
Tallmadge, William S. Orderly Book. New York Historical. No. 196, Fort Columbus, N.Y.; 1814–1815.

Manuscript

Delafield, Joseph. Letters. Mudd Library. CO391, Fort Columbus, N.Y.; 1812–1815.

47th Regiment of Infantry

Raised: March 30, 1814

On May 12, 1814, the regimental designation was changed to 27th U. S. Infantry.

48th Regiment of Infantry

Raised: March 30, 1814

On May 12, 1814, the regimental designation was changed to 26th U. S. Infantry.

RIFLES

Regiment of Riflemen/1st Regiment of Rifles

Raised: April 12, 1808
Recruited: three companies, Louisiana-Mississippi Territory; four companies, Kentucky, Ohio, and the Indiana Territory; three companies, New York and Vermont. Principal rendezvous are Shepardstown, Virginia, and Savannah, Georgia.

BATTLE HONORS

1812: Gannanoque, (det.)
1813: Elizabethtown, Ogdensburg, York, Fort George, Stoney Creek, Hoople's Creek, Massequoi Village
1814: La Colle Mill, Sandy Creek, Conjocta Creek, Fort Erie, Plattsburgh
1815: Point Petre (det.)

The Regiment of Riflemen was raised in 1808 as an outgrowth of President Thomas Jefferson's expansion of national defenses following the *Chesapeake-Leopard* Affair of 1807. It was envisioned from the outset as an elite unit specializing in forest warfare, skirmishing, and ambushes, as evinced by its green uniform with black facings. Members were also equipped with the newly designed Harpers Ferry Model 1803 rifle, a short weapon of Jaeger derivation, but highly accurate and reliable. Ten companies were authorized and recruited, and on November 6, 1811 the unit experienced its baptism under fire at Tippecanoe. Ironically, the single company present under Lieutenant Hawkins was equipped with muskets; they performed well in their first encounter, losing one dead and 10 wounded. In the spring of 1812, several companies marched from Georgia under Major Thomas Adams Smith into East Florida, where they partook of the so-called "Patriot War." Smith lacked sufficient manpower to formally besiege the Spanish bastion at St. Augustine, so he established an informal blockade. He was consequently harassed by

Bennett Riley, 1st Rifle Regiment. Kansas State Historical Society.

Spanish gunboats, Seminoles, and escaped African American slaves, and in a heavy exchange on October 27, 1812, the Indians managed to inflict three dead and 10 wounded. Soon after the riflemen were transferred from Florida to Canada to fight in the War of 1812. Well-trained, armed, and led, they proved themselves one of the best combat units possessed by the U.S. Army.

The first company of riflemen to distinguish themselves in combat belonged to a celebrated leader, Captain Benjamin Forsyth. Forsyth, whose men were the first army regulars stationed in northern New York. These men attacked and carried the Canadian village of Gananoque on September 21, 1812, suffering one killed and ten wounded. Forsyth then transferred his operations to Ogdensburg, directly astride British lines of communication along the St. Lawrence River, and continued making a nuisance of himself by storming the village of Elizabethtown on February 7, 1813. The riflemen seized 50 prisoners of the Leeds militia, along with 120 stands of arms captured at Detroit, but his success prompted a sharp British riposte. On February 22, 1813, Lieutenant Colonel George MacDonnell suddenly crossed the frozen river with 800 men, and drove Forsyth's company from Odgensburg with a loss of three killed and 17 wounded; MacDonnell's losses were six dead and 48 wounded, but the British had rid themselves of a troublesome and opportunistic raider.

Forsyth's company retreated to Sacketts Harbor where, two months later, they served as shock troops during General Zebulon M. Pike's amphibious assault on York, April 27, 1813. The riflemen landed and shot up the fine grenadier company of the 8th (King's) Regiment, at a cost of seven dead and 17 wounded. Forsyth then disgraced himself by plundering the town and releasing prisoners from jails; these most likely torched the town to get even with British authorities. On May 27, 1813, Forsyth again spearheaded the attack on Fort George, Upper Canada, inflicting numerous casualties at a cost of two killed and one wounded. At least part of Forsyth's command accompanied General John Chandler and William H. Winder to Stoney Creek where, on June 6, 1813, an entire picket was captured while it slept in the pews of a church. Forsyth himself remained active in the vicinity of Fort George, frequently skirmishing with enemy light troops and Indians. On August 16, 1813, his riflemen were part of an effective ambush that killed 15 Indians and captured 13 for a loss of two wounded. Within weeks, the riflemen were placed on boats and sailed down the St. Lawrence River as part of General James Wilkinson's offensive against Montreal. On November 11, 1813, Forsyth splashed ashore at Hoople's Creek, Upper Canada, completely dispersing a large body of Canadian militia without loss. That same day Wilkinson's main force was soundly defeated at Crysler's Farm, and the riflemen, who subsequently wintered at French Mills, New York, endured under terrible deprivation with the rest.

The riflemen also garnered fame under other commanders. On October 11, 1813, Colonel Isaac Clark of the 11th Infantry led a body of 102 riflemen on a raid against smugglers operating near Massequoi Village (Seignory of St. Armand), Lower Canada. Clark personally led a charge that netted 75 militia captives at a cost of two wounded. On February 10, 1814, Congress authorized creation of three more rifle regiments, numbered consecutively, so the

Regiment of Riflemen was redesignated the 1st Regiment of Rifles. Several companies were present at La Colle Mill, March 30, 1814, where they lost one dead and seven wounded. Other companies arrived at Sacketts Harbor under Major Daniel Appling, and on May 30, 1814, the riflemen, assisted by 130 Oneida braves, ambushed and captured two gunboats, five barges, and 133 sailors and Royal Marines at Sandy Creek, New York. British casualties in this lopsided affair also totaled 19 dead and 28 wounded to an American tally of one rifleman wounded. Forsyth, meanwhile, resumed his partisan activities throughout the Champlain Valley where, on June 24, his green jackets beat off a force of 200 British light troops and Indians at Odelltown. Four days later at this same location, Forsyth's luck finally deserted him when, disobeying orders, he refused to lure superior enemy forces into an ambush and instead, stood and fought. He was killed in the skirmish but his men wasted no time extracting revenge. On August 10, 1814, a rifle detachment under Lieutenant Bennet Riley ambushed Captain Joseph St. Valier Mallioux of the Frontier Light Infantry near Champlain Village, mortally wounding and capturing him.

By the summer of 1814 the locus of military activity along the northern frontier passed back to the Niagara sector, and that August, several companies of riflemen arrived at Buffalo, New York, under Major Ludowick Morgan. On the morning of August 4, 1814, a column of hand-picked British light troops crossed the Niagara River to the American side and attempted crossing Conjocta Creek in order to capture Buffalo. They ran headlong into Morgan's command, now entrenched along the bank, and whose accurate fire thwarted several determined charges across a bridge. At length the British drew off with a loss of 12 dead and 21 wounded, whereas Morgan had sustained only two killed, eight wounded. This was the riflemen's best-conducted and most significant action of the entire war, for it forced British general Gordon Drummond to scuttle all offensive operations concentrate on reducing the American strong point at Fort Erie. There commenced a *petit guerre* of outposts in the adjoining woods of the fort, whereby green-clad riflemen and Glengarry Fencibles routinely shot each other to ribbons. On August 13, 1814, Major Morgan, the "Hero of Conjocta," fell in a heavy exchange while a further three riflemen were killed and six wounded to skirmishing and the British bombardment. On August 15, 1814, the riflemen were closely engaged in repelling Drummond's attack upon Fort Erie, losing three wounded. Skirmishing outside the fort resumed until September 17, 1814, when General Jacob J. Brown led a violent and successful sortie against British siege lines; the riflemen sustained a further 11 dead and 19 wounded in this action.

The riflemen were also conspicuously engaged in actions around Plattsburgh, New York. On September 6, Major Appling led a detachment of 100 rifles alongside the 29th Infantry under Major John E. Wool at Beekmantown Road. American losses are not clear, but the British recorded 55 killed and wounded, including Brevet Lieutenant Colonel Willington of the 3rd (Buffs) Regiment. A week later, Appling's men distinguished themselves in combat at Plattsburgh, losing four killed and nine wounded while repulsing several British attempts to cross the Saranac River. The final action of the 1st Regiment of Rifles occurred not far from where its first protracted operations began. On January 13, 1815, Captain Abram A. Massias found that a British naval squadron was bearing down on him at Point Petre, Georgia. Massias had only his own company and one of the 43rd Infantry to oppose a combined force of 700 Royal Marines, sailors, and the 2nd West India Regiment; he was quickly overrun with a loss of one dead and four wounded. This act concluded the wartime career of these skilled sharpshooters who, in May 1815, were all consolidated into the Regiment of Riflemen. This formation performed useful service along the western frontier until 1821, when it was disbanded by Congress for reasons of economy. The U.S. Army would not again possess a unit of green-clad marksmen until the advent of Berdan's Sharpshooters in 1861.

Promotions

Major Benjamin Forsyth, brevet lieutenant colonel. February 6, 1814. Distinguished services.

Major Daniel Appling, brevet lieutenant colonel. May 30, 1814. Gallant conduct in the Battle of Sandy Creek.

Brevet Lieutenant Colonel Daniel Appling, brevet colonel. September 11, 1814. Gallant conduct at Plattsburgh.

Lieutenant Colonel James McDonald, brevet colonel. September 17, 1814. Gallant conduct, Fort Erie sortie.

Archival

RG94, Roll 32. Letters. National Archives. Thomas A. Smith, 1812–1813.
RG98, No. 439/336. Orderly book. National Archives. 9th Mil. Dist., 1813–1815.
RG98, No. 501/403. Orderly book. National Archives. Capt. Thomas Ramsey, 1813–1815.
RG98, No. 201/33. Company book. National Archives. Capt. George Gray, 1812–1815.
RG98, No. 202/34. Company book. National Archives. Capt. Thomas Ramsey, 1814–1815.
RG98, No. 200/32. Company book. National Archives. William Smyth/Sam Hamilton, 1813–1815.
RG98, No. 199/31. Company book. National Archives. Capt. Edward Wadsworth, 1812–1815.

Manuscript

Armistead, Louis G. A. Letters. Fort McHenry. Special Collection No. 35, Fort Erie; 1814.
Armstrong, William. Letters. Wisconsin Historical. Fort Erie; 1812–1814.
Fuller, John. Journal. Ohio Historical. Elk River Expedition; 1811.
Massias, Abram A. Letters. Georgia Historical. Ms. 620, Joseph W. Pinder Papers; Georgia.
Sevier, George W. Letters. Mississippi Department. John F. H. Claiborne Vol. D; 1811–1814.
Smith, Thomas A. Letters. State Historical (Mo). Sacketts Harbor, Plattsburgh, 1812–1814.

Printed Primary

Duane, William. *A Handbook for Riflemen, Containing the First Principles of Military Discipline.* Philadelphia: The Author, 1813.
Patrick, Rembert W., ed. "Letters to the Invaders of East Florida, 1812." *Florida Historical Quarterly* 28 (July 1949): 51–65.

Select Secondary

Austerman, Wayne R. "This Excellent and Gallant Rifle Corps." *Man at Arms* 3, no. 3 (1981): 18–24, 44.
Berkeley, Lewis. "Early U. S. Riflemen: Their Arms and Training." *American Rifleman* 106, no. 12 (December 1958): 30–33.
Campbell, J. Duncan. "Notes on the Insignia of the Riflemen, U. S. Army." *Military Collector and Historian* 1 (1949): 6–8.
Fredriksen, John C. *Green Coats and Glory: The United States Regiment of Riflemen, 1808–1821.* Youngstown, N.Y.: Old Fort Niagara Association, 2000.
Holt, Richard A. "Pre-1814 U. S. Contract Rifles." *American Society of Arms Collectors Bulletin* No. 47 (1982): 7–19.
McBarron, H. Charles. "American Military Dress in the War of 1812: Regular Riflemen." *Military Affairs* 5 (1941): 139–140.
Palmer, Richard. "Lake Ontario Battles, Part 3: The Battle of Sandy Creek." *Inland Seas* 53, no. 4 (1997): 282–291.
Patterson, Richard. "Lieut. Col. Benjamin Forsyth." *North Country Notes* (November 1974).
Zlatich, Marko, and Detmar H. Finke. "The Uniform of the United States Rifle Regiment, 1808–1812." *Military Collector and Historian* 50 (Spring 1998): 120–126.

2nd Regiment of Rifles

Raised: February 10, 1814
Recruited: Chillicothe, Ohio, Nashville, Tennessee, Lexington, Kentucky.

Battle Honors

Not engaged

This unit was recruited through the spring and summer of 1814, though by November it could boast only 187 members. It finally mustered around 300 men by the spring of 1815, in time for it to form part of the garrison at Detroit, Michigan, and Fort Malden, Canada. That May it was disbanded and consolidated into the Regiment of Riflemen.

Archival

RG94, Roll 20. Letters. National Archives. Anthony Butler, 1814–1815.
RG94, Roll 24. Letters. National Archives. Captain William S. Hamilton, 1814–1815.
RG94, Roll 15. Letters. National Archives. Captain Edmund Shipp, 1814–1815.

Manuscript

Butler, Anthony. Papers. Burton Historical.
Butler, Anthony. Papers. E. C. Barker. Detroit; 1814.
Croghan, George. Papers. Clements Library. Croghan Family Papers; 1814.
Croghan, George. Letters. Filson Historical. Croghan Family Papers.
Croghan, George. Papers. Library of Congress. Misc. Mss. 3005.
Croghan, George. Papers. New York Public.
Croghan, George. Letters. Wisconsin Historical. Draper 1W; 1811–1815.
O'Fallon, John. Letters. Burton Historical.
O'Fallon, John. Papers. Filson Historical. A/031; 1812–1815.
O'Fallon, John. Papers. Missouri Historical. A1151; 1814–1815.

Select Secondary

Fredriksen, John C. *Green Coats and Glory: The United States Regiment of Riflemen, 1808–1821.* Youngstown, N.Y.: Old Fort Niagara Association, 2000.
Gerber, William E. "Harper's Ferry Rifles: Comparing the Models 1803 and 1814." *American Society of Arms Collectors Bulletin* No. 38 (1978): 17–21.

3rd Regiment of Rifles

Raised: February 10, 1814
Recruited: Virginia, North Carolina, South Carolina, with principal rendezvous at Charlotte, North Carolina, Bath Court House, Virginia, and Gallatin, Tennessee.

Battle Honors

Not engaged

This unit was recruited throughout the spring of 1814 and mustered over 500 men by September. However, it never marched further north than Fredericksburg, Virginia, and Carlisle, Pennsylvania, and saw no action. In May 1815 the 3rd Regiment was combined into the reconstituted Regiment of Riflemen.

Promotions

Major Walter H. Overton, brevet lieutenant colonel. December 23, 1814. Gallant conduct during New Orleans.
Major Joseph Seldon, brevet lieutenant colonel. May 17, 1815. Meritorious services.

Archival

RG98, No. 206/38. Company book. National Archives. John G. Blount/Wm. Duffphey, 1814–1815.
RG98, No. 203/35. Company Book. National Archives. Alex W. Brandon/Wm. Parker, 1814–1815.
RG98, No. 207/39. Company book. National Archives. John E. Calhoun/Walter Coles, 1814–1815.
RG98, No. 204/36. Company book. National Archives. Captain Wyly Martin, 1814–1815.
RG98, 205/37. Muster rolls. National Archives. Thomas Robeson/Walter Coles, 1814–1815.

Manuscript

Hamilton, William S. Papers. Hill Library. Mss 1029.3167; 1812–1813.
Hamilton, William S. Papers. Southern Historical. #1471; 1814–1815.
Overton, Walter H. Letters. Library of Congress. Andrew Jackson Papers; 1814–1815.
Robeson, Thomas J. Papers. Huntington Library. BR Box 66 (3): 1814.

Select Secondary

Fredriksen, John C. *Green Coats and Glory: The United States Regiment of Riflemen, 1808–1821.* Youngstown, N.Y.: Old Fort Niagara Association, 2000.
Gerber, William E. "Harper's Ferry Rifles: Comparing the Models 1803 and 1814." *American Society of Arms Collectors Bulletin* No. 38 (1978): 17–21.

4th Regiment of Rifles

Raised: February 10, 1814
Recruited: Western Pennsylvania, principal rendezvous at Utica, New York.

BATTLE HONORS

1814: Conjocta Creek, Fort Erie, Cook's Mills

This unit was recruited through the spring of 1814 and by August several companies were in the vicinity of Buffalo, New York, under Major Jonathan Kearsley. There they operated with a larger contingent of the 1st Regiment of Riflemen under Major Ludowick Morgan. On the morning of August 4, 1814, the 4th Regiment of Rifles fought at Conjocta Creek, north of Buffalo, where a column of handpicked British light troops was decisively repulsed. Kearsley then ferried his men across to Fort Erie, where they engaged in a constant war of outposts with British light troops, most notably the Glengarry Fencibles. On August 15, 1814, a detachment of the 4th Regiment was posted near Fort Erie proper under Captain Benjamin Birdsall, where they continually peppered a contingent of the British 103rd Regiment which had seized that bastion until a huge magazine explosion terminated the affair. On August 20th, Major Kearsley was severely wounded in another scrape with the enemy and was evacuated. Leadership of the 4th regiment then devolved upon Colonel James Gibson, who arrived to take part in Fort Erie's ongoing defense. On September 17, 1814, Gibson was slain at the head of his men during General Jacob J. Brown's successful sortie, becoming the highest-ranking American regular to fall in the 1814 Niagara Campaign — his command lost a further one dead and 10 wounded. All told, the siege, bombardment, and sortie cost the regiment 19 dead and 49 wounded. Captain Irvine's company of the 4th subsequently accompanied General Daniel Bissell's brigade to Lyon's Creek, Upper Canada, where, on October 19, 1814, they were closely engaged at the battle of Cook's Mills, losing one dead. After wintering at Conjocta Creek, the 4th Regiment was amalgamated into the reconstituted Regiment of Riflemen as of May 1815.

PROMOTIONS

Captain Benjamin Birdsall, brevet major. August 15, 1814. Gallant conduct in the defense of Fort Erie.

3rd Lieutenant Richard H. Lee, brevet 2nd lieutenant. August 15, 1814. Gallant conduct defending Fort Erie.

Major Talbot Chambers, brevet lieutenant colonel. September 17, 1814. Gallant conduct, Fort Erie sortie.

James Gibson, 4th Rifle Regiment. Courtesy Delaware Public Archives.

Brevet 2nd Lieutenant Richard H. Lee, brevet 1st lieutenant. September 17, 1814. Gallant conduct, Fort Erie sortie.

Archival

RG94, Roll 49. Letters. National Archives. Lieutenant Richard H. Lee, 1814–1815.

Printed Primary

Fredriksen, John C., ed. "The Memoirs of Jonathan Kearsley: A Michigan hero from the War of 1812." *Indiana Military History Journal* 10 (May 1985): 4–16.

Select Secondary

Fredriksen, John C. *Green Coats and Glory: The United States Regiment of Riflemen, 1808–1821.* Youngstown, N.Y.: Old Fort Niagara Association, 2000.

Gerber, William E. "Harper's Ferry Rifles: Comparing the Models 1803 and 1814." *American Society of Arms Collectors Bulletin* No. 38 (1978): 17–21.

Archival and Manuscript Depositories

Alabama Department of Archives
and History
624 Washington Ave.
Montgomery, AL 36130-0100

Aldeman Library
University of Virginia
PO Box 400114
Charlottesville, VA 22904-4114

American Antiquarian Society
185 Salisbury St.
Worcester, MA 01609-1634

Bailey/Howe Library
University of Vermont
Burlington, VT 05405-0036

Beinecke Library
Yale University
PO Box 208240
New Haven, CT 06520-8240

Boston Athenaeum
10½ Beacon St.
Boston, MA 02108

Boston Public Library
Rare Books Department
Copley Square
Boston, MA 02117

Brigham Young University
Archives
Provo, UT 84602

Buffalo and Erie County Historical
Society
25 Nottingham Terrace
Buffalo, NY 14216

Burton Historical Collection
Detroit Public Library
5201 Woodward Ave.
Detroit, MI 48202

Cecil County Historical Society
135 East Main St.
Elkton, MD 2192

Center for Historical Studies
Bowling Green State University
Bowling Green, OH 43403-0001

Chicago Historical Museum
1601 North Clark St.
Chicago, IL 60614-6038

Cincinnati Historical Society
1301 Western Ave.
Cincinnati, OH 45203

Clarke Historical Library
Central Michigan University
Mount Pleasant, MI 48859

Clements Library
University of Michigan
Ann Arbor, MI 48109-1190

Connecticut Historical Society
One Elizabeth Court
Hartford, CT 06105

Cushing/Whitney Medical Library
Yale University
PO Box 208014
New Haven, CT 06520-8014

Danvers Archival Center
15 Sylvan St.
Danvers, MA 01923

Darling Biomedical Library
Special Collections/12-077CHS
UCLA
Box 951798
Los Angeles, CA 90095-1798

Dayton-Montgomery Public Library
215 E. Third St.
Dayton, OH 45402

E. C. Barker Center for American History
University of Texas at Austin
1 University Station D1100
Austin, TX 78712-0335

Feinburg Library
SUNY Plattsburgh
Plattsburgh, NY 12901

Filson Historical Society
1310 South Third St.
Louisville, KY 40208

Florida Historical Society
435 Brevard Ave.
Cocoa, FL 32922

Forbes Library
20 West Street
Northampton, MA 01060

Fort McHenry National Monument
2400 East Fort Ave.
Baltimore, MD 21230-5393

Fraunces Tavern Museum
54 Pearl St.
New York, NY 10004

Georgia Department of History and Archives
5800 Jonesboro Rd.
Morrow, GA 30260

Georgia Historical Society
501 Whitaker St.
Savannah, GA 31401

Gilder Lehrman
c/o New York Historical Society
170 Central Park West
New York, NY 10024

Hagley Museum and Library
PO Box 3630
Wilmington, DE 19807-0630

Hay Library
Brown University
Box A, 20 Prospect St.
Providence, RI 02912

Heinz History Center
1212 Smallman St.
Pittsburgh, PA 15222

Archival and Manuscript Depositories

Hill Memorial Library
Louisiana State University
Baton Rouge, LA 70803-3300

Historic New Orleans Collection
533 Royal St.
New Orleans, LA 70130

Historical Society of Pennsylvania
1300 Locust St.
Philadelphia, PA 19107

Houghton Library
Harvard University
Cambridge, MA 02138

Huntington Library
Manuscripts Department
1151 Oxford Rd.
San Marino, CA 91108

Indiana Historical Society
450 West Ohio St.
Indianapolis, IN 46202

Indiana State Library
140 N. Senate Ave.
Indianapolis, IN 46204

James Monroe Museum
University of Mary Washington
908 Charles St.
Fredericksburg, VA 22401-5801

Kentucky Historical Society
100 West Broadway
Frankfort, KY 40601

Library and Archives of Canada
395 Wellington St.
Ottawa, ON K1A 0Y4
CANADA

Library of Congress
Manuscript Division
101 Independence Ave. SE
Washington, DC 20540

Library of Virginia
800 East Broad St.
Richmond, VA 23219-8000

Lilly Library
Indiana University
Bloomington, IN 47405-3301

Louisiana State Museum
400 Esplanade Ave.
New Orleans, LA 70116

McClung Historical Collection
East Tennessee History Center
601 S. Gay St.
Knoxville, TN 37902-1629

McKeldin Library
University of Maryland
College Park, MD 20742-7011

Maine Historical Society
489 Congress St.
Portland, ME 04101

Manuscripts and Archives
Sterling Library
Yale University
New Haven, CT 06520-8240

Maryland Historical Society
201 West Monument St.
Baltimore, MD 21201-4674

Massachusetts Historical Society
1154 Boylston St.
Boston, MA 02215-3695

Minnesota Historical Society
345 West Kellogg Blvd.
St. Paul, MN 55102-1906

Mississippi Department of Archives
 and History
PO Box 571
Jackson, MS 39205-0571

Missouri Historical Museum
PO Box 11940
St. Louis, MO 63112-0040

Mitchell Memorial Library
Mississippi State University
PO Box 5408
Mississippi State, MS 39712-5408

Morristown National Park
30 Washington Place
Morristown, NJ 07960-4299

Mudd Library
Special Collections
Princeton University
Princeton, NJ 08540-2098

Nassau County Historical Museum
Hofstra University
619 Fulton Ave.
Hempstead, NY 11549

National Archives
700 Pennsylvania Ave.
Washington, DC 20408-0001

New England Historical and
 Genealogical Society
101 Newbury St.
Boston, MA 02116-3007

New Hampshire Historical Society
30 Park St.
Concord, NH 03301

New Jersey Historical Society
52 Park Place
Newark, NJ 07104

New London Historical Society
11 Blinman St.
New London, CT 06320

New Windsor Cantonment
PO Box 207
Vails Gate, NY 12584

New York Historical Society
170 Central Park West
New York, NY 10024

New York Public Library
Manuscript Department
Fifth Ave. at 42nd St.
New York, NY 10018

New York State Archives
Cultural Education Center
Albany, NY 12230

Newberry Library
60 West Walton St.
Chicago, IL 60610-7324

Oberlin College Library
148 West College St.
Oberlin, OH 44074-1545

Ohio Historical Society
1982 Velma Ave.
Columbus, OH 43211

Ohio State Library
274 East First Ave.
Suite 100
Columbus, OH 43201

Olin Library
Cornell University
Ithaca, NY 14853

Oneida Historical Society
1608 Genessee St.
Utica, NY 13502-5425

Owen D. Young Library
St. Lawrence University
Canton, NY 13616

Pace Library
University of West Florida
11000 University Parkway
Pensacola, FL 32514

Penfield Library
SUNY Oswego
Oswego, NY 13126-3599

Perkins Library
Duke University
Durham, NC 27708-0185

Philips Library
Peabody Essex Museum
161 Essex St.
Salem, MA 01970

Pierpont Morgan Library
225 Madison Ave.
New York, NY 10016

Portsmouth Atheneum
9 Market Square
Portsmouth, NH 03801

Providence Public Library
Special Collections
150 Empire St.
Providence, RI 02903

Rare Books and Manuscripts
Columbia University
535 West 114th St.
New York, NY 10027

Rauner Library
Dartmouth College
Hanover, NH 03755

Regenstein Library
University of Chicago
1100 East 57th St.
Chicago, IL 60637

Rensselaer County Historical Society
59 Second St.
Troy, NY 12180

Rhode Island Historical Society
121 Hope St.
Providence, RI 02906

Rosenbach Museum
2008–2010 Delancey Place
Philadelphia, PA 19103

Ross County Historical Society
45 West Fifth St.
Chillicothe, OH 45601

Rowan College Library
Stewart Collection
Glassboro, NJ 08028-1701

Rush Rhees Library
University of Rochester
Rochester, NY 14627

Rutgers University Library
Special Collections
New Brunswick, NJ 80901-1163

Rutherford B. Hayes Library
Spiegel Grove
Fremont, OH 43420-2796

St. Louis Mercantile Society
University of Missouri
St. Louis, MO 63121

Sheldon Museum
1 Park St.
Middlebury, VT 05753

South Carolina Historical Society
The Fireproof Bldg.
100 Meeting St.
Charleston, SC 29401

South Caroliniana Library
University of South Carolina
910 Sumter St.
Columbia, SC 29208

Southern Historical Collection
Wilson Library CB 3926
University of North Carolina
Chapel Hill, NC 27514-8890

State Historical Society of Missouri
1020 Lowry St.
Columbia, MO 65201

Swem Library
William and Mary College
PO Box 8795
Williamstown, VA 23187-8795

Syracuse University Library
22 Waverly Ave.
Syracuse, NY 13244

Tennessee Historical Society
War Memorial Bldg.
300 Capitol Blvd.
Nashville, TN 37243

Tennessee State Library
403 Seventh Ave. North
Nashville, TN 37243

Thomas Gilcrease Institute
1400 Gilcrease Museum Rd.
Tulsa, OK 74127

Ticonderoga Historical Society
6 Moses Circle
Ticonderoga, NY 12883

University of Arizona Library
1510 East University Blvd.
Tucson, AZ 85721-0055

U.S. Army Military History Institute
950 Soldiers Dr.
Carlisle Barracks, PA 17013-5021

U.S. Military Academy Library
Special Collections
West Point, NY 10996

Van Pelt Library
University of Pennsylvania
3420 Walnut St.
Philadelphia, PA 19104-6206

Vermont Historical Society
60 Washington St.
Barre, VT 05641-4209

Vermont State Archives
26 Terrace St.
Montpelier, VT 05609-1101

Virginia Historical Society
PO Box 7311
Richmond, VA 23221-0311

Western Reserve Historical Society
  Library
10825 East Blvd.
Cleveland, OH 44016

William T. Young Library
University of Kentucky
Lexington, KY 40506-0456

Wisconsin Historical Society
816 State St.
Madison, WI 53706-1417

Yarmouth Historical Society
PO Box 107
Yarmouth, ME 04096

Index

Adams, John Q. 26, 32, 50, 55
Albany 125, 223, 261
Appling, Daniel 262, 283, 284
Archer, Samuel B. 163, 171
Armistead, George 168, 171, 189
Armistead, Walter K. 189
Armstrong, John 12, 17, 19–23, 24, 30, 35, 40, 45, 48, 53, 67, 93, 106, 109, 121, 127, 139, 141
Aspinwall, Thomas 179, 212
Atkinson, Henry 133, 268, 277

Backus, Electus 179
Baker, Daniel 193
Baker, Isaac L. 276
Ball, James V. 182
Baltimore 10, 149, 225, 270
Barataria 276
Barnard, Isaac D. 228
Barney, Joshua 268, 270
Bath 277
Bath Court House 286
Baton Rouge 89, 200
Beaufort 211
Beaver Dams 37, 76, 176, 182, 206, 223, 227, 248
Bedel, Moody 218
Beekmantown Road 109, 225, 261, 284
Bennington 217
Benton, Thomas H. 271
Bernard, Simon 142
Biddle, Thomas 164, 171
Birdsall, Benjamin 288
Bissell, Daniel 20, 48, 109, 133, 205, 228, 229, 232, 263, 264, 265, 278, 288
Black Rock 216, 226, 232
Bladensburg 11, 20, 116, 151, 185, 221, 268 270
Bloomfield, Joseph 73–75, 123, 206, 229, 231
Blue Book 135
Blue Jacket 43
Boerstler, Charles G. 76, 182, 227, 228
Boston 212, 272
Boyd, John P. 36, 44, 67, 76–79, 89, 113, 145, 202, 205, 206, 221, 223, 231, 246
Boyle, James H. 168

Brady, Hugh 128, 246
Brock, Isaac 103, 203
Brooke, George M. 125, 248
Brooks, Alexander 171
Broutin, Narcissus 209
Brown, Jacob J. 20, 26, 29–34, 48, 70, 93, 109, 123, 125, 127, 133, 171, 177, 185, 189, 190, 194, 207, 229, 242, 246, 248, 283
Brownsville 32
Buffalo 30, 50, 113, 127, 171, 205, 214, 217, 248, 253, 283, 288
Burbeck, Henry 48, 79–82, 90
Burd, John A. 185
Burlington 115, 123, 203, 216, 257, 261, 262
Burn, James 85, 182, 185
Burr, Aaron 65, 83, 96, 131
Butler, William O. 276

Caledonia 163
Calhoun, John C. 32, 55, 144
Campbell, John B. 182, 194, 217, 236
Campbell's Island 194
Carberry, Henry 268
Cass, Lewis 80–84, 103, 106, 189
Castine 272
Castle Williams 187
Champlain Valley 283
Chandler, John 37, 76, 85–87, 151, 182, 212, 217, 229, 242, 248, 253, 282
Charleston 236
Charlotte 286
Chateauguay 20, 40, 48, 67, 183, 203, 205, 216, 261, 263, 265, 266
Chatham 258
Chauncey, Isaac 29, 30, 48, 127
Chazy 203, 221
Chesapeake-Leopard Affair 89, 127, 280
Cheves, Langdon 144
Chillicothe 232, 285
Chippawa 30, 113, 128, 171, 185, 214, 217, 238, 246, 263
Chippawa Creek 32, 48, 70, 171, 205, 216, 227
Chittenden, Martin 40
Chrystie, John 223, 224
Cincinnati 146

299

Claiborne, Charles C.C. 65, 89
Claiborne, Ferdinand L. 200
Clark, Isaac 217, 282
Clark, William 101
Clay, Green 44, 162
Clay, Henry 44
Clinch, Duncan L. 216
Clinton, DeWitt 10
Cockburn, George 151
Columbia 235
Concord 200
Conjocta Creek 283, 288
Cook's Mills 50, 70, 185, 205, 227, 228, 232, 288
Corps of Engineers 109, 141, 142, 190
Covington, Leonard 76, 87–90, 96, 179, 213, 231, 253
Craney Island 189, 270
Crawford, William H. 142
Creek War 52, 63, 93, 200, 271
Croghan, George 106, 113, 234, 238, 251
Crysler's Farm 20, 30, 67, 76, 89, 96, 123, 139, 141, 182, 189, 213, 221, 223, 228, 231, 242, 253
Cushing, Daniel 164
Cushing, Thomas H. 37, 81, 90–93
Cuyahoga 103

Dacres, James 113
Dallas, Alexander J. 26
Davenport, William,, 231
Dayton 112, 188
Dearborn, Henry 15, 34–39, 59, 74, 76, 79, 87, 90, 103, 117, 120, 123, 127, 150, 229, 231
Deep Creek 185
De Russy, Rene E. 189
De Salaberry, Charles 40
Desha, Robert 251
Detroit 163
Detroit 17, 35, 83, 106, 112, 146, 161, 188, 193, 203, 236, 286
Douglass, David B. 190
Downie, George 109
Drayton, William 236
Drummond, Gordon 30, 48, 70, 96, 124, 168, 190, 251, 283
Drummond, William 238
Duane, William 134, 135

East Florida 62, 131, 280
Easton 231
Easton Branch Bridge 268
Eastport 272
Eccanachaca 200
Ecole du Genie 47
Eddyville 208
Elbridge, Joseph C. 233
Elizabethtown 281
Emuckfau Creek 53
Enotachopco 53

Eustis, Abraham 176
Eustis, William 12, 15–18, 19, 24, 35, 52, 66, 103, 134, 135, 141
Evans, Frederick 171

Fenwick, John R. 176
Flournoy, Alfred 276
Flournoy, Thomas 53, 63, 93–96
Forsyth, Benjamin 221, 281, 282, 283
Fort Adams 89
Fort Bellefontaine 70
Fort Bowyer 147, 197
Fort Brown 264
Fort Claiborne 200
Fort Clark 252
Fort Covington 89
Fort Dearborn 17, 193
Fort Erie 30, 32, 70, 96, 113, 124, 125, 171, 185, 190, 194, 214, 217, 221, 238, 239, 242, 246, 248, 253, 258, 283, 288
Fort George 30, 36, 60, 76, 87, 109, 113, 120, 123, 127, 145, 150, 161, 164, 168, 176, 182, 205, 206, 223, 227, 229, 231, 242, 246, 253, 282
Fort Harrison 209
Fort Hawkins 211
Fort Jackson 53, 63
Fort Madison 193
Fort McHenry 171, 189, 221, 268, 270
Fort Meigs 44, 106, 161, 179, 182, 189, 190, 234, 237, 251
Fort Mifflin 47
Fort Mims 52
Fort Moreau 207, 261
Fort Niagara 162, 226, 237, 246, 251
Fort Richmond 189, 274
Fort St. Phillip 173, 209
Fort Scott 265
Fort Shelby 209
Fort Smith 133
Fort Stephenson 44, 182, 234, 251
Fort Stoddert 197
Fort Strother 271
Fort Sullivan 272
Fort Wayne 44, 146, 193, 233
Foster, Augustus J. 24
Franklintown 251
Fredericksburg 239
French Creek 30, 120, 168, 177, 205, 207, 246
French Mills 30, 67, 89, 96, 113, 165, 168, 189, 207, 213, 221, 224, 228, 229, 231, 240, 242, 246, 248, 253, 282
Frenchman's Creek 135, 150, 221, 223, 226, 248
Frenchtown 44, 146, 233, 236
Fulton, Robert 141

Gadsden, James 189
Gaines, Edmund P. 20, 32, 96–99, 111, 125, 253

Index

Gallatin 286
Gananoque 281
Gansevoort, Peter 76
Georgetown 267
Gibbs, Samuel 54
Gibson, James 288
Gratiot, Charles 189
Gray, Alex 251
Greenbush 135, 168, 176, 177, 205
Griffith, Edward W. 272

Hamilton, Alexander 29, 47, 109
Hampton, Wade 20, 39–42, 48, 66, 67, 115, 182, 203, 205, 216, 217, 261, 263, 265, 266
Hanks, Porter 161
Harris, Samuel D. 185
Harrisburg 204
Harrison, William H. 20, 42–47, 53, 76, 79, 83, 96, 101, 102, 106, 112, 133, 146, 189, 202, 237, 257, 258, 260
Hartford 253, 268
Hartford Convention 26, 254
Hawkins, Benjamin 63
Hayne, Arthur P. 179, 213
Heald, Nathan 193
Helm, Thomas 185
Herald, HMS 209
Hermes, HMS 197
Hindman, Jacob 164, 171
Hinds, Thomas 93
Holmes, Andrew H. 251, 260, 264
Hoople's Creek 30, 282
Hopkins, Samuel G. 182
Hopkinsville 208
Horseshoe Bend 53, 63, 271
Houston, Sam 53, 271
Howard, Benjamin 70, 99–102, 209
Hull, Abraham F. 214
Hull, William 35, 44, 83, 102–105, 106, 112, 146, 161, 189, 193, 202, 236
Humphrey, Enoch 172
Hunter, James 234

Izard, George 20, 32, 40, 47–52, 70, 80, 106, 109, 114, 127, 133, 163, 171, 177, 185, 190, 203, 216, 221, 228, 229, 231, 261, 263, 265

Jackson, Andrew 11, 20, 25, 32, 45, 48, 52–58, 63, 66, 70, 76, 83, 93, 97, 125, 142, 147, 171, 200, 209, 236, 271, 276
Jefferson, Thomas 9, 19, 24, 35, 39, 47, 65, 73, 83, 89, 102, 127, 134, 141, 142, 187
Jesup, Thomas S. 26, 128, 253
Johnson, Richard M. 44
Jones, Roger 111

Keane, John 54
Kearsley, Jonathan 288
Ketchum, Daniel 253
Kingston 20, 29

Knoxville 251, 271

La Colle Mill 67, 70, 109, 168, 177, 203, 205, 207, 216, 217, 221, 224, 228, 240, 248, 263, 265, 266, 283
Lafitte, Jean 54, 276
Lake Erie 44, 171, 189
Lane, Samuel 264
Larwill, Joseph 257
Laval, Jacint 185
Laval, William 200
Lawrence, James 119
Lawrence, William 147, 197
Leavenworth, Henry 128, 133, 214, 246
Left Division 30, 35, 96, 113, 123, 128, 171, 185, 194, 242
Leonard, John 272
Leonard, Luther 176
Leonard, Nathaniel 161, 162
Leonard's Creek 268, 270
Lewis, Andrew 272
Lewis, Meriwether 65, 100
Lewis, Morgan 36, 58–61, 87, 127, 138
Lexington 232, 285
Longwoods 251, 258
Lower Canada 40
Lowndes, William 144
Lundy's Lane 31, 113, 124, 128, 194, 214, 217, 242, 248, 253

MacDonnell, George 282
Machesney, John 206
Machias 272
Mackinac 17, 103, 161, 171, 234, 238, 251
Macomb, Alexander 20, 48, 98, 109–112, 168, 207, 224, 229, 231, 261, 264, 266
Madison, James 9–14, 15, 17, 24, 35, 44, 53, 58, 61, 73, 83, 100, 101, 103, 125, 127, 142, 145, 146, 151
Maguaga 103, 113, 161, 193, 203
Malcolm's Mills 107
Malden 103, 238, 286
Mallioux, Joseph St. Valier 283
Mann, Dr. James 30
Massequoi 282
Massias, Abram A. 275, 284
McArthur, Duncan 103, 106–108
McFeely, George 246
McIntire, Rufus 168
McNeil, John 128, 217
McRee, William 189
Melvin, George W. 177
Metcalfe, Henry 257
Michilimackinac *see* Mackinac
Military Districts: (1st) 37, 85, 90; (2nd) 80, 90; (3rd) 48, 60, 73, 76, 80; (4th) 74, 97, 122; (5th) 116, 120; (6th) 62, 93, 141; (7th) 53, 63, 66, 93, 147; (8th) 44, 70, 83, 101; (9th) 30, 40, 48, 67, 133, 139; (10th) 20, 121, 128, 151

Miller, James 103, 112–115, 124, 203, 206, 242
Miller, John 234, 236
Milton, Homer V. 205
Mississinewa 182, 236
Mitchell, George E. 168
Mobile 67, 89, 147, 197, 200, 209, 271
Monroe, James 12, 19, 23–28, 32, 50, 55, 114, 133, 151, 254
Montgomery, Lemuel 271
Montpelier 13
Montreal 20, 26, 35, 40, 67, 127
Morgan, David B. 54
Morgan, Ludowick 283, 288
Morris, William 265
Morrison, Joseph W. 76
Mullany, James R. 248
Murray, Thomas 171

Nashville 251, 276, 285
Natchez 197, 200
Natchitoches 90
Nelson, George 206
New Brunswick 193
New London 81, 90, 92, 268
New Orleans 11, 25, 35, 54, 93, 95, 97, 125, 127, 171, 200, 209, 276
New York City 19, 141, 170, 187, 188, 259, 273, 274, 278
Niagara River 30, 48, 135, 150, 163
Nicholas, Robert C. 193, 194
Norfolk 40, 116, 120
Nye, Samuel 168

Odletown 221, 283
Ogdensburg 29, 282
Olympian Springs 260
Ontario, Lake 30, 50, 168
Orders in Council 10
Oswego 168, 177
Otter Creek 177
Owings, Thomas D. 260

Pakenham, Edward 54
Parker, Thomas 115–116, 221
Partridge, Alden 141, 142, 189
Pass Christian 209
Patriot War 131–132
Patterson, Daniel T. 54
Paull, George 258
Pearce, Cromwell 231
Peire, Henry B. 276
Pensacola 25, 54, 200, 271, 276
Percy, William H. 197
Perkins, Joseph 252
Perry, Oliver H. 44, 83, 260
Petersburg 267
Philadelphia 9, 231
Pierce, Benjamin K. 168
Pike, Zebulon M. 36, 65, 89, 116–120, 206, 229, 231, 242, 282

Pimartam's Town 209
Pinckney, Thomas 61, 93, 141
Pittsburgh 76, 170
Pittsfield 179, 212
Plattsburgh 11, 20, 24, 40, 48, 74, 109, 171, 177, 182, 190, 203, 205, 206, 207, 212, 216, 225, 228, 229, 231, 240, 242, 245, 253, 258, 261, 263, 264, 265, 266, 278, 284
Point Petre 275, 284
Porter, Moses 20, 116, 120–122, 127, 151, 176, 227
Porter, Peter B. 30, 113, 136
Portland 85, 266, 272
Portsmouth 86, 272
Preston, James P. 221
Prevost, George 20, 29, 48, 109, 190
Procter, Henry 44, 83, 146, 251
Purdy, Robert 40, 115, 265
Putnam, Perley 272

Quebec 103
Queenston Heights 17, 35, 127, 135, 161, 163, 168, 206, 223, 248

Raleigh 275
Red Eagle 53, 200
Red Sticks 53
Redoubt No. 2, 266
Regulations for the Field Exercises, Maneuvers, and Conduct of Infantry of the United States 135
Riall, Phineas 30, 128, 253
Richmond 267
Right Division 40, 48, 70, 133, 171, 177, 185, 189, 231
Riley, Bennett 283
Ripley, Eleazar W. 20, 30, 31, 113, 123–126, 242, 248
Ritchie, John 165, 171
River Aux Canards 83
River Raisin *see* Frenchtown
Roach, Isaac 248
Rock River 209
Romayne, James S. 168
Ronan, George 193
Ross, George T. 276
Ross, John 151
Royal Marines 197, 275, 284
Rules and Regulations of the Army 19
Russell, Gilbert C. 93
Russell, William 209

Sacketts Harbor 20, 29, 30, 32, 48, 67, 89, 96, 109, 117, 123, 133, 141, 162, 168, 176, 177, 179, 185, 195, 206, 212, 214, 225, 229, 237, 242, 248, 278, 282
Saco 265
St. Augustine 132
St. Clair, Arthur 79
St. Lawrence, HMS 50

St. Lawrence River 67, 177, 180, 182, 189, 246
St. Louis 70, 101, 133
St. Mary's 268
Sandy Creek 283
Savannah 211, 280
Schuyler, Philip P. 223
Scott, Hercules 190
Scott, Martin 258
Scott, Winfield 20, 30, 39, 48, 60, 66, 70, 76, 79, 98, 111, 113, 120, 127, 163, 164, 214, 217, 246, 253
Senecatown 258
Shaw, John 89
Shelburne, Charles F. 203
Sheldon, Joseph 182
Shepardstown 280
Sherbrooke, John C. 272
Smith, John C. 91
Smith, Joseph L. 253
Smith, Melancthon 217, 261
Smith, Samuel 24
Smith, Thomas A. 20, 48, 70, 109, 131–134, 203, 216, 221, 224, 225, 234, 280
Smith, W.W. 177
Smith, Walter 268
Smyth, Alexander 115, 120, 127, 134–137, 149, 176, 223, 226, 239, 248
Snake Hill 171, 190, 242
Sophia, HMS 209
Southern Department 189
Spotts, Samuel 171
Sproull, John 225
Stanton Island 141, 274
Staunton 220
Stockton, George 260
Stoddard, Amos 162
Stoney Creek 37, 60, 151, 164, 176, 182, 205, 223, 227, 231, 248, 253, 282
Strong, Caleb 90
Sturgeon Creek 260
Sunbury 272
Swartwout, Robert 123, 138–139, 217, 228, 242
Swift, Joseph G. 139–143, 188, 189

Talladega 53
Tallusahatchee 53
Tatnall, Edward F. 275
Taylor, Augustine 92
Taylor, Robert 116
Taylor, Zachary 84, 98, 209
Tecumseh 44, 102, 113
Terre aux Boeufs 65
Thames 44, 83, 189, 258
Thayer, Sylvanus 142
Thornton, Arthur W. 177

Tippecanoe 44, 76, 112, 202, 280
Tompkins, Daniel D. 19, 58
Totten, Joseph G. 189
Townsend, David S. 213
Towson, Nathan 163, 164, 171
Treaty of Ghent 11, 24, 26, 54
Trenton 228
Trimble, William A. 238
Twiggs, David E. 209

U.S. Military Academy 79, 109, 141, 142, 187
Upham, Timothy 242
Utica 248, 288

Van Rensselaer, Stephen 35, 135
Villere's Plantation 54, 171, 206, 276
Vincent, John 85, 127, 151

Wade, William 209
Walsh, Michael 171
Warren, John 189
Washington, George 70
Wayne, Anthony 42, 65, 79, 87, 99, 102, 116, 120
Weatherford, William 53, 200
Wells, Samuel 233
West Florida 67, 89
West Point 47
Whitney, Eli 35
Wilkesboro 215
Wilkinson, James 20, 29, 37, 39, 40, 52, 60, 64–69, 70, 76, 89, 90, 93, 96, 109, 113, 117, 120, 127, 131, 134, 141, 164, 177, 182, 189, 197, 200, 206, 213, 221, 223, 229, 240, 242, 282
Williams, Alexander J. 165, 171
Williams, David R. 143–145
Williams, John 271
Williams, Jonathan 47, 141, 187
Winchester, James 44, 145–149, 233
Winder, Levin 151
Winder, William H. 20, 24, 37, 76, 85, 121, 128, 135, 149–152, 182, 205, 223, 226, 227, 231, 268, 270, 282
Wollenstonecraft, Charles 172
Wood, Eleazar D. 189, 190, 242
Woodford, John T. 182
Woodstock 263
Wool, John E. 223, 261, 284

Yeo, James L. 168
York 36, 118, 123, 127, 176, 206, 228, 231, 242, 282

Zanesville 236

www.ingramcontent.com/pod-product-compliance
Lightning Source LLC
Chambersburg PA
CBHW021347300426
44114CB00012B/1108